The War Between Mentalism and Behaviorism

On the Accessibility of Mental Processes

SCIENTIFIC PSYCHOLOGY SERIES

Stephen W. Link and James T. Townsend, Series Editors

MONOGRAPHS

William R. Uttal • The War Between Mentalism and Behaviorism: On the Accessibility of Mental Processes

William R. Uttal • Toward a New Behaviorism: The Case Against Perceptual Reductionism

Gordon M. Redding and Benjamin Wallace • Adaptive Spatial Alignment

John C. Baird • Sensation and Judgment: Complementarity Theory of Psychophysics

John A. Swets • Signal Detection Theory and RC Analysis in Psychology and Diagnostics: Collected Papers

William R. Uttal • The Swimmer: An Integrated Computational Model of a Perceptual–Motor System

Stephen W. Link • The Wave Theory of Difference and Similarity

EDITED VOLUMES

Jonathan Grainger and Arthur M. Jacobs • Localist Connectionist Approaches to Human Cognition

Cornelia E. Dowling, Fred S. Roberts, and Peter Theuns • Recent Progress in Mathematical Psychology

F. Gregory Ashby • Multidimensional Models of Perception and Cognition

Hans-Georg Geissler, Stephen W. Link, and James T. Townsend • Cognition, Information Processing, and Psychophysics: Basic Issues

The War Between Mentalism and Behaviorism

On the Accessibility of Mental Processes

William R. Uttal
Arizona State University

2000

LAWRENCE ERLBAUM ASSOCIATES, PUBLISHERS
Mahwah, New Jersey London

Lawrence Erlbaum Associates, Inc., Publishers
10 Industrial Avenue
Mahwah, New Jersey 07430

Library of Congress Cataloging-in-Publication Data

Uttal, William R.
The war between mentalism and behaviorism : on the accessibility of mental processes / William R. Uttal.
p. cm.
Includes bibliographical references and indexes.
ISBN 0-8058-3361-7 (hardcover : alk. paper)
1. Behaviorism (Psychology) 2. Cognitive psychology. I. Title.
BF199.U77 1999
150. 19'43--dc21 99-29247
CIP

Books published by Lawrence Erlbaum Associates are printed on acid-free paper, and their bindings are chosen for strength and durability.

Printed in the United States of America
10 9 8 7 6 5 4 3 2 1

BOOKS BY WILLIAM R. UTTAL

- Real Time Computers: Techniques and Applications in the Psychological Sciences
- Generative Computer Assisted Instruction (with Miriam Rogers, Ramelle Hieronymus, and Timothy Pasich)
- Sensory Coding: Selected Readings (Editor)
- The Psychology of Sensory Coding
- Cellular Neurophysiology and Integration: An Interpretive Introduction
- An Autocorrelation Theory of Form Detection
- The Psychobiology of Mind
- A Taxonomy of Visual Processes
- Visual Form Detection in 3-Dimensional Space
- Foundations of Psychobiology (with Daniel N. Robinson)
- The Detection of Nonplanar Surfaces in Visual Space
- The Perception of Dotted Forms
- On Seeing Forms
- The Swimmer: An Integrated Computational Model of a Perceptual–Motor System (with Gary Bradshaw, Sriram Dayanand, Robb Lovell, Thomas Shepherd, Ramakrishna Kakarala, Kurt Skifsted, and Greg Tupper)
- Toward A New Behaviorism: The Case Against Perceptual Reductionism
- Computational Modeling of Vision: The Role of Combination (with Ramakrishna Kakarala, Sriram Dayanand, Thomas Sheperd, Jaggi Kalki, Charles Lunskis Jr., and Ning Liu)
- The War Between Mentalism and Behaviorism: On the Accessibility of Mental Processes

For Mit-chan

Contents

Preface

The Evolution of a Theoretical Perspective

My theoretical point of view, as a scientific psychologist, has evolved substantially over the years. I was trained as a physiological psychologist, with an interest in sensory processes, by Professors Donald R. Meyer and Philburn Ratoosh at Ohio State University, both of whom recently died. I find myself in the unexpected position of being a critic of neurophysiological and cognitive reductionism and increasingly in support of what is today, at best, a minority and, at least, a very unpopular point of view—a modern version of classic behaviorism. The change in my thinking is virtually a complete reversal of my early training. How could this happen?

It really does not matter very much why one individual (in Winston Churchill's words) "ratted." It does matter if there is a strong empirical, technical, logical, and philosophical argument to suggest the psychological community consider taking another pendular swing between reductionism and mental accessibility and molar behaviorism, that has characterized its history. I am convinced that our science is in a period of theoretical reorientation and have taken on the task of detailing why some form of behaviorism is the most plausible and scientifically coherent course to take.

New developments suggest that a discussion of basic assumptions of our science may be extremely timely, and necessary for it to survive. In the predecessor to this book, *Toward a New Behaviorism: The Case Against Perceptual Reductionism* (Uttal, 1998), I discussed the forces at work that have altered the answers that scientific psychology have given to some of its core questions in recent years. These forces have been the result of powerful intellectual currents driven by new technologies and perspectives emerging from computer science and neurophysiology. The successes in those fields sometimes overshadowed the application of their theories, techniques, and findings to psychological problems. This is not without its own logical, philosophical, and theoretical complications. The purpose of this book is to examine a foundation premise of psychology—Are mental processes accessible?

The extreme poles toward which theory in psychology has always been attracted are a radical mentalism and a radical behaviorism. Stripping away intellectual decorations and secondary assumptions, the key criteria dividing mentalism and behaviorism are their respective answers to the questions of accessibility and reduction. However, there is no sharp line of demarcation between theories of one genre or another. There have been many intermediate positions, clearly not situated at these extreme poles, that have been of importance in the history of scientific psychology. Furthermore, many sciences and scholarly traditions, other than scientific psychology, contributed to the ways in which psychologists have formulated their individual perspectives. Influences have come from biology, computer modeling, evolutionary theory, psychoanalysis, and speculative philosophy. Embedded in the different forms that psychology has taken over the last century is the conundrum of mental process accessibility. It is one of the main, if not the main, dimensions, or axes, or criteria defining a psychological school of thought. It is also what this book is about.

However explicitly unconcerned modern cognitive psychology may be about the accessibility issue, the specific response to this core question is undeniably a root assumption of each theoretical approach. The mere substitution of the word *information* for *drives* or *goals* (which themselves replaced *minds, consciousness,* or *thoughts*), does not ameliorate the fact that cognitive psychologists are talking about more than the relations between stimuli and responses; they are also assuming that valid inferences can be made concerning what is happening in the organism. Of course, some behaviorists make the same assumptions (see, e.g., the subsequent discussion of drives and goals by Hull [1943, chap.1]). This reminds us that the separation between mentalisms and behaviorisms is not a sharp line, but may be better characterized in terms of the relative positions along a continuous axis anchored by a radically affirmative answer to the accessibility question and by its equally radical, but negative, antithesis.

Behaviorism as we know it today arose in the 1920s mainly as a response to the mentalism of E. B. Titchener, a pioneering psychological scientist who used introspection as his primary research method. Titchener believed that mental processes could be accessed and, even more fundamentally, analyzed into components. There were other forces that led to J. B. Watson's creation of a new kind of psychology. The revolution in the biological sciences stimulated by Darwin and Mendel, among others, the problems of animal behavior and cognition, and the difficulties that other psychologies (such as functionalism) generated, all added to his desire to develop a truly scientific psychology devoid of the "ghost in the machine"—conscious mind. The influence of such movements as American Pragmatism and other archetypical American approaches to our interaction with the natural environment also had strong influences on the emergence of Watsonian Behaviorism. As we see in chapter 1, Watson's personal attitudes toward religion also contributed to his invention of *behaviorism.*

Subsequently, a new mentalism, which explicitly has as its goal the exploration and analysis of mental processes and mechanisms, evolved in the 1960s as a counterrevolution to what many considered to be uninteresting, if not sterile, evolutionary descendants of Watson's behaviorism. The counterrevolution was reinforced by what were perceived by many psychologists to be the failures of an extreme methodological behaviorism that eschewed virtually any kind of interpretation or theorizing beyond the raw statement of the obtained experimental findings. Such a constrained and narrowly defined science, if it did really exist and was not just a red herring, did not survive as the modal form of scientific study in psychology. There was considerable debate concerning whether the goal of a scientific psychology should be measurement and control as opposed to explanation and explanatory understanding (and, at another level, whether or not the two had to be exclusive). It was just too much to demand of an inquisitive group of scientists that they avoid interpretations of the meaning of their data. Whether such an extreme caricature of behaviorism is justified is another one of the questions examined in this book.

The counterrevolutionary, antibehavioral, empirical, modern version of mentalism came to be called cognitive psychology. Its goal was specifically to delve into the cognitive or mental structures and functions; it explicitly concerned itself with consciousness in a way that was anathema to behaviorists. Its aim was to do nothing less than measure and dissect the mind itself. The success of the cognitive approach as the prototype of modern psychology in the past decades has been extraordinary. There are more cognitive scientists and more kinds of cognitive scientists at work today than could have been imagined only a few years ago.

Some of us feel that the revolutions of the past have been guided by criteria other than scientific ones. Some of us would have preferred to use the agreement between data and theory as the criteria for defining the nature of the science. Psychology, in particular, has long been plagued by the introduction of personal values, societal needs, theological implications, and unarticulated, but deeply held, assumptions about conflicts that are difficult to resolve at a dispassionate and objective level. Perhaps psychology is too close to the human condition to avoid the introduction of such secondary influences. It would be preferable if we could define our theories in terms of a more objective set of criteria. Some social philosophers and historians may claim that all human endeavors, science included, are driven by what I consider to be extraneous criteria. This book is an attempt to shift the balance of the various criteria from the extraneous to the objective.

That the choice of a psychological theory has not been objectively driven in the past may be a disconcerting thought to both committed behavioral and cognitive psychologists. This does not mean that we have not progressed. As these theoretical controversies and revolutions were taking place, the database continued to accumulate. No responsible cognitive psychologist rejects the validity of most of the empirical operant literature however much the conceptual approach of the behavioral experimenters may have been repellent. Earlier behavioral findings were rarely shown to be "wrong" nor were they supplemented by new findings that rejected the scientific perspectives that underlay their protocols. Rather, behaviorism became unsatisfactory and incomplete (just as the introspective structuralism of its predecessors had become unsatisfactory) to cognitive psychologists for reasons of scientific styles, social values, jostling for position, and other such extraneous criteria. Often, it was not new findings, but changing social conditions (both in the sense of the general and scientific communities) that dictated the most fundamental changes in the history of psychological theory.

There is a fundamental difference in this regard at the present stage of our scientific discussion. The forces that direct us toward a new form of behaviorism are in large part different kinds than those that gave rise to previous intellectual and conceptual revolutions in psychology. For the first time, empirical and technical issues are in a position to dominate the debates between mentalists and behaviorists. This is a very positive development. Empirical and technical arguments are the favored and normal kind in science: They are to be preferred over any kind of speculative arguments and certainly over any matter of style or taste. To develop a theory independent of empirical findings would eventually lead to the rejection of any such theory.

This is the main theme of any modern science—observe and explain, and then perhaps re-explain. It has been so since the Middle Ages when science emerged from theology and the speculation of "natural philosophers." Irrefutable theories devoid of controlled observations are the substance of other forms of human thought, but should not be of science. No matter how esoteric the mathematics may be, the ultimate arbiter of a theory's utility and acceptability is its compatibility with empirical observations. Occasionally, some inspired intuition may anticipate an observation and theories can lead us into selecting or inappropriately interpreting observations. Nevertheless, a theory that contradicts observation must ultimately be rejected.

As we progress through this book it will become clear that a substantial body of psychological literature rejecting the assumption that the mind is accessible and that mentalisms of all kinds are untenable has already been published. Much of it has been continuously available for many years, even from the 19th-century beginnings of scientific psychology. However, much of it was simply ignored. To continue to do so is guaranteed to produce theoretical absurdities.

I am aware that some philosophers (e.g., Hanson, 1958) look askance at this simple criterion of theory–observation compatibility. Additional concerns such as simplicity and the effect of one's theory on the interpretation of one's observations cannot be overlooked. However, once agreement is achieved concerning some measurement, a theory that predicts otherwise is in deep peril.

Another form of argument against mentalism has long been ignored in scientific psychology, or in any other form of psychology that attempts to infer from behavior what is happening in the mind. It is the interdisciplinary interaction between the goals and aims of this science with developments in other natural sciences. Simply put, it is that scientific psychology has set for itself some goals that cannot in principle be achieved for reasons that are well understood and appreciated in other sciences, but although relevant, are ignored in ours. It is only by contrasting our goals with these known constraints and limits in those other sciences that a rational, revitalized version of scientific psychology can be developed.

Another goal of this book is to consider the future of scientific psychology. To espouse such a major reorientation of our science without appreciating the evolution of the term *behaviorism* would be incomplete. This book, therefore, briefly reviews the past, examines the present, and outlines my estimate of the most desirable future. The task I set for myself is going to be a difficult one in a zeitgeist that is so strongly dominated by the mentalist (which assumes that mental processes can be accessed) and reductionist (which assumes that once accessed, mind can be reduced to subcomponents) forces at work in scientific psychology today. There are many reasons for this pessimistic view. First, the topics of concern to scientific psychology are so important to all levels of humanity it is likely they will always be subject to pressures from extrascientific influences. My target audience is not those with casual or parochial interests in scientific psychology, but rather the generalists who define (or the protogeneralists who will define) the future scientific nature of this field of research.

Second, it seems that many cognitive psychologists are not deeply enough concerned with the fundamental issue of accessibility. Usually, the issue is finessed and ignored.

Third, the language that is available for this discussion is woefully inadequate. The key term "behaviorism" is so festooned with emotional and historical connotation that, even after all of the study and research that I have done for this book, I am not sure what it means.

Fourth, although I am concerned with the scientific role of cognitivism and behaviorism and am writing mainly for psychologists from the point of view of a psychologist, there are many others (including historians and sociologists of science as well as an army of scholars from many different fields) who have an interest in "consciousness" who may find my view incomplete and my arguments uncompelling. To reiterate, my goal here is to examine the empirical and technical bases for choosing between the two alternatives, not to explore the entire social sphere of science.

Fifth, make no mistake—this is a tough problem. I have no delusion that whatever I say in this book, it will go away. Although I am uncomfortable with them, there are extrascientific values that do influence our theoretical perspectives. It is unlikely that even the most objective and compelling logic will overcome decades of conviction and commitment.

Finally, I want to emphasize that this book is concerned with the conceptual foundations of scientific psychology and not with its extrapolations to social causes of practical admonitions to educators. The emphasis in my discussion of behaviorism is how it can instantiate this scientific endeavor. The eminent psychologists B. F. Skinner and J. B. Watson were probably chastised more because of their social extrapolations than because of their research methodology or scientific approaches. These social extrapolations from a scientific theory may have cost behaviorism more than is generally appreciated. The free will-versus-determinism issue that was at the crux of so many of Skinner's humanistic controversies lies outside of the domain of science. We cannot expect behavioral science to solve all of the social or theological problems of the world any more than can, for example, materials science. It is reasonable for critics to argue that the microscopic behavioral details of a laboratory experiment, highly controlled as they are, need not be good indicators of how a child should be schooled.

In conclusion, I am somewhat now more humble. I no longer believe it is possible that a "killer" argument against any mentalism will emerge from these discussions. Nor that a totally new behavioral science will be kindled by this book. If just a few of my colleagues pause to reconsider some of the fundamental premises of our science, my aims will be fulfilled.

ACKNOWLEDGMENTS

In writing this book, I have benefited from the writings of others who share the feeling that all is not well with contemporary psychology. To the maximum attempt possible, I cite the source of my ideas and concepts. However, I am sure many others have contributed to my current opinions in ways that are less direct. A sentence that did not ring true can sometimes be as influential as a positive impulse toward a new perspective.

I am also indebted to many others who have directly or indirectly supported the career-long project of which this book and its predecessor are a part. This book is really the sixth that I have written in an effort to clarify what is happening when we "perceive." The series started with two patently neuroreductionist efforts—*The Psychobiology of Sensory Coding* (Uttal, 1973) and *The Psychobiology of Mind* (Uttal, 1978). These were followed by a transition volume in which I realized the limits of neuroreductionism and the necessity for a molar approach to many high-level visual phenomena (*A Taxonomy of Visual Processes*, Uttal, 1981). The next volume, *On Seeing Forms* (Uttal, 1988), was the one in which I became aware that the cognitive explanations were unsatisfactory. Even more profoundly, researching the 1988 book alerted me that it was not only our theories that were malleable, but our data were also quite fragile. In the fifth and immediately preceding volume in the series, *Toward a New Behaviorism: The Case Against Perceptual Reductionism* (Uttal, 1998), I dealt directly with the idea of reductionism, from both the point of view of neurophysiology and cognition, as well as the role of formal modeling in contemporary perceptual science. This very critical effort laid the groundwork for the present book and its consideration of the accessibility issue. I could not have left the task incomplete. The urge to finish the project would have gratified the good Professors Zeigarnick and Ovsiankina who both pointed out that incomplete tasks are remembered better than completed ones.

In spite of the idea of collegial interaction at a university, in fact, the writing of this book was very much a private matter. I was, however, supported and encouraged, as well as enlightened and tutored, by my colleague, Professsor Peter Killeen of Arizona State University's psychology department. Peter has been a behaviorist for a long time. I am newly come to this point of view. At one point Peter suggested that our paths were crossing as he became more of a cognitivist and I became more of a behaviorist. I am not sure that this is exactly what happened (and I do hope I can retrieve him), but I do know that I am very grateful for the intellectual support he provided. Both Peter and professor Jay Klein read and commented on an early draft of this book vastly improving the final version. I am also extremely grateful to my editor, Sondra Guideman, who helped so much and with such good humor, in bringing this book to publication.

Finally, no project of mine would ever have been possible if it had not been for the love and companionship of my dear wife, Mit-chan.

Chapter **1**

The Issue—Mentalism Versus Behaviorism

Can the mind be observed, measured, and then analyzed into its parts? In other words, is it accessible to scientific examination? These are the questions that motivate this book. Anyone who has had the audacity to ask these questions must acknowledge at the outset that there are not likely to be simple answers to what is obviously a collection of related and profoundly complex queries. Nevertheless, these are among the most important of the fundamental issues that drive psychology, whether it be classical and speculative or modern and empirical. These questions also underlie the foundation of the historical and continuing conflict between mentalism and behaviorism—the two great contending approaches that have divided and destabilized as well as energized scientific psychology, in particular, for the last 120 years. Although one cannot make a judgment about the value of this destabilization in the history of this science (it is yet to be determined whether it has been detrimental or seminal), it is clear that this dialog, this debate, this controversy, has been ubiquitous during the intellectual development of our diverse attempts to understand psychological processes.

Make no mistake, although there have been many other matters of import that have risen to the attention of psychologists from time to time, the development, extinction, and reemergence of the various schools of psychology has been based on their respective answers to these fundamental controversies. Methodologies have come and gone and will come and go as new technologies are developed. Theories of one or another phenomenon of this science have been offered, debated, and ultimately have disappeared within the context of a newly emerging perspective or point of view. For that matter, some of the most popular theories of psychology's history have been shown to be misinterpretations and have been discarded. Alternative models of relatively limited extent arise, compete, and then more often than not are merged into a more global explanation than had been used to describe either theory. However, the fundamental questions I have just raised remain at the deepest conceptual core of our science.

The swing from one point of view to the other (concerning the issue of whether the *intrapersonally* privileged awareness of our own mental life is amenable to the same techniques that characterize *interpersonally* observable empirical science) continues, and the controversy remains unresolved. Unresolved, perhaps, but not without influence. In fact, as I just suggested, the scientific accessibility of "mind," or "cognition," or "consciousness," or whatever else one wishes to call this "stuff of self-awareness" has been the main historical force behind the evolution of the various psychological schools and general approaches that have emerged over the years.

There are several important points that must be made clear at the outset of this book. I am approaching this problem from the point of view of a natural scientist. My arguments will mainly be those based on the same kind of scientific standards that characterize any other science. Psychology is a subdivision of biology and as such is subject to all of the standard criteria that would be required to resolve any controversy there. For example, standards of compatibility between theory and observation, standards of mathematical and computational logic, standards of simplicity, and, to an important degree, standards of elegance all must play their part. The problem for psychology is that its content matter impacts on so many other important aspects of human existence that these scientific standards are often subjugated to the constructs and values of other aspects of our life. This book is about the science of psychology, not about the arguable implications that it may have for society or the influence that society may have on it.

It is also important as we begin this discussion to appreciate that it is not the "reality" of mind or consciousness that is being debated here. Even the most radical behaviorist can not easily reject the ontological existence of personally experienced awareness. To do so would be tantamount to not only rejecting the reality of the world around us but of ourselves as well. The focus of the present discussion is on a far more specific point—how far can psychological science go in the kind of systematic analysis and reduction that was characteristic of other, if I may say, simpler scientific subject matters?

As the history of this problem is reviewed, it becomes evident how the epistemological issues of the accessibility and analyzability of mind, not the ontological issue of its existence, were truly at the focus of the evolution from one school of psychology to the next. Early in the history of what we now consider to be modern science, the notion that mind was inherently physical in origin led quite easily to the analogous idea that it was just another process that could be observed and analyzed as well as any other. This point of view evolved into mentalistic associationism, structuralism, and cognitivism as well as some behaviorisms that assumed, at least in principle, that mind could be reduced to its components. A reaction to these philosophies led to the global and molar and antiatomistic approaches that characterized some other behaviorisms and such related psychologies as Gestaltism.

Currently, a new form of mentalism called cognitive science or cognitive psychology has captured the attention of most experimental psychologists. As with previous forms of mentalism, it is characterized by premises of mental observability, accessibility, and functional analyzability. These are the basic ideas espoused by cognitive psychology, as well as all of its predecessor mentalisms. Whatever modern methods may have or will evolve, the classic assertion remains—the subject matter of psychology is mental activity itself and it can be studied.

Opposed to such a mentalism has traditionally been a collection of behaviorisms asserting that it is not mind, but rather, only the interpersonally observable behavior resulting from a complex of different driving forces, some internal and some external, that must be the target of a valid psychological science. The key difference of opinion between the two points of view concerns whether or not the observed behavior can be used to infer the nature of the underlying mental states and mechanisms. In the baldest of terms, the question posed is—is mind accessible?

The metaphor of a pendulum going back and forth between two extreme conditions is probably inadequate to describe what has really happened in the history of psychology. Each successive pendular swing did not return to the same behaviorism or the same mentalism that was its predecessor, but rather to a new and modified version of it. In another perhaps more illuminating metaphor, Amsel (1989) suggested that advanced versions of the alternating approaches to psychology could vary considerably from earlier ones. The model he suggested is represented by a cone standing on its narrow tip—the tip representing a time at which there was little scientific information. As time goes on and our knowledge increases, however, the alternation goes upward from one version of either mentalism or behaviorism to a more advanced version of the other on a wider portion of the cone. The width of the cone, of course, represents the knowledge available at each historical epoch of the psychology. As psychological history runs its course, the knowledge base grows and the cone widens. The point of this metaphor is that both behaviorisms and mentalisms come in many different varieties.

Whatever the conceptual model, some of us now feel that the mentalist–behaviorist pendulum is ready to swing back to some kind of behaviorism. Perhaps it won't be as radical as some of its predecessors, but there is an increasing appreciation that the cognitive mentalism of the recent past is deeply flawed for logical, empirical, philosophical, and technical reasons.

The questions of the accessibility and analyzability of mental functions are complex. Accessibility, of course, is assumed a priori by many different systems of psychology. Analyzability or reductionism has also been a tenet of many different schools of psychological thought. To understand the impact of the question of the analyzability of "mind" on our science, it is necessary to understand the positions taken by and interpretations made by both mentalists and behaviorists in their classic and contemporary versions.

In this chapter, I have chosen to undertake a brief historical analysis of the intended meaning of some of the more notable mentalisms and behavior in the past. It seems very clear that the fundamental nature of the respective positions of the two schools has been clouded by secondary issues other than the ones that are at the scientific core of their intellectual structures.

It is mainly with regard to their respective positions on the twin issues of accessibility and analyzability that differentiates the theories of mentalists and behaviorists. The key to understanding the mentalist program has always been their foundation assumption of cognitive accessibility and the corollary idea that, in actual fact, there exist fundamentally real elements of mental activity that can be inferred from behavioral observations. This is the essence of both the concepts of analyzability and elementalism, two sides of the same coin, and two ideas that are inextricably intertwined through the history of mentalist psychology.

Analyzability (i.e., the property of being separable into parts) is closely related to reductionism, the latter generally referring to the explanation of one level of discourse in the language, terms, and measurements, especially as they define the components, of a lower level. The classic reductionism for our times is neuroreductionism—the explanation of psychological functions in neurophysiological terms. I also use the term reductionism to refer to the attempts by psychologists, for example, to reduce reaction time to subcomponents such as detection time, decision-making time, and response-selection time. As another example, attempts are now being made to reduce perceptual processes such as apparent motion to "matching and parsing" subprocesses. These examples of attempts to go from the global or molar phenomenological level to a level of more elemental mental processing components is also a kind of reductionism.

This elemental reductionism is nowhere more evident than in the study of memory. Watkins (1990) called our attention to this phenomenon when he reminded us of Underwood's (1972) comment that:

> Memories now have attributes, organization, and structure; there are addresses, read out rules, and holding mechanisms . . . our memories are filled with T-stacks, implicit associational responses, natural-language mediators, images, multiple traces, tags, kernel sentences, markers, relational rules, verbal loops, and one-buns. (p. 1)

Watkins (1990) pointed out that along with these mechanisms, there is also a superabundance of learning and memory theories that seem to perpetuate themselves, proliferate, yet not enlighten us. He argued that all of this theorizing about memory and all of these hypothetical constructs (and those that have come forward since) are due to our tendency to seek a "mediational" explanation—that is, to seek out the component traces or mechanisms that underlay the behavior. Watkins' assertion is essentially a criticism of reductionism to elements and an argument against searching for mediating internal mechanisms. He concluded by pointing out that the attempt to reduce memory to its neural substrates or to computer models exacerbates the microscopic, elemental approach. His conclusion is a behavioral one, although he does not use the word.

The antithesis of an accessible and analyzable mind is to assume that mental processes are private (i.e., interpersonal, inaccessible). Of course, mind is not inaccessible in one sense—some facets of its content can be communicated through speech and writing, by means of facial, postural, or other motor responses and even, to at least a modest degree, by means of physiological indicators.

However, behaviorists generally argue that all responses (or behaviors) are measures of the totality of the experience or awareness of the behaving organism and are the resultant of a combination of many different stimulus, organism, and response variables as well as the past experiences and (to an unknown, but usually lesser, degree) the genetic heritage of the individual. The combination is irretrievably tangled, according to behaviorists, and little if anything can be done to disentangle the combination. According to this viewpoint, behavior cannot tell us anything about the component processes or mechanisms that underlie the mental events. Indeed, because many possible mechanisms could lead to the same psychological event and there are many obscuring and transforming factors between behavior and mental processes, the barrier between the two domains is impenetrable as a matter of both deep principles and practical considerations.

Furthermore, consciously or unconsciously, people can and do obscure their true mental processes. Actors are trained specialists in separating their behavior from their thoughts; sociopathological liars succeed in their scams and cons; and even normal people are not always in touch with their own motives and the causes of their own behavior. Therefore, it is not inappropriate to suggest that behavioral responses may be as neutral with regard to these underlying processes as is mathematics to the systems it represents.

This does not mean that all behaviorisms are totally molar in basic principle; some behaviorists have assumed that, in principle at least, that molar behavior is made up of inferable, if not directly accessible, components. Most, however, have rejected the practical accessibility of those components. Analyzability in principle, on the other hand, has been a part of virtually all versions of the mentalist point of view from its earliest origins. I believe that to the degree that behaviorisms accept this concept of analyzable cognition, they are polluting their doctrinal purity with mentalist concepts.

The idea that the actual subcomponents of mind can be inferred from behavioral measurements is based on an assumption of accessibility that is far more contentious than many cognitivists seem willing to acknowledge. Hardly restricted to scientific psychology, this is an example of one of the great historical debates of natural science—how far should one go in hypothesizing the existence of internal or hidden mechanisms from external observations?

In summary, it is important to emphasize that the essential disagreement between the two schools of psychology does not concern the reality of mental events themselves, but rather is based on an assertion of putative limits on their accessibility and analyzability. This, as I have noted, is an epistemological statement, not an ontological one dealing with the reality of mind. Indeed, many of the classic "schools of psychology" can better be understood in terms of their differences concerning this basic assumption than in the terms of any other criteria that may have been incorrectly used to characterize them. The following brief review of some of what I consider to be the major mentalisms is presented to flesh out this skeleton assertion.

1.1 MENTALISM AND ELEMENTALISMS

1.1.1 Associationism

From its earliest days the associationist school of psychological theory assumed that the analyzability of mental events was possible. Indeed, the basic premise of associationism was that more complex thoughts, ideas, and percepts were built up out of simpler elements that had been sensed or experienced previously. The antecedents of the associationists were to be found among the British empiricists (e.g., Thomas Hobbes [1588–1679], John Locke [1632–1704], George Berkeley [1685–1783], James Mill [1773–1836], and John Stuart Mill [1806–1873]). These philosophers rejected the notion of innate ideas, and argued that the growth of mental experiences depended specifically on the concatenation or association of previously experienced sensory components. Whether they gave ontological to mind (e.g., Berkeley) or to matter (e.g., Hobbes) there was assumed to be both a macrostructure of mental processes and microstructure of the components that had to be connected together to create that macrostructure. Their emphasis on the connection of ideas through experience is a qualitative precursor to the pseudoneural, quantitative connectionism of contemporary psychology. Indeed, comparable physical models were prevalent throughout the associationist tradition. James Mill proposed a mechanical model of mental processes that evolved in John Stuart Mill's writing into a chemical model of the mind. What could be more patently "elementalist"? How conceptually close these models are to contemporary "neural network" or connectionist models!

The empiricist philosophical assertion (that we had to learn how to think by assembling previously sensed components) obviously stimulated the development of one of the earliest schools of scientific psychology—associationism. The common thread among all philosophers and psychologists of this persuasion was the way each sought to explain the way in which the components of ideas became literally associated with each other. Adhesives of contiguity and similarity linked ideas together, with some investigators emphasizing the necessity for some kind of *effect* or *reinforcement* and others simply alluding to the fact that mere *concomitancy* could account for the strengthening of associationist bonds.

A major transition, of course, was the emergence of scientific psychology from its philosophical antecedents. Although the questions asked were very much the same, the methodologies of philosophy and the emerging scientific psychology could not have been more different—speculation was replaced by experimentation. Admittedly, the early psychologists, such as Weber, Fechner, and even Wundt himself, were very often more philosophers than empirical scientists. Nevertheless, the move from the armchair to the laboratory represented an important development for those interested in studies of the mind.

Early laboratory evidence for the associationist point of view came from the experiments of physiologists such as Ivan Pavlov (1849–1936) and Valdimir Bekhterev (1857–1927) in Russia. However, the American Edward L. Thorndike (1874–1949) may best be considered the leading proponent of what was not so much a formal school of psychology as a psychological tradition or principle. To him, as to many subsequent mentalists, the principle that mind could be analyzed into its components was the foundation assumption. The associationist goal of psychology was and is to determine the laws that combined simple ideas into complex ones and that linked stimuli to responses. Clearly this is an approach that not only accepts the analyzability of mental structures but reifies it as the main theme of mental action as it seeks to determine the rules and laws that guide the association. Even though he is sometimes included among the protobehaviorists,

Thorndike appears to be quite willing to accept both the accessibility and the analyzability of mental functions. For example, in an early major work (Thorndike, 1907) he makes it quite clear that the objects of psychological inquiry are "mental facts," a classification of data that is juxtaposed to "physical facts," but of no less consequence. Specifically, he says:

> Psychology, as the psychology of mental facts or of mind, deals with . . . the thoughts and feelings of men and other animals; ideas, opinions, memories, hopes, fears, pleasures, pains, smells, tastes and so on through the list of states of mind. (p. 1)

Thorndike was also an explicit neuroreductionist. Sixty-four of the 350 pages of his book were dedicated to describing the anatomy and action of the nervous system. The major portion, however, both in terms of goals and page count, was concerned with determining and describing the rules governing the establishment and development of the connections between the component mental states—in other words with the associations developed as a result of experience. Today we have a common term to denote this process—we call it learning.

Associationist ideas are ubiquitous in modern neuroreductionisms. The growth of synaptic junctions as a model of learning incorporates exactly the same sorts of functional concepts that classic psychological associationism did, albeit with a different set of components and linking processes. The common principle in each case was that exercise produces increased strength of function. The ideas that the growth of synaptic efficacy depends on use and that learning proceeds by laws of *effect* or *reinforcement* (ideas central to Thorndike's associationism) are virtually indistinguishable in a conceptual sense even though one is framed in a more molar psychological terminology and the other in an elemental neurophysiological one.

Thorndike's associationism never really was displaced or replaced. Cognitive psychology and behaviorism both still accept the importance of the Laws of *Primacy*, *Recency*, *Exercise*, *Contiguity*, *Belonging*, *Effect*, and *Intensity*. Many of these major empirical laws simply became a part of later thinking in psychology, sometimes within a new medium or expressed in different words, but still conceptually unchanged. How the components in a system came to be connected was the main motivating question in associationism just as it is in that portion of modern neurophysiology directed at the question of how we learn. As such, both are inherently and fundamentally elementalist.

1.1.2 Structuralism

Predating to a degree, but also overlapping with the associationism of Thorndike and his followers, was the school of psychological theory called structuralism. Classic structuralism, like associationism, was also clearly and explicitly an analytic elementalism, the main goal of which was the search for and identification of the most primitive elements of mental experience. The main ideas of this kind of mentalism were originally developed at the University of Leipzig in Germany by Wilhelm Wundt (1832–1920), one of the first scholars who can be specifically identified as a modern scientific psychologist.[1] Wundt published an early text of physiological psychology in 1874 (the English translation of the fifth edition was translated by Titchener in 1902). He also was an active experimenter quite committed to a well controlled kind of introspection. Historians have quibbled over whether or not Wundt actually was as committed to introspection as was his successor Titchener, but Leahey (1997) made it clear that may have been nothing more than a translation error. Wundt rejected the old kind of "armchair" introspection of speculative philosophers, but was firmly committed to what he believed was a well controlled, repeatable, form of laboratory introspection using standard conditions and relatively simple responses.

The main theme of Wundt's approach to psychology was that it was a natural science and it could be studied with the standard approach of science as well as any other domain. His psychological goal was to seek out the most primitive and early forms of mental activity (i.e., immediate experience), define them, and measure them.

Wundt's student, Edward B. Titchener (1867–1927), brought a vision of psychology as a natural science to the United States, named it structuralism, and greatly expanded the use of introspection. To Titchener, as to any other mentalistically oriented psychologist, mind, consciousness, the objects of our current attentiveness, or whatever other equivalent terms one chose to use, were the appropriate subject matters of psychology. To him, the determination of the elements of these mental experiences was the main agenda of the science.

The central idea that distinguished structuralism from many other psychologies was that mental states were considered to be aggregates or a collection of many basic and very primitive psychological experience components that could be classified as sensations, images, and feelings. According to the structuralists, these elements could be accessed and analyzed in the same manner, if not with the same methods, that physical objects could be measured and analyzed. Mental units had qualitative and quantitative properties and could exist for measurable amounts of time or for measurable distances in space. Mind could be dissected in a manner analogous to the way in which anatomists, for example, picked apart a cadaver

[1]Although psychologists look on Wundt as one of them, he was always academically identified as a philosopher. The breadth of his interests, like the other great polymaths of history makes any simple classification inappropriate.

or a chemist determined the atomic components of a molecule. In short, the structuralists were extremely analytical.

It was implicit throughout the structuralist's entire program that the mental actions and their structure could be determined in detail. This, I maintain, clearly indicates that theirs was a psychology based on the fundamental assumptions of mental observability, accessibility, and analyzability. There is, however, little suggestion in the basic structuralist text (Titchener, 1899) that he considered these mental elements to be even further reducible to neural ones in practical terms. Titchener's book has few neural or other physiological allusions. It was not, it seems quite clear as his work is retrospectively examined, a physiological reductionism or analysis that Titchener championed, but a purely psychological one.

Titchener argued that the most powerful method that could be used to carry out the agenda of identifying these basic components of mentation was introspection. Effortful self-reports, controlled by careful training of subjects and fine-tuning of procedures, permitted the direct examination of their own mental processes by subjects. Titchener's commitment to the method of introspection was complete even if Wundt's had been only partial. Indeed, he believed this method to be so powerful that he argued (Titchener, 1899) that:

> There is no fact of mind, as we have defined mind, which has resisted our methods of investigation; no process of which we have been compelled to say "We cannot see any hope of accounting for this; it contradicts what we have previously said." (p. 340)

And:

> . . . within the sphere of psychology, introspection is the final and only court of appeal, that psychological evidence cannot be other than introspective evidence. (p. 341)

Interesting, Titchener was so confident of this method that he rejected any evidence of mental activity behind the stream of consciousness. Although acknowledging that there may be such entities ("many psychologists believe in their existence," p. 341) he also suggested that they are inaccessible to the science.

However strong his commitment to introspection, the major weakness of the entire structuralist approach ultimately lay in this method itself. Many criticisms have been leveled at the introspective method, but they were all manifestations of the same basic criticism—self-analysis (in the structural sense of self-discovery or self-analysis of the component acts or processes of mental action) was not feasible. This basic criticism may have been worded in many ways, but they all have the same meaning. For example:

1. Introspective subjects cannot appreciate the processes or mechanisms of their own mental processes.
2. The fundamental elements proposed by the structuralists are not available to the self-observing subject even if they do exist.
3. Introspection is not available as a research method to the student of animal or infant psychology. Nor could a scientist use introspection to study the "unconscious" mental processes that were highlighted by such popular concepts as Helmholtz's unconscious inference or Freud's repressed memories.

In spite of the fact that some forms of this basic criticism must have been known to Titchener, he totally committed the structuralist approach to the introspective study of mental states and their underlying structures. This remains a highly charged subject and perhaps the greatest weakness in the contemporary framework of the kind of cognitive psychology that dominates experimental psychology currently. Cognitive psychology attempted to ameliorate the great difficulty engendered by the introspective methodology by offering as an alternative, an objective experimental approach. Unfortunately, the methodological alternative they suggest does not resolve the fundamental issues of accessibility and analyzability any better than does introspection for some equally fundamental reasons. Sometimes, the methods used by these latter-day mentalists even obscured insight and understanding by providing answers to questions that are not what they (the questions) seem to be. In some situations, the method used to study mental processes may drive the obtained answer more than the properties of the mind they purport to probe. Those interested in digging deeper into the impact of method on results should look at the interesting book by MacKenzie (1977).

1.1.3 Cognitivism

Of all of the words in the recent lexicon of psychology, perhaps the most hapless (in the sense of unfortunate) is "cognitive." Books have been written in efforts to explain what modern cognitive psychology includes and how it is different from other earlier kinds of scientific psychology. In my opinion most such efforts fail because this neologism does not really denote anything very different from earlier schools of scientific psychology other than the new technologies and terminologies that had emerged since the second world war. It is, in other words, a word that has many predecessor synonyms.

Cognitive psychology, from the point of view of some of us, is just the current term for what has long been called experimental psychology as defined by its classical methods and content and as modified by the addition of new theoretical metaphors and techniques of investigation. It is hard for many contemporary scientific psychologists to distinguish the subject matter of this new mentalist version of our science from that of others that preceded it. It seems almost as if its introduction was more of an effort to renew (with the new and modern tools provided by information theory, cybernetics, neurophysiology, and computer science) the structuralist and associationist mentalisms that preceded behaviorism rather than to define a new intellectual approach.

The history of the cognitive revolution has been discussed and well documented in a number of books. Among the most notable of these is Gardner's (1985) treatise. Gardner not only names the psychologists who were instrumental in the development of this new point of view and the places where many of the influential meetings took place, but also details the discussions that were important to the changes that occurred in psychology and related fields at that time. I do not attempt to recapitulate that history here; it was done well enough by Gardner. However, a rhetorical question is in order. Throughout Gardner's book there is repeated allusion to the impact of the new technologies. Perhaps, it might be asked—was what distinguishes modern cognitivism from its predecessors nothing more than the adsorption of new ideas and terms from outside of psychology?

Nevertheless, let us continue the search for the essential definition of the new mentalism—cognitive psychology. Attempts to define any kind of psychological term are usually terribly strained and the results are usually very unsatisfactory. One way is to simply say it is the science that studies cognitive processes. We are then confronted with defining the term cognition. One dictionary definition is:

> **cog•ni•tion** *n.* **1.** The mental process or faculty of knowing, including aspects such as awareness, perception, reasoning, and judgment. **2.** That which comes to be known, as through perception, reasoning, or intuition; knowledge.

Clearly, cognitive psychology, both from the point of view of this lay definition and from those of the more formal professional definitions, is a mentalism and is primarily concerned with the mental processes and faculties. It deals with thought and self-awareness and "intuition" as well as "perception." Cognitivism, at its most fundamental level, accepts the reality of these mental entities as well as their accessibility and analyzability according to most modern interpretations of the field.

However, this simple lexicographic approach to defining a field of inquiry as complex as cognitive psychology leaves much to be desired. The mental terms that are invoked in the dictionary definition, as I have already noted, are themselves notoriously difficult to define and attempts to delimit their denotation usually end up being circular. Indeed, the classic first line of more than a few texts in the field is "Cognitive psychology is the study of cognitive processes" (or some equally tautological paraphrasing of this sentence).

In this context, it is quite clear that cognitive psychology is hardly either revolutionary or evolutionary. It is but another swing of the pendulum back to many of the ideas expressed by William James (1842–1910). In his magnum opus (James, 1890) James expresses the same mentalistic outlook:

> Psychology is the science of Mental Life, both of its phenomena and their conditions. The phenomena are such things as we call feelings, desires, cognitions, reasonings, decisions and the like; . . . (p. 1)

Alternatively, cognition is defined for the novice as the aggregate of all mental processes and cognitive psychology as the study of cognition. In several of my earlier books (e.g., Uttal, 1988, 1998) I apologetically offered some definitions of these terms. The lexicographic difficulties I encountered were enormous and I make no claim that I even came close to solving the problem of defining this denotatively and connotatively loaded word. Precise definitions require precise antecedent referents and conceptual anchors; unfortunately, such precision is notoriously absent when attempts are made to define mental terms.

Beyond lexicographic-type definitions, an alternative way to define any field of science is to seek out some central concept or content matter that is unique or distinctive. As is well known, one of the major forces that stimulated the emergence of modern cognitive psychology was the development of the digital computer. The computer not only provided a powerful tool for carrying out experiments and analyzing data, but it also contributed a powerful metaphor for mind and thought. The metaphor was that of the information processor—a system of sequential (and, presumably, isolatable) processing elements (both physical and procedural) that transformed information from one form to another. The brain, like the computer, was deemed to have inputs and outputs and processors that could select adaptive and appropriate responses to current stimuli and previously stored contexts. The message represented by a stimulus "input" was successively translated from one coded language to another at different stages of the process as precise transformations were applied in neat order until it emerged as a response "output." The concept of mental *information*—amounts of knowledge measured in bits (binary digits)—helped to quantify and solidify some of the earlier less quantitative ideas championed by the structuralists, in particular, but by mentalists in general.

The concepts of process and transformation themselves provided an alternative dynamism to mental processes that both included and transcended the notion of change implicit in the emphasis on learning by the traditional behaviorists. Not only could change be conceptualized and measured in behavior, but also the mechanisms of change could be dealt with inside the cognitive system by inferring hypothetical internal mechanisms. Information processing, thus, became a model for mental processing. Not only was it à la mode, but it came completely equipped with measures of quantity, quality, time, and space that were beyond the wildest aspirations of the earlier mentalist structuralists. Notions such as representation, attention, message, media, content, codes, decision making, and memory hierarchies, were added to the lexicon of sensations, perceptions, emotions, and memory.

The new vocabulary, the new technology, and perhaps most important, the new metaphor had an enormous impact. Mentalism arose from the darkness in which it has been suspended throughout the era of Behaviorism like Lazarus from the grave. Indeed, some would eventually come to define cognitive psychology entirely as "information-processing psychology" in which the main goal is to work out the details of the "program" of transformations and operators and the amount of information involved in, for example, making a decision. Thought was to be dealt with in the same way one would observe and analyze the design of a computer program.

Unfortunately, two difficulties, of which much more is said later, arise. First, a metaphor, although descriptive and perhaps even a useful heuristic, has no properties that must *necessarily* be transmitted to the analogized system. In fact, the metaphor may mislead by injecting its own properties into the discussion. By conceptualizing the mind as a computer program, the methods and techniques of that science were all too casually transferred to psychology. This is hardly unusual; virtually every prior mechanistic metaphor for mental processes (hydraulic, pneumatic, chemical, electrical, or telephonic) created the same situation and allowed the properties of the model to be erroneously introduced into the contemporary theory of mind.

Second, even if something like the mind can be functionally analogized by a mechanical model, it is not clear that it can be disassembled in the same manner as can be the model. The computer was an engineering construction built by humans from known components arranged in a manner and according to a priori rules. Even then it is considered to be difficult to reverse engineer a computer system without the head start provided by the circuit diagram and information concerning the rules of combination that had been used in its construction. The brain–mind complex provides neither a circuit diagram nor knowledge of the rules of organization and combination. There remains, furthermore, a serious question whether or not such information can be made available (see chap. 2) even with the best possible neurophysiological and psychological research tools.

Its constituent subject matter is another way to define a science. Although the selected content may differ in the emphasis given to various topics by various authors, examination of some of cognitive psychology's most important texts suggest what was fair game for its practitioners to study. For example, in what many consider to be the original text of cognitive psychology and one of the earliest explicit statements of what the field was all about, Neisser (1967) delimited the field in his Table of Contents to include:

- Iconic storage and verbal coding
- Pattern recognition
- Focal attention and figural synthesis
- Words as visual patterns
- Visual memory
- Speech perception
- Echoic memory and auditory perception
- Active verbal memory
- Sentences
- A cognitive approach to memory and thought

Twenty-seven years later, Matlin (1994) tabulates the content matter of Cognitive Psychology as follows:

- Perceptual processes
- Models of memory
- Sensory memory and short-term memory
- Long-term memory
- Imagery
- General knowledge
- Language comprehension: Listening and reading
- Language production: Speaking, writing, and bilingualism
- Problem solving, creativity, logical reasoning, and decision making
- Cognitive development

The words differ over time; some old terms have been dropped and some new words have been added, but there is surprisingly little difference in the content incorporated into cognitive psychology in these two books. One additional aspect of these tabulations is that they both cover virtually the same range of topics in which psychologists have been interested throughout the history of the science.

The attempt to define cognitive psychology in terms of its content or from a dictionary should not be used as a substitute for the identification of its foundation axioms, however. As one looks over these definitions and tabulations it is clear that the main theme that distinguishes cognitivism are its answers to the question of whether or not high level mental processes are accessible and can be analyzed into their components by experimental procedures. Not only is the observability and accessibility of mental processes accepted by cognitivists but so, too, is the ability of their methodology to reduce mind to the smallest components of which mental experience is constructed. If any single premise (beyond the central idea of cognitive accessibility) characterizes modern cognitive psychology, it is its near universal acceptance of the possibility of reducing mind to mental processing elements.

Another way to help us toward an understanding of the nature of contemporary cognitive psychology is to look at its intellectual roots. Two books, in particular, are usually identified as having been seminal in the creation of the modern version of this school of psychology. They are Neisser's (1967) book (already mentioned), and a much less "texty" tome entitled *Plans and the Structure of Behavior* by Miller, Galanter, and Pribram (1960).

Before I discuss these two books, which were so influential in determining the course of modern scientific psychology, it is of interest to note that there was another book of a very similar genre that seems to have had absolutely no influence. Surprenant and Neath (1997) wrote a very interesting article pointing out that there had been another book entitled *Cognitive Psychology* published 28 years earlier than Neisser's (1967) book. T. F. Moore (1939) was the author of this forgotten work. According to Surprenant and Neath, Moore's book covered much of the same material, anticipated many of the same ideas, and expressed a point of view that was generally quite compatible with contemporary cognitive theory.

One must ask, then, why was it not an important milestone in the history of cognition? The answers are the obvious ones. According to Surprenant and Neath, the book was, first, an anachronism. It was simply unsupported by the technological and theoretical advances that provided a foundation for the modern version of cognitive psychology. Second it had the unfortunate timing to be published in 1939 between Woodworth's (1938) and McGeoch's (1942) texts, both of which were very well received. Third, behaviorism was at its peak of popularity at this time and the alternative approach suggested by Moore simply fell on deaf ears. Fourth, there was all too much philosophy in Moore's book (he was a Benedictine monk) for a science that was still trying to separate itself from its philosophical ancestry.

Now, with this piece of historical esoterica noted, let us consider the more influential origins of what was ultimately to be the transformation to the new cognitivism. Miller, Galanter, and Pribram (1960) were aware of and concerned with the changes that were occurring in scientific psychology at a time that in retrospect we now realize was actually the interface between behaviorism and cognitivism. They were dissatisfied with the prevailing behaviorist zeitgeist and the limited range of topics that was considered by behaviorists of that time to be acceptable objects of psychological study. The key idea of their new conceptualization was that there had to be "some mediating organization of [past] experience" (p. 8) to account for the complexities of human behavior. These three psychologists named that mediating organization the *image*. The image in their model plays much the same role as the *schema* proposed earlier by Bartlett (1932) or the various forms of psychological *framework* theories suggested by many other theoreticians over the years.

The image and its accouterments—*plans* and the *TOTE* unit were their proposed hypothetical mechanisms. The TOTE unit (Test-Operate-Test-Exit) was a cognitive generalization and elaboration of the Sherringtonian reflex arc. It was not intended to represent a physiological unit but, rather, a psychological or mental building block that mirrored some of the important ideas of the time—cybernetics, information, control—developed by Shannon and Weaver (1949) and Wiener (1948) among others. If the TOTE unit, was a metaphorical cognitive building block, the *plan* was a equally hypothetical structure built up from an aggregation of those units. Obviously, another influence on their work was the pioneering conceptual model of the nervous system provided by Hebb (1949) in which he proposed the physiological mechanisms of the *cell assembly* and the *phase sequence*. These mechanisms were directly analogous to the TOTE unit and the plan even though the incipient cognitivism of Miller and his colleagues was not, in any sense of the word, a neuroreductionism.

Miller, Galanter, and Pribram appreciated that the impossibility of direct observability of such cognitive processes as the TOTE unit, but were convinced that something had to be said about the internal mediating organization of cognitive processes. To reconcile these almost antithetical ideas, they took a middle ground and identified themselves as "subjective behaviorists." It is not clear exactly what they meant by this term, but their intent was obviously to reject both classical behaviorism as well as structuralist introspection. In their place they specifically adopted an approach that required multilevel analysis and extrapolation from the "action" (behavior?) to the "processes lying immediately behind the action" (mental mechanisms and activities?). They argued that their idea of subjective behaviorism was hardly anything new, but was what all psychologists must do if they have any desire to go beyond the "what" of raw behavior to understanding the "why" of the underlying cognitive processes. In so doing, they committed both themselves and most of the rest of the next half century of scientific psychology to the grip of a new mentalism.

From my point of view, Miller et al. (1960), although well aware of the great dilemma eternally faced by psychology, were retreating from the positivist and operationalist standards of the then current behaviorism to something that is hardly distinguishable from any other mentalism. All of the features of more classical mentalisms are there—the accessibility of mental activity, the possibility of mental reductionism, the extrapolation from behavior to hypothetical constructs such as the image, and even, although I think they would have denied it, a modified kind of introspection. With regard to the latter, they say ". . . we are willing to pay attention to what people told us about their ideas and their plans" (p. 211).

Once these compromises were made it is hard to see how the term "subjective behaviorism" implied anything more than a strong commitment to an observational and empirical paradigm for collecting data—the sine qua non of any endeavor presenting itself as a science. Nevertheless, the core concepts of behaviorism are simply no longer present in their protocognitive psychology. The compromises made in their theory took them across the fuzzy dividing region between the extreme psychological poles and dropped them unequivocally among the mentalists.

It would be inappropriate, whether one agrees with them or not, to not appreciate that their decision to embrace (and to preach) some of these nonbehaviorist criteria was one of the most important milestones in the history of modern scientific psychology. Many, many of their contemporaries were influenced by their opinions in spite of what now appears to be the intellectual inconsistencies in their logic. In doing so they helped psychology slip back along the path of least resistance—one that inevitably led to a rebirth of mentalism and an endless stream of nonsensical theories and useless therapies. However much modern cognitive psychologists would prefer not to be tagged as mentalists, it seems clear that their basic assumption of mental accessibility is consistent with other earlier schools of thought that more comfortably accepted such a designation.

Neisser (1967), in writing his comprehensive text, was able to discern in the contemporary literature a trend away from behaviorism toward something quite different; something even more mentalist and reductionist. Following the lead of Miller et al.'s (1960) influential book and Miller's (1962) subsequent text, Neisser's text mobilized an enormous amount of dissatisfaction with the then current behaviorist consensus and probably influenced more young psychologists than any other book of that time.

Neisser's book was an integration of many emerging points of view and an explosion of new research findings. Like most historically significant introductory texts it appears on the surface to be primarily a review of empirical findings, classical phenomena, and current microtheories. However, it was more than that; it expressed and consolidated a system of conceptual changes driving a major swing of the mentalist–behaviorist pendulum. Neisser helped many scholars and students to understand some of the intellectual origins of the revolution that was to become cognitive psychology. He pointed out, for example, that "Psychology, like economics, is concerned with the interdependence among certain events rather than their physical nature" (p. 7). This permitted him to ignore any neurophysiological theories and explanations throughout the book. What Neisser offered instead was a new development—the motivating, vitalizing, and central metaphorical theme of the computer program as the theoretical mechanism for the emerging cognitive psychology. Astutely, and yet curiously given this acknowledgment of the computer metaphor, Neisser rejected the computer program as a theoretical mechanism saying of computer programs that ". . . none of them does even remote justice to the complexity of human mental processes" (p. 9). It is, rather, the flow of information in and among a system of modules that provides "philosophical reassurance" for his reconceptualization of scientific psychology.

In retrospect, given the enormous amount of attention given to computational modeling in recent days by cognitive psychologists, Neisser seriously underestimated the role of this kind of theory for the science he was midwifing. On the other hand, he may have been presciently expressing a point of view that I share, namely that models and psychophysical data are neutral with regard to the underlying processes or structures. In an article (Uttal, 1990) 23 years later and in my most recent book (Uttal, 1998), I spelled out an argument asserting there were impenetrable barriers between models of all kinds and the psychological processes they purported to simulate. The main idea on which both of us apparently agree is that *simulation is not tantamount to reductive explanation.*

The basic tenets and premises of Neisser's version of the new mentalism that has come to be called cognitive psychology were provided by him (1967) in a final chapter. Specifically he postulated:

1. Stored information consists of traces of previous constructive mental (or overt) actions.
2. The primary process is a multiple activity, somewhat analogous to parallel processing in computers, which constructs crudely formed "thoughts" or "ideas" on the basis of stored information.
3. The secondary processes of directed thought and deliberate recall are like focal attention in vision. They are serial in character.
4. The executive control of thinking in the secondary process is carried out by a system analogous to the executive routine of a computer program.
5. The secondary processes themselves are mostly acquired through experience.
6. Failures to recall information which is actually in storage are like failures to notice something in the visual field. (pp. 303–304)

Implicit in this list are the fundamentals of a nonbehaviorist mentalism. These include:

1. An empiricism akin to that of the British empiricists, the associationists and the structuralists.
2. Analysis of thought processes into different types, some serial, some parallel.
3. The unwritten assumption that these mental processes can be either observed or inferred from carefully designed experiments. That is, that acceptance of mental accessibility and analyzability.

In his thoughtful history of the cognitive revolution, Gardner (1985) also attempts to define cognitive psychology by tabulating what he sees as its fundamental beliefs. Based on an extensive series of interviews with both proponents and opponents of the cognitive "revolution' Gardner lists the following characteristics of the field. In so doing, he clearly points out that although not all cognitive psychologies fit this set of criteria exactly, most share agreement with most of them. In the following paragraphs I have paraphrased and abstracted Gardner's (1985) five criteria:

1. Cognitive psychology invokes mental representations "wholly separate" from biological, neurological, sociological, or cultural levels of analysis.
2. The computer is the essential tool for both theory building and experimental testing.
3. Cognitive science deemphasizes emotions, historical, cultural, and background context effects.
4. Cognitive science gains from its interdisciplinary approach.
5. Cognitive science is a modern day epistemology growing out of the philosophical tradition. (pp. 6–7)

From my point of view, all of the last four of Gardner's criteria are secondary and incidental, as well as not being uniquely definitive of cognitive science. They mainly deal with tools—the computer and interdisciplinary interaction—that can be and are being used by virtually all spheres of human interest, inquiry, and concern—scientific or otherwise. The facts that cognitive psychology was also swept along in this great current tradition of intellectual inquiry and that cognitivism minimized the importance of emotions and other forms of consciousness certainly do not distinguish it from many other versions of scientific psychology.

Gardner's suggestion that interdisciplinary interaction is of special import for cognitive psychology also has an implication that is questionable, if not rigorously rejectable. It implies that converging results will magically allow us to penetrate that which is otherwise impenetrable. As I discussed in my recent book (Uttal, 1998) and briefly abstract in Chapter 2 of this book, we must consider that there exist barriers to explanation and bridge building that are likely to make such chimeras beyond capture, no matter how many different ways one may build a chimera trap.

Thus, we are left with Gardner's first criterion. That, of course, is the familiar and essential one. Cognitive science or cognitive psychology is a mentalism emphasizing mental terms and concepts driven by the basic assumption that the interpersonal, private cognitive processes of a human being are both accessible and analyzable into their components.

Finally, in searching for the essential identity of cognitive psychology, I turn to a finely tuned and succinct definition offered by a philosopher, Churchland (1988), who is certainly neither a mentalist nor a behaviorist, but is an astute commentator on the essence of this science. Although imperfect and leaving many loose undefined ends itself, it captures the essence of modern cognitivism perhaps as well as any single paragraph:

> The aim of cognitive psychology is to account for the various activities that constitute intelligence—perception, memory, inference, deliberation, learning, language use, motor control, and so on—by postulating a system of internal states governed by a system of computational procedures, or an interactive set of such systems governed by a set of such procedures. (p. 92)

Churchland's definition, succinct as it is, highlights all of the weaknesses and vulnerabilities of both classical and modern mentalisms. However, his defining goals are all subject to counterarguments including:

1. It (i.e., cognitive mentalism) invokes hypothetical constructs that may not exist.
2. It questionably metaphorizes mind as computation.
3. It hypothesizes internal states that are likely to be unobservable.
4. It invokes procedures and interactions that are unlikely to be unique.

This brief sketch provides an insight into the nature of cognitive psychology and some of its intellectual roots. It is clearly and indisputatively a mentalism of the same sort as structuralism and associationism, but one encrusted with new tools and methods and, perhaps even more significantly, ennobled by a wealth of new data. In their search for the mechanisms of and transformations that are carried on our thoughts or cognitions, cognitive psychologists accept the basic mentalist premise that these mental processes are both accessible and analyzable. As the relevant technology and the science have matured, the breadth of topics included in modern cognitive psychology has expanded greatly—just as would have any experimental psychological science of an older vintage. In addition to the Tables of Content listed earlier, Neisser (1967) also notes that "Such terms as sensation, perception, imagery, retention, recall, problem solving, and thinking among many others, refer to hypothetical stages or aspects of cognition." Despite Neisser's early concerns, formal models of cognitive information processing, mainly computational ones, have flourished in the belief that these models cum theories can also add insights into the mechanisms of the mind. This premise of inferentiability thus raised, however, mires us once again in that most controversial issues in psychology—the accessibility of mental processes.

Make no mistake, the last 3 decades in which cognitive mentalism has held sway has been a time in which an enormous amount of progress has been made in the psychological sciences. Of this, there is no question. However, just as enormous amounts of empirical data have accumulated, there has also been some misdirection, some invalid progress, and some apparent (rather than valid) insights into the nature of human mind–brain function and activity. Much of the empirical progress would have occurred without the cognitive program in place; some of it may not have. Still, it is not the data that is the issue here. Rather, it is the meaning of these findings and the theories to which they lead that is the issue at hand and the main concern of this book.

Now, however, let us turn our attention to the loyal opposition—the behaviorisms and related philosophical positions and psychological theories that emphasize that psychology is a science of behavior rather than of mental processes.

1.2 BEHAVIORISMS

1.2.1 A Brief Taxonomy of Behaviorisms

Many intellectual movements, traditions, and philosophies, sometimes directly and sometimes indirectly, contributed to the emergence of the predominantly nonmentalist, nonanalytic approach to psychology that came to be called behaviorism. Behaviorism did not arise *de novo* solely as a doctrinaire reaction to introspection as is sometimes asserted. Rather, it was the culmination of a long evolutionary history and a point of view that has deep roots in the history of normal science.

Kantor (1971a), one of the most prolific writers on psychological theory in this century, lists some of the most important intellectual movements that contributed to the emergence of behaviorism. His list includes:

1. The Corrigibility of Science. By this term, Kantor is referring to the fact that science, among others forms of human endeavor, is most susceptible to being corrected or modified on the basis of its experiences. Direct experience ultimately will refute the unobservable or unrepeatable in a way that is unmatched by any other human endeavor where false ideas may remain indefinitely.

2. The Materialistic Tradition. Here Kantor refers to the historical fact that materialism places mentalistic ideas into a secondary or "subservient" role leading to an emphasis on observables.

3. The Theory of Evolution. By linking humans directly to animals, the special role of such constructs as souls or minds tended to be eschewed.

4. The Development of Conditioning. The ideas and techniques of conditioning provided a model for the hierarchical development of processes that could ultimately lead to complex mental processes without any special internal processes or mechanisms that transcend plausible physical ones. (Abstracted from Kantor, 1971a, pp. 523–524)

The behaviorist approach has waxed and waned in its influence in scientific psychology in step with the prevailing attitudes concerning the nature and accessibility of the mind. If I were to continue this discussion of what behaviorism is in its simplest form, it would be to spell out "the" dictates and premises of "the" behaviorism. However, this can not be done simply because there are many different approaches to the problem that have come and gone and which could lay claim to at least a part of the connotation of what we mean by the term.

I know of three authors, Zuriff (1985), Staddon (1993), and Kantor (1971b) who have attempted the difficult task of building a taxonomy of behaviorisms. Accepting the subtle nature of the views of the various schools and the arbitrariness of any such taxonomy, Zuriff's (1985) outline is useful and I now present his list in a slightly shortened and paraphrased version.

1. *Eliminative behaviorism* hypothesizes that as scientific accounts of behavior develop, mentalistic accounts will simply be abandoned as were prescientific beliefs in demons.
2. *Methodological behaviorism* suggests that mentalistic language applies only to the private phenomenal world beyond the scope of science.
3. *Logical behaviorism* translates mentalistic statements in terms of the publicly observable conditions used to test their truth.
4. *Operational behaviorism* defines a mental concept by the operations used to measure or detect that concept. Tolman, for example, suggests that mental concepts can be identified with certain intervening variables in behavioral theories.

5. *Analytic behaviorism* refers to behavior and dispositions which serve as the criteria for the application of mental terms. (As modified from Zuriff, 1985, p. 201)

The second, equally arbitrary, taxonomy of behaviorisms I have encountered is the one offered by Staddon (1993). His classification system differs enough from Zuriff's to add to the difficulty of organizing the many different approaches to behaviorism and the ambiguity of the term. Staddon's taxonomy includes the following types:

1. CLASSICAL: The behaviorism of Watson; the objective study of behavior; no mental life, no internal states; thought is covert speech.
2. METHODOLOGICAL: The objective study of third-person behavior; the data of psychology must be intersubjectively verifiable; no theoretical proscriptions. Has been absorbed into general experimental and cognitive psychology.
3. NEO-: Hullian and post-Hullian, theoretical, group data, not dynamic.
4. RADICAL: Skinnerian behaviorism; includes behavioral approach to "mental life"; not mechanistic; internal states not permitted.
5. TELEOLOGICAL: Post-Skinnerian, purposive, close to micro-economics.
6. THEORETICAL: Post-Skinnerian, accepts internal states (the skin makes a difference); dynamic, but eclectic in choice of theoretical structures. (From Staddon, 1993, p. 17)

The details of these two taxonomies are sometimes cryptic and sometimes anachronistic (Tolman's teleological behaviorism can hardly be considered to be post-Skinnerian). Nevertheless, these two authors help move us toward an intuitive appreciation of what is generally denoted by the term behaviorism. It should also be noted that Staddon provides much more extensive analyses of the meaning of these various behaviorisms later in his book.

The taxonomic system that I like the best, however, is an older one proposed by Kantor (1971b). His classification system is much more linear historically. In his system of classifying behaviorisms he does not attempt to draw fine distinctions between contemporary versions that are only slightly different versions of each other. Rather, he emphasizes the great historical stages of this approach to psychology.

1. Archaic or Naive Behaviorism. Kantor describes Aristotle as an archaic and pioneering behaviorist. The classic Greek philosophers described

behavior in a very naturalistic way that predated any notion of mental representation.

2. Antibehaviorism. Dating from the days of Alexandria, Kantor sees a dark age of antibehaviorism emerging that lasted until the renaissance. This was the age of religion and spiritualism, of souls and gods, and of dualistic distinctions between minds and bodies. Questions of morality and the metaphysical displaced science during this epoch.

3. Prebehaviorism. The latent behaviorism of this period consisted, according to Kantor, of three distinct stages. The first stage consisted of the works of the philosophers such as Hobbes who suggested that the spiritual might also be a result of natural events. The second stage was typified by the English Empiricists who made knowledge and learning into processes that were the results of "human activities." The third stage was the Enlightenment in which man himself became the centerpiece of inquiry rather than the constructs of metaphysics and religion.

4. Protobehaviorism. This category of primitive behaviorism emerged in the 19th century and included the approaches of the classic psychophysicists (e.g., Weber and Fechner). Their essential contribution to behaviorism was to introduce the experimental method into psychological science. Although many of these early psychophysicists were still concerned with spiritual and religious issues, their methodological innovations were essential for the development of modern behaviorism.

5. Watsonian Behaviorism. Although Watson had intellectual predecessors, it is he who must be credited for laying the cornerstone and building the basic structure of what we now consider to be modern behaviorism. Nevertheless, Kantor believes that his version was still not modern behaviorism since Watson still incorporated mental concepts in his work.

6. Authentic Behaviorism. Kantor denoted the ultimate form of behaviorism as interbehaviorism, field behaviorism, or authentic behaviorism. What ever the terminology, this contemporary version was characterized as being antimentalistic in the sense that it ignored mental constructs. It also ignored the physiological underpinnings and thought of behavior as being the result of a complex interaction between the organism and many different (field) aspects of its environment. (Abstracted from Kantor, 1971b, pp. 534–548)

The bottom line of this excursion into these minitaxonomies is that there are (and have been) many varieties of behaviorism. As these taxonomies demonstrate, they do not all share the same premises and criteria. Therefore, the word *behaviorism*, like so many other terms in psychology, is a poorly defined concept.

As we did for cognition, we can search for a conventional dictionary definition, but it also does not help very much either.

> **be•hav•ior•ism** *n. Psychology* **1.** A school of psychology that confines itself to the study of observable and quantifiable aspects of behavior and excludes subjective phenomena, such as emotions or motives.

Only a few of the behavioral systems offered in the past are adequately encompassed by this simple rubric in all of their foundation premises. The definition of the term *behavior* is itself fraught with difficulties as is the loaded term "excludes" (see chap. 3). Furthermore, any attempt to define in a precise manner what is meant by "subjective" may be more of a challenge than defining behaviorism itself.

One curious fact is that the span of content covered by behaviorism is not that much different from that one suggested by the more mentalistically oriented authors. The main difference was pre-1960s behaviorism's all too heavy emphasis on learning, a topic that increasingly dominated the behaviorist's attention from the time of Watson. In his first book, however, Watson (1914) spent almost a third of his pages on sensory processes. His later work (Watson, 1924) expanded the range of topics to include emotions, talking, and thinking. Tolman (1932)—the mentalist behaviorist—was more concerned with speech and introspection, and such esoterica as "inventive ideation." Some of the older words are archaic and have been replaced by the terms found in the tables of content I presented earlier in this chapter; the technology has certainly changed—computers are now ubiquitous; the emphasis is somewhat different; but, the content of the science of psychology has remained relatively constant in terms of its subject matter regardless of the dominant point of view throughout its history.

We can also, once again, turn to Gardner (1985) for a tabulation of possible criteria that may help us to define behaviorism. Abstracting and condensing his arguments, we find the major criteria that Gardner believes characterize behaviorism.

1. Behaviorism restricts its techniques to those that are "public methods of observation."
2. Behaviorism restricts it target phenomena to observable behavior and "eschews such topics as mind, thinking, or imagination and such concepts as plans, desires, and intentions." (p. 11)
3. Behaviorism is essentially an empiricism, emphasizing the influence of the environment and early experience.

Each of these criteria, of course, also raise questions. What does "public" really mean? If we "eschew" a topic like mind, does that mean it does not exist? If it does exist, are there distinct properties that deny it the same kind of accessibility as other natural entities? If it does exist, what kind of an influence can it exert on behavior? What is the exact balance between experience and the innate forces that drive development? Is it possible to untangle them?

An interesting characterization of behaviorism was offered by Day (1980). He suggested a definition based on the following "salient features":

a. A focal interest in the study of behavior in its own right;
b. antielementalism;
c. a commitment to biological evolutionism; and
d. a commitment to materialistic determinism.

Day's list of features is not incompatible with the others and adds some new twists. However, it is not completely satisfactory because at least some of the features he highlights might be challenged by at least some behaviorists.

In sum, none of these efforts to define behaviorism help us very much in our search for understanding of both the evolution of the term—behaviorism—or a consensus meaning of it (if such a thing as a consensus can occur in this contentious field). What this particular brand of psychology *is* can probably best be approached by examining what the most significant theorists in the field said in their most important works. It is this biographical and historical method that I now use in the search for the essential aspects that define this branch of the tree of psychological theory.

1.2.2 Watson's Methodological Behaviorism

We have already seen that behaviorism, in its modern form, has a much longer history of precursors than many current psychologists appreciate. There are, furthermore, additional strands of this history that have not yet been mentioned. Biologists who were concerned with the overall behavior of the organisms they studied were clearly in this school. Jennings (1906), a well-known turn of the century zoologist, wrote in words that were clearly and indisputatively aligned with some of the latter day behaviorists when he said:

> The conscious aspect of behavior is undoubtedly more interesting [than behavior itself] but we are unable to deal directly [with such mental processes] by methods of observation and experiment. (p. v)

There was also an active school of philosophers whose intellectual stances were close to the behaviorism of later times. Consciousness was rejected as a special domain of science that could be accessed by introspection. Rather, such "neorealist" philosophers as Holt (1914) suggested that our relationship to the outside world were direct and immediate and that consciousness was always going to be private and inaccessible to external observation. A complete history of other precursors to behaviorism can be found in Leahey's (1997) excellent history of psychology.

The most appropriate psychologist, however, with whom to begin this discussion of the modern science of behaviorist psychology is certainly John B. Watson (1878–1958). Watson probably had many motives and goals that stimulated his development of his behaviorist psychology, but whatever they were, he was from all points of view the first to articulate the shape of modern behaviorism. It is, furthermore, fascinating to read his works and to observe the factors that led him to his thinking.

Perhaps it would be best to let Watson himself describe what he believes were the fundamentals of his new approach to psychology. In the first chapter of his first book (Watson, 1914) he succinctly characterized his view of Behaviorism in the following ways:

> Psychology as the behaviorist views it is a purely objective experimental branch of natural science. Its theoretical goal is the prediction and control of behavior. Introspection forms no essential part of its methods, nor is the scientific value of its data dependent on the readiness with which they lend themselves to interpretation in terms of consciousness. (p. 1)

and

> The time seems to have come when psychology must discard all reference to consciousness; when it need no longer delude itself into thinking that it is making mental states the object of observation. (p. 7)

and

> It is possible to write a science of psychology, to define it as Pillsbury does (as the "science of behavior") and never go back on the definition: never to use the terms consciousness, mental states, mind, content, will, imagery, and the like. . . . It can be done in terms of the stimulus and response, in terms of habit formation, habit integration, and the like. (p. 9)

In his introductory chapter, Watson went on to attack three other problems that he perceived to be constraining and misleading the then prevailing psychology. The first was reasoning by analogy; the second was the use of the concept of the image (i.e., a "centrally aroused sensation")—something that Watson considered to be the "most serious obstacle in the way of a free passage from structuralism to behaviorism" (p. 16); and the third was the concept of "affection." By "affection," Watson was referring to feelings and emotions in general. He believed that in spite of some efforts to merge the concepts of sensation and feeling, any attempt to do so would be futile.

As one rereads the eloquent statement of the behaviorist position presented in his first book (Watson, 1914; which was really more a text of comparative psychology than either a polemic or a logical analysis supporting his philosophy of a behaviorist psychology), one might infer that the genesis of his ideas was a purely technical reaction to the methods and limitations of structuralism. The conventional view is that Watson had directed his attention mainly at the introspective techniques and mentalist speculations of the structuralist tradition that was dominant when he began the 1914 work. However, a careful reading of his later works suggests that this may not be the entire story. It now seems clear that there were other motives driving his work of a much more personal nature. Virtually the first comment in Watson's (1924) book (where he was speaking more freely and in a somewhat less formal manner than in the 1914 text) is one in which he refers to the "religious background of current introspective psychology" (p. 3). He went on to assert that "If the fear element were dropped out of any religion, that religion could not long survive" (p. 4). In the very next paragraph he vehemently argued against the concept of the "soul" and indicated that its new incarnation in the form of the concept of consciousness is nothing more than a resurrection of classical dualistic thinking. Finally, in the latter pages of this introductory chapter, Watson made clear his point of view when he referred to the fact that religion is in the process of "being replaced among the educated by experimental ethics" (p. 18).

Watson's psychology was, therefore, quite obviously motivated by more than abstract scientific principles.[2] His is not simply a technical rebellion against the scientific status quo but another step in the centuries old debate between pluralistic and monistic philosophies. Cloaked in its scientific terminology, it is also an ontological statement in the long tradition of physicalist and positivist thinking that attempted to bring psychology into the realm of scientific analysis and physico-chemical materialism. To do so, he argued that some of the supernatural (i.e., "metaphysical" in his lexicon) and unobservable elements had to be removed from the discussion. Consciousness (the subject matter of introspective structuralists) was to Watson nothing other than the newest manifestation of the "unprovable" and "unapproachable" soul.

If this analysis of his writing is correct, Watson, whatever he was otherwise as a scientist, was also a philosopher dealing with the age-old dualism–mo-

[2]Also, see my comments on the other social and intellectual forces on Watson that led to his scientific formulation of Behaviorism later in this chapter.

nism issue. His "methodological behaviorism" is really an academically respectable materialist monism, a neo-critical alternative to traditional theological points of view. No wonder that he was confronted with such enormous critical hostility in the 1910s and 1920s in the United States when his books and other writings became well known to the public as well as to the academic community. Watson was attacking some of the most fundamental beliefs of at least some of his colleagues and certainly most of the members of the nonacademic society in which he lived. Atheism had then and has now few friends in a crypto-theocracy!

Once Watson's philosophical and theological premises were set, the logical chain to the ultimate technical nature of behaviorism was straightforward. It was not just introspection that was the target of Watson's behaviorism, it was the fundamental ontological conception of the nature of our minds that he seeks to revolutionize. Speaking of his predecessors' assumptions, Watson (1924) said:

> As a result of this major assumption that there is such a thing as consciousness and that we can analyze it by introspection, we find as many analyses as there are individual psychologists. There is no way of experimentally attacking and solving psychological problems and standardizing methods. (p. 4)

As we see later in this same book, this is a precursor to the argument that different methods all-too-often produce different answers to the questions asked by the newest mentalism—cognitive psychology. Indeed, one of the most compelling arguments against current cognitive psychology is that its findings reflect its observational methodology rather than the fundamental underlying psychobiology of the observed mental processes. This emerging fact (and its predecessor corollary in Watson's statement just quoted) adds a strong foundation to the argument that Watson may have been right in general principle and that his behaviorism (or a newer version of it) must be the way of the future.

Throughout his 1924 book, Watson presents in various places what he believes are the basic ideas of behaviorism.

- Behaviorism should study only that which can be observed.
- Consciousness is not interpersonally observable.
- We should observe only what the organism does or says.
- What the organism does or say should be observed in terms of stimulus and response.
- Observation should be conducted by means of controlled experimentation.
- We should observe the whole behavior of the organism—"the overall functioning of the parts."

- Man and animals differ only in the quantity and complexity of their behavior.

But, then, given how the behaviorist school has been interpreted over the years and the nature of his earlier statements, Watson made one of the most remarkably inconsistent assertions in the history of psychology:

> . . . saying is doing—that is behaving. Speaking overtly or to ourselves (thinking) is just as objective a type of behavior as baseball. (p. 6)

This extraordinary pronouncement makes it clear that one of the most oft heard criticisms of behaviorism—that it rejects the reality of mind and mental processes—was not a part of Watson's original thesis any more than it has been of many of the more recent versions. Thinking, cognition, thought-processes were not rejected by him as "unreal." His behaviorist viewpoint accepted their reality, but his emphasis on the "overall functioning" excludes any hope of analysis just as his emphasis on interpersonal observability minimized any hope of accessing mind.

It should be noted as we pass through this point in our argument that it was not the first expression of such in-principle barriers in science. The 19th century physiologist Emil Du Bois-Reymond (1818–1896) had repeatedly asserted that some grand problems posed by nature could not be solved. He argued that we could never know the answers to some of these "world riddles" and that the "nature of mind" was among the most intransigent. His argument was not based on some theological mystery, but rather grew out of his extreme mechanistic approach to science and his appreciation of the complexity of organic systems.

Watson obviously did not originally reject the reality of thought or other mental processes in any way. He alluded to the fact that there are two kinds of responses—the explicit and the implicit. Explicit behaviors are the obvious muscular and secretory ones that can be observed and measured directly by a suitably trained scientist. The implicit responses, which presumably include not only the hidden neurophysiological responses of the brain as we think, but thought itself, are impossible to measure. Thought processes are "difficult to observe, not because they are inherently different from the external or overt [i.e., explicit] responses, but merely because they are hidden from the eye" (Watson, 1924, p. 15). The problem of accessibility is, therefore, an epistemological one and not an ontological one. The path to direct knowledge of the mind is blocked, but the existence of mind is not denied.

There is, it must be acknowledged, the stuff of internal consistency in Watson's rejection of consciousness but acceptance of implicit "saying." Was he only asserting the inaccessibility of consciousness or was he succumbing to the same profound dilemma faced by all humans, scientists or otherwise, and failing to deal adequately with it? This great issue, not yet adjudicated by science or theology, is—how do we reconcile our passions for scientific objectivity with our own personal subjectivity? This conundrum permeates the entire history of behaviorism and, for that matter, all of scientific psychology and perhaps most of biology. The influence of our individual self-awareness is so great that it has acted like a "greased skid" for psychologists of many persuasions, forcing even the most positivist and objectivist of us back into making some kind of a Faustian deal with mentalism.

There is no question, however, that Watson's original form of behaviorism was extreme, even if he had veiled references to various kinds of mental processes scattered through his works. He suggested that behaviorists must use a scientific vocabulary that does not include even such quasi-subjective terms as "sensation, perception, image, desire, purpose, thinking, and emotion. . . ." (Watson, 1924, p. 4). In doing so he sought to remove much of the subject matter that is, from the point of view of many, essential for the understanding of human experience. "Implicit saying," however, remains an ambiguous part of his science and his philosophy.

Another somewhat disconcerting aspect of Watson's behaviorism was the inconsistency between one of his criticisms of Wundt's structuralism and his own reductionistic elementalism. Watson's early research was in the field of comparative psychology. He seems to have accepted the Pavlovian ideas of association between stimuli and responses and the development of complex patterns of these conditioned responses. His behaviorism was, in principle at least, as much an elementalist associationism as was Wundt's or Titchener's even though his methodology was very different and he did not believe that an analysis could actually be carried out. Associationism of this kind on his part is inconsistent with his assertion that observations should based on "overall functioning." His associationism, however, was an ontological statement of the fundamental nature of cognitive processes and not a part of his epistemology. As a researcher, he was more or less true to his call for a psychology that concentrated on the overall functioning of the parts.

In practicing his science, Watson thus rejected the observability of the mind and the measurability of consciousness. However, as I have just noted, this did not imply a parallel rejection of the reality of mental experience. Like all other humans, he had first-hand evidence of the existence of at least one mind. Neither, did he reject the basic psychobiological premise that mind was a function of the brain. To Watson, as to all other material monists, mind was a direct manifestation of the physiological apparatus, as real as both the measurable aspects of behavior and the physical brain itself. It was just not directly accessible to measurement.

There were many others, of course, who had contributed earlier to the evolution of this same mechanistic point of view. Jacques Loeb (1859–1924), Herman v. Helmholtz (1821–1894), Du Bois–Reymond, and Rudolf Virchow (1821–1902) were among the most famous 19th century physiologists who asserted that nonmechanistic concepts had no place in a truly scientific study of life. It was their rebellion against vitalisms and dualisms of all kinds that played an important role in the development of an objective behavioral science.

Of this group, perhaps the most interesting was the biologist Loeb. Loeb was among the most important biologists of his time in championing the idea that all biological processes had physical–chemical causes. The work for which he is best known, ingenious studies of parthenogenetic reproduction of such simple animals as sea urchins, helped us to understand the way in which sperm and eggs interact to produce higher organisms. His prescient intuitions about the role that chemicals must play in heredity ring especially true in these days of DNA and RNA.

However, it was Loeb's studies of tropisms that brought him closest to the problems faced by psychologists. Tropisms are tendencies of plants and animals to move toward particular stimuli; in other words, they represent primitive behaviors. Loeb's successful explanations of tropisms in terms of the physical and chemical forces operating to determine the behavior of simple organisms could not help but make him of relevance to the psychological community. Indeed, one of his most important papers was entitled "The Significance of Tropisms for Psychology" (Loeb, 1909/1964). Here he stakes out the mechanistic argument for physical–chemical explanations of mental phenomena. Although it is clear that his full physico-chemical and reductive agenda has not yet been achieved and may not be in the future, he still strongly influenced the thinking of many contemporary psychologists. Certainly the goals of neuroreductionists are heavily indebted to the kind of mechanistic theories that Loeb and the others championed. Equally obviously, this same kind of mechanist thinking also influenced Watson and the other behaviorists.

What, then, were the novel axioms of Watson's behaviorism. I believe that its unique and essential aspects were two in number if not one in meaning.

1. The rejection of our ability to measure consciousness and mental processes by introspective means—not their existence.
2. The reinforcement of the positivist idea that psychology could best proceed by means of an objective study of interpersonally observable behavioral responses.

Many of the other tenets of Watsonian Behaviorism turn out to be very much in the tradition of the previously existing scientific milieu. He supported elementalism, in principle, even as he asserted that analysis could not be achieved in practice; he accepted verbal responses as valid data; and he invented the concept of implicit responses (i.e., "thinking is covert saying"). None of these ideas was incompatible with earlier schemes. Indeed, they suggest that his psychology—behaviorism—was hardly revolutionary, but rather was evolutionary.

It should be noted, furthermore, that Watson's own views also evolved. In his later years, he was reputed to have taken some very extreme positions as his view of behaviorism evolved. According to some historians of psychology, Watson did subsequently deny the existence of mental processes altogether. Whatever his ultimate view of this particular issue was, it is clear that Watson' original conception of behaviorism had an enormous impact on psychology. It ultimately led to an emphasis on behavioral change, that is, learning, because changes in behavior could be measured by direct observations. It deemphasized sensation and perception because these mental experiences, it was thought at the time, required some kind of verbal mediation to be measured and, therefore, transcended the capabilities of the methodologies thought to be available to psychologists.

Finally, like many other great intellectual innovators, Watson was also a person of his times. The previous decades of American and world history were filled with other scientific and social ideas that must have influenced his thinking. John Dewey's (1859–1952) progressive effort to produce new educational methods, Charles S. Peirce's (1839–1914) and William James' (1842–1910) psychological pragmatism, and the work of the Russian behavioral physiologists Ivan M. Sechenov (1829–1905) and Ivan P. Pavlov (1849–1936) studying animals, all contributed to a changing psychological (in both senses of the word) environment.

My goal here is to concentrate on the scientific logic and arguments that led to behaviorism. I leave to professional historians such as Leahey (1997) the duties of explaining these other influences in detail. Leahey, however, in a cogent and insightful statement, did usefully summarize the social and intellectual forces that must have worked to produce Watsonian behaviorism.

> Philosophical idealism, which made the study of consciousness so important, had been replaced by pragmatism, realism, and instrumentalism, all of which denied consciousness a special, privileged place in the universe. The concept of consciousness had been reworked, becoming successively motor response, relation, and function, and could no longer be clearly differentiated from behavior. . . .
>
> Lurking behind all of these changes was the desire of psychologists to be socially useful, implying the study of behavior—what people do in society—rather than the socially useless study of sensory contents. (p. 315)

There is little to be found in Watson's original writing to indicate that he was aware of these forces. He concentrates on his disdain for the study of consciousness and the method of introspection. Nevertheless, this was the nature of the intellectual ferment out of which behaviorism was born.

1.2.3 Tolman's Mentalistic Behaviorism

Watson's strong views on the proper nature of behaviorism soon were disputed by other psychologists, some of whom claimed to be behaviorally oriented themselves. Among the most notable of these was E. C. Tolman of the University of California at Berkeley. In 1932, Tolman published his magnum opus entitled *Purposive Behavior in Animals and Man* in which he sought to alleviate some of the concerns that had been created by Watson's stringent and strict formulations of the science. By that time, of course, behaviorism was already under heavy and sustained attack by mentalist-orientated psychologists. Indeed, in the series editor's introduction to Tolman's book, Richard M. Elliot pointed out that by the 1930s:

> no psychologist today hesitates to stigmatize some of its [i.e., behaviorism's] phrases as puerile, cocksure, *simpliste*, strident, precipitate, or bootless. (p. vii)

This is probably an understatement concerning the attitudes of some psychologists of the time, particularly those who were caught up in the urge to understand human mental activity. However, it is an overstatement if it is interpreted to mean that behaviorism was dead: Behaviorism clearly had its champions, even if they were not Watsonian in a classic sense.

Tolman is usually included among the behaviorists when taxonomies of this science are developed. However, it appears that the reasons for this was more due to his appreciation that an objective science was the only hope for psychology than that he ascribed to a nonmentalist philosophical foundation. His methodology was behaviorist, in the sense that it was intended to be objective and depend on direct observables. However, the essence of his version of behaviorism was framed in terms of interaction among what can hardly be differentiated from the mental components of Thorndike's associationism or Titchener's structuralism. The emphasis in Tolman's behaviorism was quite obviously on the hypothetical constructs that had been introduced only with reluctance by Watson and other stricter behaviorists. It was in this regard that Tolman's behaviorism begins to look more like a mentalism than the austere behaviorisms that preceded it.

Tolman was clearly not an elementalist even in the ontological manner accepted by Watson, nor did he reject mental concepts. Rather, he invoked a kind of holism that incorporated motives and perceptions in an irreducible fashion. As some said, Tolman "gave the mind back to psychology." This is a strange legacy, indeed, for someone who claimed to be a behaviorist.

The question that immediately arises is—given this context, why should Tolman be considered to be a behaviorist? Or, more properly—what was his conceptualization of behaviorism? Happily, he was an indefatigable lexicographer and has left us with precise definitions of the conceptual foundations of his version of behaviorism. In the glossary of his 1932 book, we read:

> *Behaviorism.* Any type of psychology which, in contrast to mentalism, holds that "mental events" in animals and human beings can, for the purposes of science, be characterized most successfully in terms wholly of the ways in which they function to produce actual or probable behavior. (Tolman, 1932, p. 439)

Here, it must be noted that although he distinguished between behaviorism and mentalism, Tolman was clearly acknowledging at least the indirect accessibility of "mental events." What I believe he was really doing was asserting the basic objectivist argument that observation of the behavior of the organism (as opposed, for example, to introspection) is the best way to approach psychological issues. However, it was not behavior that he wanted to understand, it was the mental events that he believed could be inferred from it.

It is important to also observe here that there was no rejection of the reality of "mental events" in Tolmanian behaviorism, simply an assertion of what he believed was the best strategy with which to approach them. However, he then went on to put his personal brand on a new form of behaviorism that he believed could overcome some of the difficulties encountered by the Watsonian version. Continuing on in his glossary, we find:

> *Purposive Behaviorism,* the specific brand of behaviorism defended in this treatise, asserts that these "mental events" are to be described further as a set of intermediating variables, "immanent [*sic*] determinants" (*q.v.*) and behavior-adjustments (*q.v.*), which intermediate in the behavior-equation between environmental stimuli and initiating physiological states on the one hand and the finally resulting behavior or behavior-adjustments, on the other. (Tolman, 1932, p. 439)

With these words, Tolman clearly diverged from the conventional Watsonian behaviorism of his day and reintroduced mental processes in the form of "immanent determinants." Later he goes on to more specifically characterize this term and it becomes clear that his behaviorism was, in fact, a crypto-mentalism. His "immanent determinants" equivalents of mind became, once again, the goal of psychological science, rather than irrelevant epiphenomena of behavior. It was this new conceptualization of the mind, not the behavior, that was of primary interest to Tolman. When he particularized the meaning of "immanent determinants," it becomes even clearer that this was the case. Not only the concept, but the vocabulary as well, became mentalistic in a very conventional sense. Immanent determinants were of two kinds to Tolman—*purposes* (or, as he also refers to them—demands) and *cognitions*. Both are indisputatively mentalist terms

If there was any ameliorating escape hatch for Tolman from this crypto-mentalism, it was that he dealt with these immanent determinants not as the actual operations that produced behavior but, rather, as states of the organism that helped to clarify what the effect of a stimulus had been. To some behaviorists such as Hull, this would amount to an acceptance of unseen hypothetical constructs. To other more extreme behaviorists, however, this was a subtle distinction that came all too close to invoking mental states. The only remaining behaviorist characteristics of Tolmanian behaviorism were the methodological ones—the collection of data by behavioral observations that are available to all observers—and the molar approach. The ultimate goal of Tolman's behaviorism, therefore, was not behaviorist; it was the identification and measurement of the "immanent determinants," in other words—mental states.

The central assumption in Tolman's psychology, therefore, was his assertion that these internal states can be inferred from behavioral measurements; that they are not only real but also observable and accessible. In doing so, he joined Watson in specifically rejecting what he considered to be the sine qua non of structuralism—the idea that ". . . minds are essentially inner happenings primarily available to introspection only" (Tolman 1932, p. 451). Tolman now substituted behavioral measures for the introspective ones. However, it must be noted that the pendulum had thus swung back from Watson's rejection of the accessibility of mental processes to what had been Wundt and Titchener's and what was now Tolman's acceptance of it, albeit by means of "behavioral" rather than introspective measurements.

The rejection of introspection by Tolman, of course, was not a trivial matter; it was one of the key issues that had led from classic structuralism to behaviorism. However, this is mainly a methodological dispute over whether behavioral observations, rather than first person reports, should be the tools used to measure mind and thought. Nevertheless, it is hard to escape the inevitable conclusion of this retrospective examination. Tolman was obviously more in accord with mentalism than with behaviorism in terms of what he considered to be the "proper" subject matter of psychology.

There was another important way in which Tolman diverged from his predecessors. It had to do with the nature of the entities uncovered by behavioral observations. Watson was, like Wundt and Titchener, an elementalist in principle if not a reductionist in practice. That is, Watson believed that the behaviors he observed were, in ontological fact, composed of more microscopic or molecular, although inaccessible, elements.

Tolman, on the other hand, had a much different notion of both the observables and the inferred "immanent determinants." To Tolman, Watson's behaviorism was a "twitch-ology." Tolman held this view in spite of Watson's repeated assertion of the need to study "overall functioning." For Tolman, mental reality consisted of molar wholes with ". . . certain emergent properties of their own" (Tolman, 1932, p. 7). Psychology was now to have molar, unanalyzable mental entities as its fundamental targets of inquiry rather than microelements of sensation that characterized the approaches of Wundt, Titchener, the British Empiricists, and, to a degree, even Watson. The molar entities included both behavioral responses and the inferred internal states.

The other great theme in Tolman's system was the concept of purpose. Organisms were not simply reflexive automata. Rather, their behavior was controlled and directed by meaningful goals. Responses were characterized as being influenced by purposive or goal-directed driving forces, interactions between the goal and the behaving organism, and a preference for the short and direct over long and indirect behavioral sequences. In this regard Tolman added a version of teleological thinking to his scientific philosophy. In so doing, he raised another extremely difficult philosophical question: How does one distinguish between a purposive system and the operation of an automaton that is simply playing out either its predesigned or evolving (in response to environmental stimuli) role? The question comes in many guises, both scientific and theological, including whether or not Darwinian evolution with its "survival of the fittest" criterion represents a purposive thrust toward humankind or merely a series of random events. I have no intention of attempting to resolve this age-old debate in these pages; the point being made is that even some of the most academic issues of psychology impinge on and are impinged on by issues of enormous complexity and uncertainty from the other sciences.

This brief survey of Tolman's behaviorism only begins to introduce what obviously was later to become a major force in American psychology. Tolman, like Watson, was primarily trained as an animal psychologist. Like Watson's early book, much of Tolman's 1932 volume is filled with discussions of his research on rats. In his rejection of introspection and support of objectivism, he was clearly following in the footsteps of the earlier behaviorists. In his implicit acceptance of both the reality and the accessibility of mental processes, however, the rubric of behaviorism is stretched beyond the breaking point.

Perhaps, the main contribution that Tolman added to the behavioral tradition and thus to an expanded psychology was his molar or holist approach. He specifically noted the similarity between his concept of "mean-end-field" and the Gestalt notions of "Topologie" (Tolman, 1932, p. 179). He even goes so far as to say that the system that he presents is ". . . a sub-variety of the Gestalt Doctrine" (p. 319). Elsewhere, Tolman gives specific credit by acknowledging his debt by such phrases as ". . . we owe primarily to the Gestalt psychologists." Clearly he was both influenced by and may in return have influenced the Gestalt tradition of Kohler, Koffka, and Werthheimer.

There is another point that is usually ignored but may help to understand the changes that occurred in behaviorism. Tolman, like Watson, alludes to his own personal attitude toward religion. He points out that "I have, I believe a strong anti-theological and anti-introspectionistic bias" (Tolman, 1932, p. xviii), thus conceptually linking religion and introspection in what is clearly intended as a pejorative comment. It was in this context that he went to such an effort to define the teleological, as opposed to theological, nature of the word "purpose." Tolman extensively discussed how the term is used in his theory in a purely objective manner. Nevertheless, it is obvious that the tension between psychology and religion was a major part of the objectivist, positivist, behaviorist tradition that emerged in the first half of the 20th century in the United States. It is equally likely that it played a role in the antibehaviorist revolution just as it did in the antistructuralist one. Both Watson and Tolman made both explicit antitheological and implicit statements challenging popular beliefs. It is not too much of a stretch to interpret the m-word as the s-word. If any one has any doubt about the tension between behaviorism and religion at that time, one should take a look at the articles by Mark (1930) and Rawl (1930). Mark, for example, states that:

> The issue between Behaviorism and Religion is clear cut and definite. It resolves itself down the question, "Does man live by bread alone?" The answer of the Behaviorist is a positive "yes," while the reply of the Religionist is an equally unequivocal "no". (p. 273)

Rawl (1930) is equally emphatic, if less allegorical:

> Point by point, the central convictions of [such] a religion are negatived [sic] by radical behaviorism. (p. 298)

I believe that this tension still exists and still plays a role in defining the dominant psychology of our time.

1.2.4 Hull's Formal Behaviorism

Clark L. Hull (1884–1952) summarized his approach to behaviorism in his book *Principles of Behavior: An Introduction to Behavior Theory* (Hull, 1943). As with Watson, I find that the mature summary of one's philosophy sometimes provides the best possible and most thoughtful reconsideration of general principles. One of Hull's main points was that there is a difference between scientific empiricism (observation and description) and scientific theory (interpretation and explanation). Theories can emerge either from both induction of empirical observations or from deduction based on logical principles. The impact of this epistemological distinction on psychology in the 20th century has been profound.

Hull's own statement of the goal of his behaviorism is succinct and helps us to understand the differences that existed between his approach and those of Watson:

> It is the primary task of a molar science of behavior to isolate the basic laws or rules according to which various combinations of stimulations, arising from the state of need on the one hand and the state of the environment on the other, bring about the kind of behavior characteristic of different organisms. (p. 19)

A few key indicators in the quotation are worth discussing. First, Hull's use of the word "molar" is very important in understanding both his approach and what was a constant theme in all other behaviorisms. Once again, we read the words of a behaviorist who was *not* rejecting the existence of mind. However, he was an ardent ontological reductionist. Hull emphasized that if there were a neurophysiological science that was capable of providing reductive answers to behavioral issues, it would be mandatory, not just desirable, to incorporate it into any theory of mind and/or behavior. Unfortunately such a body of scientific knowledge was not available to him (and may never be available according to some like Du Bois-Reymond) and, therefore, for practical epistemological reasons, psychological science has to be a molar and nonreductive one. Hull was clearly not rejecting the ultimate physiological basis of any behavioral state, but rather was suggesting (as did and as will many others) that it seemed unlikely that the bridge between behavior and the essential parts of neural activity will ever be built. His argument was the same as that of the others; this impenetrable barrier was simply due to the complexity of the neural structures. Here, once again, we see evidence of the difference between the ontological stance (materialist monism) and the epistemological one (a molar theoretical, nonreductive approach) that is characteristic of many of the pioneering behaviorists. In this regard, Hull's analytic predispositions were extreme. Even though the neurophysiology of his time was too primitive to be applied more than at the grossest levels to psychology, one has the feeling that he might have easily accepted the current hyperreductionist, even eliminative, approach to psychological research.

The next key indicator of Hull's theoretical position is the term "state of need." A state of need is an intraorganism variable, or in Hull's, as well as in MacCorquodale and Meehl's, terms a "hypothetical entity" or "intervening variable." Whether conscious or not, these inner states played an important role in his conceptualization of his behaviorist psychology. In the light of the harsh and unsupportable criticism on the part of cognitive psychologists that behaviorism had rejected consciousness and thought, it must be appreciated that the hypothetical entity, not directly observable but inferable, was an acceptable part of Hullian theory. All that he required was that these inferred internal states be functionally linked to the stimulus and the response by deductive (i.e., mathematical) models.

Hull, however, specifically rejected the use of unverifiable intervening variables. Here, once again, we see a thoughtful scientist confronted with what is possibly the crux of the greatest dilemma faced by all psychologists—the determination of what is verifiable and what is convenient and desirable, but unverifiable. Indeed, Hull's functionally defined "needs" in humans were not all that conceptually distant from the assumption of consciousness in one's pet dog. Hull, apparently oblivious to this analogy, was also one of the principle psychologists who strongly argued against the scientific "sin" of anthropomorphization—the attribution of consciousness to animals because of observed analogs between their behavior and that of humans. Nevertheless, he did accept something that was operationally very close to anthropomorphization when it came to defining what could be considered to be intervening variables in humans. This set of inconsistencies in his system is, unfortunately, typical of most other psychologies as well. It is a direct result of the tension between our own self-awarenesses and the inaccessibility of the minds of others. This is the crux of the dilemma faced by all psychologies and the root source of the continuing theoretical swings between mentalisms and behaviorisms.

The word "combination" was also central to the Hullian system. Hull, the behaviorist, was, as I noted previously, like some of his predecessors, an in principle neuroreductionist. He also sought to develop formal models that summarized and organized the observations of his behavioral science in terms of the component parts of behavior—an example of what I have called cognitive reductionism. Thus, he was particularly concerned about the "theoretical despair" introduced by such "pseudo-remedies" as *emergentism* (Hull, 1943, p. 26). To Hull, emergentism was a philosophy that suggested that there was an innate kind of unanalyzability of complex systems. This view ran strongly counter to his commitment to a reductionism elementalism, again in principle if not in practice.

In philosophical summary, like many other behaviorists, Hull was an ontological monist who was well aware of the theoretical barriers that exist between neurophysiology and psychophysical measurement. In principle, he was an analytical reductionist even though he held to the necessity of the molar approach as a practical necessity at the time of his work. His work was replete with citations and examples from the physiological world. He was ambiguous with regard to the nature of internal "intervening" processes which he both believed could not be observed directly and yet which in some cases could be inferred from behavioral observations. His highly negative opinion about anthropomorphization was in contrast to his acceptance of analogous "hypothetical entities" when discussing human behavior.

Hull's major contribution was not the philosophical position he took, however. Rather, his legacy was in his emphasis on formal expression of the "basic laws or rules" of behavior. This led him to develop a mathematical representation that defined and described the action of such "intervening variables" as habit strength, stimulus generalization, and extinction. Hull was a prolific definer of inferred internal states and variables (e.g., excitatory tendency) in his system. His mathematization of many of these variables was carried to a point that was far beyond that of any of his predecessors; his formal theorizing was a harbinger of the many types of statistical, mathematical, and computational models that were developed in the decades after his work. Although the use of mathematics in psychology was not entirely novel (we must not forget either Weber or Fechner) nor was Hull's implementation of it at a level that came close to that in the physical sciences, it did set off a new wave of formal modeling in this science.

The nature of his particular mathematical approach, however, had a severe impact on the kind of topics that he believed he could study. Once again, psychology limited and constrained itself by its methodology to study only the topics that were amenable to that particular methodology. Hull's approach added to the constraints placed on psychology by his predecessors to study only the variables that were involved in the dynamic change of behavior, habit strength, and reinforcements—in other words, the variables involved in learning. It was a constraint that took psychology decades to overcome.

1.2.5 Skinner's Radical Behaviorism

B. F. Skinner (1904–1990) remains one of the most controversial figures in contemporary psychology. The reasons for this are simple. He carried behaviorism to an extreme that many other psychologists and other social scientists simply could not accept. To Skinner the essential problem faced by psychology was the scourge of "mentalism." In one of the most eloquently expository of his books (Skinner, 1974), he states:

> In its search for internal explanation, supported by the false sense of cause associated feelings and internal observations, mentalism has obscured the

environmental antecedents which would have led to a more effective analysis. (p. 165)

and

Almost all versions [of mentalism] contend that the mind is a nonphysical space in which events obey nonphysical laws. (p. 32)

What Skinner offered us in its place is his version of behaviorism, an approach that has come to be called the *Experimental Analysis of Behavior.* There are several essential characteristics of his approach that should be immediately identified. First, according to Skinner (but contrary to the attacks of many of his critics) his system did not reject the reality of mental functions, in spite of the fact that he denied mentalism a role as a satisfactory basis for a valid psychological science. Thus, although criticizing mental processes as the appropriate target of psychology, like many of his predecessors, he did not reject their reality. Second, Skinner preferred to carry out experiments on the basis of controlled stimulus conditions and observed behavioral responses. Third, he preferred to use the data obtained from single subjects rather than to pool data from many subjects.

It must be emphasized, however, that there seems to be no essential disagreement between Skinnerian behaviorism and contemporary mentalisms with regard to the reality of mental processes.[3] Nor was there anything in the Skinnerian system that denied the fundamental ontological foundation that neurophysiological mechanisms provide for mentation. Rather, his approach to psychology differed only with regard to his attitude toward the accessibility of underlying mechanism through input–output (i.e., behavioral, stimulus–response, psychophysical) experiments and the ultimate practical reducibility of mind to neurons, both of which he rejected. For example, in 1963 Skinner said:

An adequate science of behavior must consider events taking place within the skin of the organism, not as physiological mediators of behavior, but as part of behavior itself. (p. 951)

With regard to introspection, Skinner (1974) made his position clear:

Introspective knowledge of one's body—self knowledge—is defective for two reasons: the verbal community cannot bring self-descriptive behavior under the precise control of private stimuli, and there has been no opportunity for the evolution of a nervous system which would bring some important parts of the body under that control. (p. 220)

[3]Some of the material in this section is updated and adapted from my earlier work (Uttal, 1998).

Other criticisms of Skinner's behaviorism (e.g., that it was not theoretical) seem quaint in light of many of the theoretical constructions that Skinner himself used in his written work. There is no question that Skinner's radical behaviorism did not make much of a commitment to the kind of formal theorizing that typified Hull or so much of modern cognitive psychology. Indeed, his work was often presented in terms of operant conditioning curves that were not that distant from the raw data. However, another important modern behaviorist Killeen (1988) clarified the falsity of this criticism when he emphasized both Skinner's deep theoretical intuition and his repeated use of concepts such as the "reflex reserve" as models of the forces that drive behavior. Killeen also pointed out that Skinner (1953) does not deny the existence of inner states, but rather places them in another scientific context:

> The objection to inner states is not that they do not exist, but that they are not relevant in a functional analysis. (Killeen, 1984, p. 35)

From this perspective, therefore, it must be appreciated that Skinner was simply designating both mental and physiological mechanisms as being irrelevant to the study of behavior, not denying the reality of either domain. It was the epistemological issues concerning the inappropriateness of the strategies of mentalism and neuroreductionism, not the ontological issue of the existence of the mind or the brain, that were the foundations of his behaviorism. In this light, it is clear that the essence of Skinnerian behaviorism was that theories should be formulated in the concepts, terms, and logical units (i.e., the language) of the same level whence came the empirical observations. The influence of his logical positivist and operationalist philosophical heritage is apparent when viewed from this point, as is, of course, the influence of his behaviorist predecessors.

To Skinner, physiology was an important but generally invisible intermediate stage of processing interspersed between the ultimate source—the forces exerted by the physical substrate—and behavior. If one keeps the two issues—materialist monism and reductionism, one reality and one strategy—separate, one can accept the former although rejecting the latter. It is, in other words, possible to have materialism without reductionism. The task is to keep our ontology and our epistemology separate.

In concluding this review of some of the better known proponents of the approach to psychological science that has come to be called behaviorism, it should also be pointed out that although these psychologists are among the best known, there were many others who identified themselves as behaviorists. The interested reader is directed to Marx and Hillix (1973), Boring (1950), Day (1980), Smith (1986), Lee (1988), Leahey (1997), and others for a fuller rendition of the many contributors to this field and its history. Therefore, make no mistake, this approach to scientific psychology was not the result of the idiosyncrasies of a few eccentrics, but it was the main theme of scientific psychology for much of this century and probably back much further into our protopsychological history.

It is also important to appreciate that behaviorism is not dead today in scientific psychology. There are many proponents of the approach including Staddon (1993), Kimble (1996), Killeen (1992, 1995), others mentioned throughout this book, and, of course, your current guide through some of the conceptual intricacies of this field. Some of us also think that it may be the main theme of the next wave of scientific psychology.

1.3 SOME RELATED SCHOOLS OF THOUGHT

There is no question that throughout history the dominant solutions proposed by the majority of laypersons, contemplative philosophers, and scientific psychologists have been various versions of analytic mentalism. For centuries it was taken as divinely bestowed that the mind or soul was real and that it could be observed and analyzed, indeed dealt with in many different ways, separately from the physical body. In more recent times, without necessarily accepting these dualistic ideas from earlier times, the perception of our own individual consciousness has been a powerful force that has led many serious scholars to consider the study of mental events to be both timely and of great import. Not only has our own self-awareness been influential, but so, too, has been the conceptualization of the mind as an aggregate of relatively independent functions and parts. Human qualities of intelligence, talent, acquisitiveness, pain, and emotion as well as perception, learning, and decision making, all were part of the folk philosophy of virtually all cultures. At an even finer level, conduction times, decision times, and stimulus identification times on the one hand and, short-, medium-, and long-term memory on the other have been a part of the lexicon of scientific psychology throughout most of its recent history. This elementalist approach persists, indeed dominates, to this day and dictates much of what we currently do in psychological research. This has not always been the case, however, and to understand what contemporary psychology is today, we must examine more of the past.

In addition to those already discussed, the distant roots of modern behaviorism can also be discerned in the emergence of the scientific method in the 16th and 17th centuries with the works of Francis Bacon (1561–1626), Rene Descartes (1596–1650), Galileo Galilei (1564–1642), and, somewhat later, Isaac Newton (1642–1727). Although these great men of science are not usually specifically linked with what later came to be called behaviorism, they certainly laid the conceptual groundwork for their successors by stressing the objective scientific method as a more powerful approach to understanding the nature of nature than the philosophical speculations of the past. A new way of thinking about science in general and ultimately about psychology in particular arose from the scientific revolutions that each of these influential scholars created. For the first time in human history the foundations were laid for a scientific approach to this central aspect of human existence—our thoughts as well as our behaviors. The essence of this new approach was its replacement of the speculative with the experimental. Such an approach to mind was, at first, anathema even to some of these great scientists who, in accord with their times, were often religious zealots if not spiritualists. Eventually the step was taken toward a nontheological approach to mind by a number of philosophies.

The specific historical influences on behaviorism of the philosophies that I now consider is sometimes disputed. All of these perspectives and world points-of-view do, however, share some common features with behaviorism as it developed in the United States. Some historians argue that Bridgman's operationalism or the Heisenberg uncertainty principle, as two of the most notable examples, had no direct impact on psychology. Others feel they had a strong influence. I must leave the final resolution of these controversies to others. But, the varieties of positivisms I now discuss certainly share with behaviorism the championing of an objective approach to any science. As we shall see, objectivity has direct implications for both the accessibility and the analyzability questions.

1.3.1 Positivism

Among the earliest of the positivist philosophies, influential or merely analogous, was positivism itself. The term *positivism* seems first to have been used by Auguste Comte (1798–1857) in the early part of the 19th century. Comte was particularly concerned about the evolution of explanatory thought. The progression, he asserted, originally started with the earliest theological or religious theories of existence. At this stage behavior was assumed to be driven by entities with psychologies much like our own, although much more powerful. Tree-sprites, demons, angels, gods, and many other supernatural but personalized entities fill out the *dramatis personae* of this initial approach to explaining human nature and its interactions with its environment. This first stage was followed by a "metaphysical" (his use of the term) approach to explanation in which inner psychological forces of a less personal kind were assumed to drive behavior. These forces (e.g., curiosity, hunger, and lust) were inferred from what the organism was doing, that is, from its behavior. Finally, in the last and ideal stage of explanation—Comte's positivist stage—science sought to explain without inferring the existence of any of these mysterious underlying forces. Rather, the goal of this ultimate stage of explanation was merely to describe the relations among the observable antecedents and resultants. No longer, at this ultimate stage of explanation, Comte suggested, was there any need for what he believed was a futile search for "first causes." Nor were scientists required to futilely seek complete reductive explanations of events that could only be indirectly observed.

The conceptual, if not the specific historical, links between this philosophy of science and behaviorism are obvious. Nevertheless, it is interesting to note that although his impact on psychological thinking (as the father of positivism) was enormous, Comte felt it was impossible to have a science of psychology. Perhaps it was because most "psychologies" (or at least the philosophies of mind then prevalent) were introspective and clearly violated his notions of what the highest stage of science should be like.

1.3.2 Objectivism

As usual, nothing arises out of thin air and there were predecessors that incorporated many of the ideas of Comte's positivism. Positivism was an evolutionary continuation of even earlier efforts to standardize science. Objectivism—the idea that one should ignore anything that depended on subjective judgments from the observer (or in the case of psychology—the self-observing subject)—had been emerging as a central idea in philosophy and natural science. Pierre-Jean Cabanis (1757–1808) was the leader of a group of French philosophers—the *ideologues*—whose philosophy was based on the rather modern idea that mental processes were manifestations of the action of the material brain. It seems clear that the ideologues should be placed in the tradition that led from Hobbes and his "mechanical" approach, to the British empiricists, and thence to the intellectual stream that led to the positivists, and on to Wundt and Titchener's elementalist mentalism as well as to behaviorism. Cabanis was one of the first to express the idea that all mental processes could be understood in terms of simple sensations. In adhering to their neuroreductionist ideas, clearly members of the Cabanis school were both physicalist and reductionistic.

1.3.3 Empirocriticism

Another important personage in the succession to what was to become the behaviorist tradition was the 19th-century philosopher Richard Avenarius (1843–1896). Avenarius was one of the first to specifically eschew the introspective method and suggest that only the most basic direct perceptions, unmodified by either the subject's or the scientist's interpretations, were useful in any attempt to understand human thought. To the followers of Avenarius' "empirocriticism," only the most direct indicators of perception were acceptable as data. Subjective interpretations of one's thought processes, it was asserted would be, at best, misleading and, at worst, false. Although he was certainly an early protopositivist, Avenarius seems to have been willing to accept verbal reports of direct perceptions, only asserting that any elaboration of these basic experiences was not satisfactory as scientific data.

1.3.4 Mach's Eclecticism

Ernst Mach (1838–1916), an extraordinary polymath and contemporary of Avenarius, may be considered to be the next significant figure in the historical trail leading to modern behaviorism. Mach was a scientist of extraordinary breadth; his name is now attached to phenomena in the physical (e.g., the Mach number) as well as the perceptual sciences (e.g., the Mach band). Like many of these other precursor and pioneer contributors to behaviorism, Mach does not fit exactly into its modern definition. From one point of view, he was a neuroreductionist who provided one of the first neural network models. He suggested that the illusory bands occurring at the edge of a brightness ramp were caused by inhibitory interactions between discrete neurons in the retina. Ratliff (1965) described this neural model in great detail.

In spite of this neuroreductionist contribution, Mach's main philosophical stance has always placed him among the positivists (Leahey, 1997). In the context of the present discussion, this meant that he believed that science cannot make inferences about internal mechanisms. In his most important works he repeatedly refers to the idea that the goal of science is to describe, predict, and control nature and not to hypothesize about internal, but invisible mechanisms. In so doing, Mach was rejecting the role of the kind of *ex post facto*, hypothetical, reductive analysis that permeates past and present mentalisms. Mach's attitude toward theories was prototypically modern. For him, theories were merely temporary substitutes for more direct kinds of explanation—the direct relation between our sensations and the observed phenomena that is measured in a psychophysical experiment. The descriptive theory was not intended by him to be a reductive explanation, but rather only a formal description or metaphor that may (or may not) help us to predict or to understand or to control. I have earlier (Uttal, 1990, 1998) asserted general agreement with this point of view; there are barriers of profound and numerous kinds between models and mechanisms. Perhaps, if Mach were with us today, he too would be championing the need for revitalizing behaviorism.

In conclusion, for Mach it was only necessary to describe the phenomena by providing analogues to our sensations or mathematical models that related variables and described processes in a compact form. Clearly, this is one of the most important issues in science and is at the heart of discussion in this book. It is necessary to acknowledge that most scientists today accept the fact that we can and do make inferences about the invisible, inaccessible, and unobservable. It is not necessary, however, to accept the fact that the argument is settled.

1.3.5 The Uncertainty Principle

If modern physics was not positivist by definition or antecedent, it certainly had practitioners who were at the same time developing ideas that could support the trend toward an objective behaviorism. Werner Heisenberg (1901–1976), for example, provided one of the most persistent icons of modern thought when he proclaimed the *uncertainty principle.* There, he (Heisenberg, 1927) proposed that the position and energy (or momentum) of a subatomic particle could not be simultaneously measured. This uncertainty arose because the measurement of one attribute affected the measurement of the other. On the basis of this principle, he proclaimed that the internal structure of subatomic particles could never be definitively evaluated. The Heisenberg principle was one of the first to define an in-principle barrier to accessibility and analysis in any science.

The uncertainty principle proposed by Heisenberg is about ultramicroscopic events that are far removed from the psychological domain. Nevertheless, the uncertainty principle cum principle has managed to make its way from physics to psychology in a remarkable manner. One of the reasons that the transition from one field of science to the other was so easy was that the germ of the idea was already there. Philosophers like Comte had suggested that, in order to study one's own thoughts, one had to stop thinking what one had been thinking and think *about* what one had been thinking. Obviously, therein lay a latent psychological uncertainty principle.

Heisenberg's postulation of the physical principle of uncertainty provided a cogent and compelling example of the external effects of the measuring process on the measurement itself. Deeply impressed by the apparent generality of this concept, some nonmentalist psychologists went on to assert that there may be boundaries to and limits of the potential measurement of cognitive processes, just as there are to physical ones. How can you ask a subject a question without affecting the subject's state of mind? Having suggested in the physical world that there are some unanalyzabilities because of fundamental principle, is it not possible that there are some equally impossible goals at the psychological level? This may have been another one of the intellectual steps in the chain of logic from the earliest positivisms to the behaviorisms.

Given the differences in scale between the two levels of discourse—the ultramicroscopic and the psychological, there can be no rigorous proof of such a psychological uncertainty conjecture based specifically on the one available in fundamental particle physics or, for that matter, any other set of formal principles. Nevertheless, the heuristic is compelling. Given the possibility of impossibility in one science, and particularly in one as fundamental as basic particle physics, why should not the general principle apply at other levels?

The germ of the idea that the measurement can affect the measured can also be found in earlier psychological times. William James (1842–1910) described a similar problem—the "psychologist's fallacy." James (1890) saw two versions of this difficulty. The first version is the psychologist's confusion of his own mental processes with the mental process he is studying. He says:

> He himself, meanwhile, knowing the [mental] object in *his* way, gets easily led to suppose that the thought, which is *of* it, knows it in the same way in which he knows it, although this is often very far from being the case. (p. 196)

James sums up the second version of the psychologist's fallacy as follows:

> Another variety of the psychologist's fallacy is the assumption that the mental state studied must be conscious of itself as the psychologist is conscious of it. (p. 197)

One can argue whether these somewhat cryptic comments have exactly the same meaning for psychology as Heisenberg's uncertainty principle did for physics. There is no question, however, that both ideas suggest a fundamental barrier to accessibility for their respective sciences.

1.3.6 Operationalism

Another physicist who may have played a later, but significant, role in the evolution of psychological thinking was P. W. Bridgman (1882–1961). Bridgman (1927) early on argued that all scientific concepts were strictly equivalent to the operations or procedures that are used to measure them. He states that:

> In general, we mean by any concept nothing more than a set of operations; *the concept is synonymous with the corresponding set of operations.* If the concept is physical, as of length, the operations are actual physical operations, namely those by which length is measured; or if the concept is mental, as of mathematical continuity, the operations are mental operations, namely those by which we determine whether a given aggregate of magnitudes is continuous. (p. 5; italics added)

Bridgman asserted that if these operations cannot be defined, then the measurements as well as the concept are meaningless. The implication is what should by now be a familiar assertion—science should not create or infer entities that cannot be measured by well-defined procedures. On the other hand, he points to two other important implications of the operational approach—all knowledge is relative and that it is terribly easy, if one ignores operational definitions, to invent "meaningless questions."

Operationalism, of course, leaves a lot of leeway in its interpretation as does any other approach. What is a well-defined operation? Are atoms, for example, measured by well-defined operations or are they hypothetical constructs invented or inferred to add tangibility to our thoughts? The emphasis, however, is important.

How conceptually compatible this point of view is with the teachings of the behaviorists, the logical positivists, and others who also sought a more objective approach to science! Although Bridgman himself only applied this principle to physical entities, his philosophy immediately became of interest and relevance to discussions of the nature of psychological inquiry. Stevens (1935) was directly influenced by Bridgman's work to introduce it as a panacea for the pendular swings and continuous series of intellectual revolutions that regularly afflicted psychology. A more complete discussion of the implications of operationalism on psychology is given by Leahey (1997).

Not all scholars agree, however, that operationalism has actually played or should have played a significant role in psychology. Koch (1992) was particularly critical of how most psychologists had misinterpreted Bridgman's analysis. He pointed out that Bridgman was really trying to formalize methods to study entities that already existed in physical science. Bridgman, according to Koch, was interested in developing a means of analysis and not in defining objects or constructs that had no other reality. It was only the superficial similarity between psychologists' misreading of Bridgman and the behaviorist emphasis on objectivity that led him to become an icon for psychologists. It was also important to psychologists that Bridgman was a physicist. According to Koch:

> Experimental psychologists have traditionally suffered from a syndrome known as hypermanic physiophilia (with quantificophrenic delusions and methodico-echolalic complications). (p 264)

As a result of the collective susceptibility of my colleagues to this syndrome, he argued that they uncritically and without careful reading of what Bridgman really said, adopted a distorted idea of what his operationalism meant.

It is also important to remember that Koch was, at the end of his career, an arch foe of behaviorism. One cannot read his article without some amusement as well as respect for his inventive command of the English language. Clearly his view of the interaction between psychology and operationalism deserves attention. Furthermore, Koch was not the sole voice crying in the theoretical wilderness. Green (1992) also argued that operationalism has been rejected, in his opinion, by most philosophers, yet continues to be taught by psychology. The problem, he asserted, is special to psychology because of the difficulty of defining psychological entities such as thought, emotion, perception, or decision making. Behavioral psychologists offered what they saw as a way out of this dilemma—definition in terms of the methods (i.e., operations) rather than in terms of any intuitive insights or specious inferences into the real nature of the mental process. Today, at least a few of us contend that although some psychologists may have misinterpreted Bridgman's intent, psychological operationalism still has some utility as the pendulum swings back from mentalism to some revitalized and revised behaviorism.

Operationalism, like most of the other ideas I have been discussing, did not spring full blown from nothing. We must also acknowledge the earlier contribution of the mathematician J. H. Poincaré (1854–1912) to a related, but earlier, line of thought. Poincaré's contribution lies in his expression the difference between mathematics and the physical world. He pointed out the that logic of mathematics and that of the physical (including the biological) world may be very different. Mathematics may allow for some kinds of analysis of symbolic representations that may not be achievable in a finite length of time with real physical systems.

This theme—that mathematics and physical–biological reality cannot be approached in the same way—has been recently re-expressed by Casti (1996) in a slightly different, but reversed, form. Casti points out that although some *mathematical problems* describing real systems are intractable (i.e., for either practical reasons, such as combinatorial complexity, or reasons of fundamental principle, such as the actual unavailability of the necessary information) real *physical systems* can and regularly do carry out the very same operation that was deemed to be mathematically unsolvable. This is probably more due to the fact that real systems are true parallel processing entities unencumbered by any limits on processing complexity or intercomponent communication times than to the logical limitations of mathematics per se. Real systems, therefore, can be considered to represent parallel processing, self-representing "computers" of virtually unlimited power. No matter how inadequate some other representation may be (e.g., a mathematical or computational model) the thing itself may be considered an analog computer in which the relations among the components are physically instantiated and the "problem" allowed to run its course.

Thus, both Poincaré and Casti saw differences between formal mathematical models based on both the inductive accumulation of empirical data and a set of rules, on the one hand, and the actual physical entities that gave rise to the phenomena being measured, on the other. This is also one of the main themes of a nonanalytic behaviorism and may possibly have been significant in some indirect way to later conceptualizations of psychological problems. Certainly the interplay between these philosophical inquiries into the nature of the relationship between mathematics and reality are germane to the topics I consider in this book.

1.3.7 Logical Positivism

Among the contemporaries of modern behaviorism were the logical positivists of the so-called Vienna circle. This most interesting group of philosophers included such eminent names as Moritz Schlick (1882–1936), Otto Neurath (1882–1945), Herbert Feigl (1882–1988), Rudolf Carnap (1891–1970), and Kurt Godel (1906–1978) as well as others who have not been dealt with quite so well by history. Other important contemporary philosophers, including Ludwig Wittgenstein (1889–1951) and Karl Popper (1992–1994), actively interacted with the Vienna group. The logical positivists were active from the early 1900s until the late 1930s and thus overlapped with the behaviorist revolution.

The central ideas of this group of philosophers are very similar in many regards to those characterizing the behavioral revolution. One of the central tenets of logical positivism was what was referred to as the *verifiability principle*—the idea that the truth of some observation was equivalent to the method used to obtain it. This, of course, is also close to the concept of operationalism suggested by Bridgman (1927). It is also very close to some of the behaviorist ideas that I have been discussing that argue externally observed behavior and its control and measurement are all that can be accomplished in psychology. Skinner, even if not identified as such, came close to this concept in defining his radical behaviorism as little more than the operant data itself and the methods used to measure them. Operationalists, behaviorists, and logical positivists all sought to remove as many unobservable mentalist, internal, and supernatural concepts, entities, and events from the discussion as possible.

The logical positivists also distinguished between logical and factual truths. This subtlety has persevered (even though the school itself has passed from the scene) in the form of arguments concerning the neutrality of theories, percepts, and models as discussed earlier in this chapter. Curiously, given the many formal similarities between behaviorism and the logical positivist school of philosophy there is little evidence that American behaviorism was directly influenced by the Vienna circle or any other proponent of logical positivism. Behaviorism antedated the development of the logical positivist school by several years. Nevertheless, it is hard to discuss one without the other given how parallel were their fundamental assumptions and premises. The main principle that ties them together is a shared commitment (along with Bridgman's operationalism) to objectivity that assumes that "things" are either verifiable by observation or they are "metaphysical nonsense." The likelihood is that both were influenced by some of the common intellectual ancestors we have already described.

Smith (1986), in one of the best considerations of the interactions between the two traditions, pointed out the following additional similarities:

1. The thrust of both movements was more methodological than substantive.
2. The proponents of both behaviorism and logical positivism depicted their movements as turning points in the history of their disciplines.
3. The common conviction ... that eliminating historical problems from consideration would clear the way for the achievement of steady piecemeal progress. (p. 4)

Although these "personality" characteristics of the two movements don't define their common fundamental principles, another similarity is that they both declined at approximately the same time for reasons that may have been very similar.

For more discussion of their mutual decline, my readers are referred to pp. 114–115 in Chapter 3.

1.3.8 Gestaltism[4]

I have shown earlier in this book how the holism–elementalism issue was instantiated in debates concerning the analyzability of mental processes. Some behaviorists, such as Watson, deviated very little from an "in principle" acceptance of the earlier structuralist elementalism. Others, such as Tolman, responded to what were certainly strong pressures from other areas of psychology (other than comparative) to reintroduce molar concepts. The timing is certainly relevant in this case: Watson's immediate predecessors were members of the Titchenerian school. Tolman, on the other hand, as we have seen, was a contemporary and heavily influenced by the German school that came to be known as Gestaltism.

The concept that complete understanding of a complex event could only be achieved by analysis of the event into ever simpler components was a key premise of the associationist, structuralist, and at least some behaviorist theories of perception. In so doing, they adhered to an ele-

---

[4]Some of the material in this section on Gestaltism is updated and adapted from my earlier work (Uttal, 1981).

mentalist and reductionist philosophy that has long influenced psychological thinking. Developing parallel to this analytical theme, however, was a diametrically opposed viewpoint that stressed the overall configuration of the stimulus pattern rather than the elements of which it was composed. Immanuel Kant (1724–1804), for example, stressed the idea that the act of perception was not a passive concatenation of individual ideas to produce perceptions but rather an active processing of the information communicated by the overall stimulus pattern. In other words, he stressed the "melody" rather than the "notes" of the symphony of perceptual experience. In doing so he implicitly suggested the vital importance of the pattern itself without rejecting the fundamental elementalism implicit in the associationist philosophy.

Similarly, Ernst Mach (1838–1916) and Christian von Ehrenfels (1859–1932) both made singularly important contributions by suggesting, more or less independently, that, in addition to the elemental sensory qualities and properties already considered by the associationist and elementalist tradition, there were other properties that could be defined in terms of the overall spatial and temporal form of stimulus patterns and sequences. Both Mach and von Ehrenfels alluded to the emergentist idea that these global properties contained more information than did the sum of their parts. Thus, they asserted that the properties of patterns transcended any simple arithmetic summation of the properties of the separate components.

Another important antecedent of modern holist psychology can be discerned in the writing of Thomas Reid (1710–1796). According to Robinson (1976), Reid was one of the earliest to develop the idea of the relations among the parts as a central theme in perception. Another who argued that we perceive by a process of analysis "from the whole to its parts" was William Hamilton (1788–1856) thus also contributing to the molar tradition that came to be called Gestalt psychology.

The essence of this emerging new configurationist school of thought revolved around the radically different (compared to the associationist–structuralist tradition) approach their molar philosophy took with regard to the problem of the nature of the relationships between the whole and the parts in determining perceptual experience. The molar school of thought ultimately crystallized in the Gestalt (best translated as "pattern" or "structure") theories under the leadership of Max Wertheimer (1880–1943), Kurt Koffka (1886–1941), and Wolfgang Kohler (1887–1967) in the first half of the 20th century, first in Germany and then, after the dismal days of 1933, in the United States.

The essential premise of this new Gestalt school of thought, which most sharply distinguished it from the structuralism of Wundt or Titchener or even Watson's Behaviorism, was its vigorous adherence to the notion that the global configuration of the stimulus was neither just another property of the stimulus nor the sum of the parts of which it was composed. Rather the central dogma of Gestalt psychology was that the overall form of a pattern was the foundation of not only perceptions but also all other mental processes and acts. In this regard the Gestalt theory was obviously a strong reaction to the associationist and structuralist idea that combination of the sensory elements, the features of a stimulus, or the details of the retinal mosaic were the most influential determinants of perception. It was, also in principle, totally antagonistic to any reductionist aspirations exhibited by the structuralists.

The Gestalt psychologists carried out a large number of experiments demonstrating the important role of the global stimulus pattern and what they believed to be the lesser role played by the individual components. Many of their experiments were nonquantitative, however, in that they were often unique demonstrations that made some point concerning the global pattern without exploring the effect of varying the salient dimensions. Often these demonstrations were not suitable for parametric experimental manipulation nor did the experimental protocol provide an adequate degree of control over the full range of the salient stimulus dimension. The most challenging problem faced by the Gestalt psychologists, however, was the definition and measurement of a Gestalt itself. "Form," unfortunately, was as poorly quantified then as it is now, and thus this centerpiece of Gestalt theory was never adequately quantified in their experiments. As a result, this configurationist approach was at odds in many ways with the quantitative and reductionistic tradition of modern cognitive psychology. Theory was terribly inhibited when both definition and units of measurement were obscure or unavailable. Efforts (Attneave & Arnoult, 1956; Brown & Owen, 1967; Leeuwenberg, 1971) to quantify, and thus to rigorously define form, remain unsatisfying. These methods typically do not uniquely define a form; they usually only classify categories of forms. Thus, Gestaltism of the kind practiced in the heady days of the 1930s and 1940s was primarily a phenomenological and descriptive science.

What the Gestalt psychologists did contribute, and what remains their major legacy to modern scientific psychology, is their emphasis on the global, holistic, or molar (all synonyms as I use them here) attributes in a science that had previously been so heavily dominated by an elementalist tradition. Whether or not the particular Gestalt data base or theory was totally incorrect or not is almost beside the point; the Gestaltists called attention to an important alternative way to explore not only perception (their main interest) but all of the many topics now of concern to both cognitive and behavioral psychology.

Beyond their well known and widely accepted set of descriptive principles governing grouping, Gestalt perceptual theory also made one colossal theoretical error in a neuroreductive sense. It associated itself with a specific molar physiological model that proposed that the actual neural representations of perceptual processes were nothing other than isomorphic electrotonic brain fields. There are two main premises of this holistic neural theory of perception that should be kept separate—(1) the physiological idea of neuroelectric fields and (2) the linking hypothesis asserting the necessity of isomorphism of the percept and the brain field.

First, in accord with the general adherence to molar processes, the standard Gestalt brain theory strongly supported (with very little hard evidence that this was so) the idea that it was the overall field of brain action, rather than the action of individual neurons, that was critically important in the representation of psychological function. However, it was later definitively shown (Lashley, Chow, & Semmes, 1951; Sperry, Miner, & Myers, 1955) that these fields of electrical activity in the brain could not possibly account for perceptual phenomena. Metal foils and pins inserted into the brain in a way that would certainly have short-circuited any neuroelectric field seemed to have little effect on any behavioral measures of perceptual responses in experimental animals. This argued strongly for the modern view that networks of discrete neurons, rather than fields of activity, were the correlates of perceptual awareness.

The second premise of the Gestalt brain field theory, which asserted that the relevant brain responses must be isomorphic to the associated psychological processes, still exerts a powerful, though usually unacknowledged, influence on thinking with regard to models of perceptual process, in particular, in contemporary thinking. The Gestalt theoreticians accepted the fact that neural isomorphism did not have to be rigid and inflexible. They knew enough about the nature of brain representation to accept the important fact that topological distortion of the neural representation of a stimulus shape need not necessarily deform the perceptual experience.

Unfortunately, Gestalt isomorphism did not accept any coded or symbolic representation of mental events—the brain field had to share the same topology as the perceptual experience, not be congruent with it. This belief in at least a topologically constant spatial and temporal isomorphism is a hidden premise of many current neuroreductionistic theories of perception, especially ones emphasizing the activity of single neurons as the codes for complex mentation and those that suppose that imagery is the result of low level retinotopic reconstructions. However, strict isomorphism (as opposed to symbolic or even linguistic representation) is totally contrary to the ideas of neural coding and nonisomorphic representation that seems to be a much more likely interpretation of the relation between perception and modern neurophysiological data. The conflict between the concepts of isomorphic and symbolic coding remains one of the most perplexing issues of contemporary theory. (A more complete discussion of this issue can be found in my previous book—Uttal, 1998.)

Thus, although it led 20th-century theory astray with regard to its neural models and its reification of the isomorphism criterion, Gestalt psychology was one of the main contributors to modern thought with regard to its emphasis on the global, the molar, or the whole attributes of both neural representations and mental events. The Gestalt argument was straightforward—something essential is lost from a stimulus or a response if we push reductive analysis too far. In other words, the very act of combining or concatenating adds something new to the components that was not present in them individually or at least ignored if one did not include the effects of the process of combination itself. It is not possible yet to resolve the issue of whether molar phenomena are due to the emergent properties that arise unpredictably as a result of extensive concatenation of components, or to the fact that the ways in which they interact must also be considered as additional properties in any complete description of the components. Regardless of its source, a holistic or molar approach is essential to a revitalized behaviorism and, thus, its acceptance is a necessary next step in the evolution of modern psychology.

Modern scientific developments have added a new twist to this argument. There is increasing evidence that, however we may long for it, the analysis of complex systems is simply not possible for very fundamental reasons from other sciences. If this view is correct, then all hope of a practical analytical approach to neural-perceptual bridge building must be forever abandoned. Chapter 2 speaks more to this issue.

1.4 THE FUNDAMENTAL ISSUES IN THE HISTORIC MENTALISM–BEHAVIORISM CONTROVERSY

It is always fascinating to go back to the original writings and thoughts of the pioneer psychologists whose names have become associated with a particular approach to understanding human mentation. Very often, when the original sources are examined, it turns out that the secondary sources interpreted the original material in ways that seem to a fresh reader to differ from the original intent of the pioneers. This is especially problematic in psychology because so many of the ideas that must be used to characterize the various schools and approaches are among the most controversial and challenging issues of human existence.

Perhaps it is for this reason that one comes away with a sense of disappointment concerning many of the seminal works that I have cited here. Many of them were primarily textbooks that briefly presented their fundamental assumptions and points of view and then went on to review, organize, and discuss the findings and theories of their time. The works of Thorndike (1907), Watson (1914), Tolman (1932), Hull (1943), and the earliest of Skinner's (1938) works all fall into this category. It is almost as if there had not been any extensive thought given to the position that would be taken or the critical arguments that supported it. A firmly held position was arrived at rather quickly, and then once presented, it became axiomatic. It was left to philosophers and historians of science to infer what were the influential intellectual forces at work. (Then, of course, the question of the accessibility of the minds of these pioneers arises.)

Of course, most of these scientists were primarily laboratory workers and not philosophers or historians of science. That may be a partial explanation for what seems to be this curious omission on the part of the people who are acknowledged to have invented their own versions of psychological science. Nevertheless, there is an unsatisfied gap as one reads these wonderful books—the explicit statements of the essential logic and propositions that led each of them to their novel perspectives during the evolution of psychology are often missing.

This section of this book isolates what appear to me to be the fundamental issues that are of concern to psychology. By understanding these fundamental issues and controversies and the positions taken by various psychologists, it is possible to compare and contrast the individual works on a common ground. It also alerts us to the fact that some of these issues, however important they may be in other contexts, do not discriminate between any of the schools—they all share some common beliefs and not all consensus views are controversial, even between mentalists and behaviorists.

Before I begin that process of isolating what I believe are the fundamental questions and issues that are being dealt with by scientific psychology, I must make a few comments about a very important side issue. That is the matter of the theological or religious theme that appears in several places in the discussion. It is explicit in the writing of Watson and Tolman and implicit in others. The battle is not drawn over anything as heady as the existence of God, but rather over what I believe is a surrogate for the dualistic notion of a separate kind of reality for the mind. The ideas of soul, free will, ego, self, and consciousness are all tied together as Skinner (1974) made clear. His critique of commencement addresses by university presidents in which such terms as "fruits of faith," "spiritual face," and "moral power" are used leaves no doubts about his attitude toward conventional religious beliefs.

The point is that all of these mentalistic and religious synonyms for consciousness have a collective past that probably extends back to the most primitive glimmerings of our own awareness. Make no mistake, these ideas (and the reactions against them) play powerful roles in the formal scientific theories offered by the mentalists and the behaviorists alike. It is not without a cost to one's own ego that a commitment is made to materialist monism or that one rejects the accessibility and analyzability of mental mechanisms and processes.

Furthermore, even without a religious commitment, each of us has the undeniable self-awareness of our own mental life. What could be more compelling than one's own firsthand experience that the mind exists? In fact, self-awareness is the one irrefutable argument each of us has that we (and others) are not automata! The logical leap from this self-awareness (and the fear of losing it) to the idea that mind is real and separate was the impetus to much, if not most, of human thought about human thought. Philosophical and theological dualisms that invoke any one of the variety of synonyms for mind that I listed previously were and are the basis of the personal philosophies of most of the people who have lived and who now live on the face of the earth. It is undeniable that such a powerful social and intellectual force has had a significant impact on our scientific outlook—particularly in psychology. Whatever logic and science may be called on to support material monism, however, it is still a minority point of view.

Dualistic notions of the nature and role of mind may not be just a popular historical solution to the problem of human nature. Some authors have suggested that it may be a logical necessity, even when one accepts the material monist view that mind is nothing more than a process of the brain. Minsky (1963), for example, made an extremely interesting argument in suggesting that dualisms are the normal self-analytic outcome when a machine or an organism arrives at a level of complexity that permits it to consider its own nature. Minsky's argument that dualism is unavoidable goes this way:

> The argument is this: our own self-models have a substantially "dual" character; there is a part concerned with the physical or mechanical environment with the behavior of inanimate objects—and there is a part concerned with social and psychological matters. It is precisely because we have not yet developed a satisfactory mechanical theory of mental activity that we have to keep these areas apart. We could not give up this division even if we wished to—until we find a unified model to replace it. (p. 449)

Then, speaking of a newly created, sentient robotic machine, Minsky went on to say:

> Now, when we ask such a creature what sort of being it is, it cannot simply answer "directly"; it must inspect its model(s). And it must answer by saying that it seems to be a dual thing—which appears to have two parts—a "mind" and a "body." Thus, even the robot, unless equipped with a satisfactory theory of artificial intelligence, would have to maintain a dualistic opinion on this matter. (p. 449)

Minsky's logic, even after 35 years seems impeccable. If we accept his thesis that that any thinking machine would thus be driven to a dualism and ultimately to accepting the separate reality of its mind (from its "body") it becomes understandable how such a logic would play such a large part in any philosophy—no less so for the pioneering psychologists than for any of their fellow humans. Therefore, dualisms and their associated mentalisms are very compelling foundations when one sets out to develop psychological theories.

Between the lines of most mentalisms are the same kind of assumptions that guide Minsky's thoughts on intelligent robots. That is not meant in a pejorative sense to reduce so many great minds to the levels of robots, but rather to point out that that there are compelling intellectual and logical forces at work that make mentalism the "easy way out." It is not only traditional theologies and other related philosophies, but also the insistent logic of thoughtful entities, be they robots or human, that makes mentalism so popular.

The countervailing force to the mentalist *easy way out* comes from the much more difficult-to-intuitively-justify objectivist, positivist, and behaviorist traditions. From this alternative point of view, if something cannot be publicly observed directly by independent observers, then it is beyond the pale of scientific consideration. Mind, proponents of this side of the controversy argue, is not directly accessible and it true nature can be viewed only vaguely through the clouded glass of cognitive reinterpretation and filtering.

Herein lies the heart of the continuing war between behaviorism and mentalism—*intra*personal self-awareness versus *inter*personal and consensual observability. It is a battle of considerable significance, and one that will probably be with us for quite a while. Although it is unlikely that this book solves the problem to everyone's satisfaction, I believe it is possible to tease apart the great controversy into a number of specific issues that may help us to classify and define the essence of the two great contending points of view. The respective answers to some of these questions not only help us to understand the past, but also help us toward a more realistic evaluation of what the most appropriate kind of psychological science should be in the future. Some other traditionally asked questions, however, turn out to be ineffective in helping us to understand the differences between behaviorism and mentalism. It may come as a surprise to some vigorous proponents of particular views, but there is substantial agreement among all kinds of psychologists concerning many of the foundation premises and goals of the science.

In the following brief list, I tabulate what I believe are the main questions that have energized the behaviorism–mentalism controversy.

1. Are mental processes real?
2. If mind is real, is it accessible?
3. Can verbal responses access mental processes?
4. Can other forms of behavior access mental processes?

5. Are mental processes analyzable?
6. What is the role of theory in psychology?
7. What is the role of experimentation in psychology?
8. Is the goal of psychology understanding or control?
9. Can neurophysiology replace psychology?
10. Can a behaviorism ever not be a crypto-mentalism?

Discussions, if not answers, of all of these questions are presented in subsequent chapters.

1.5 SUMMARY

This chapter has been a discussion and review of the origins of and the distinctions between behaviorism and mentalism. This primarily historical and philosophical review has attempted to clarify what are the natures of the opponent theories and how the ideas that led to each have developed over the centuries. It should be clear to my readers by now that there is no sharp line between the two camps. Rather, individual scholars have positioned themselves at various points along a continuum anchored at one end by a radical mentalism that assumes that mind is accessible and at the other by a radical behaviorism that assumes that mind is not accessible. Philosophical, religious, and methodological criteria have all been invoked by various proponents in support of their particular version of what psychology can or should be. In spite of their firm commitments to their own particular schools of thought, few of the pioneer psychologists spelled out the empirical, logical, and scientific reasons and premises for their original choice to support either the mentalist or behaviorist points of view.

The residual controversy is concerned with whether or not psychology can be a complete science if it does not make some attempt to go beyond description of behavior to reductive explanation and cognitive inference. The ultimate questions, therefore, are—is the mind accessible? And—is such a reductive analysis possible?

It is important to appreciate that this controversy in psychology is not unique to this science. It is only one example of a more general debate that has been carried on between positivist scholars and those who assumed that we could go beyond observation to make valid inferences about entities that could only be indirectly be observed. The particular issue at Mach's time was the significance of atoms—were they real entities or only inferences that could be used to model or depict what might be? In physics, this question may be considered analogous to the conundrum of mental accessibility and inferentiability posed by psychologists.

The issue has other names—it was denoted as the controversy between realists and antirealists. Although most modern historians of science feel that the realists won—and, therefore, that atoms are real, one of the goals of this book is to at least raise this issue anew.

The most specific challenges to a revitalized behaviorism consist of how well it provides a convincing negative answer to the question—is it possible to validly infer the nature of the central processes from behavioral observations? This is the question of mental accessibility and the purpose of this book. I am aware that this question can be asked in many different ways. Philosophers and psychologists have been preoccupied with related issues for most of this century. For example—can a relevant explanation of behavior be produced without reference to central states? If mind exists, can intentional states be characterized in a satisfactory matter. In my opinion, however important, these are secondary issues that must be confronted after the accessibility question is resolved. Without that resolution, sufficient ambiguity remains (e.g., "relevant," "satisfactory") to make these questions difficult to answer.

Times change and new knowledge provides additional arguments in what remains one of the great controversies of modern science. In the next chapter, we see how modern scientific developments add substance to the discussion in a way that was not possible even in the recent past.

Chapter 2

The Critics Speak Against Mentalism

Mentalist approaches to scientific psychology have had a pervasive persistence that is remarkable. The reasons for their endurance are not too difficult to understand. Mentalist concepts permeate all societies for no more subtle reason than the firsthand evidence that each human being has of their own personal consciousness. Mentalist terminology and concepts are explicit in all human languages and most popular notions of one's personal existence and meaning. It is virtually impossible for humans to speak to each other without using mentalist terms. It is this very uniformity and commonality of meaning that binds us together and that transcends any differences in regional vocabulary or local variations in syntax. Our literature, our therapies (both medical and psychological), our commerce, our religions, in fact all aspects of our lives are expressed in the terms of personal awarenesses, experiences, and perceptions, of cognitive decision making, of emotions and feelings, and of a consensual acceptance of the existence of each individual's mind.

Thus, as scientific psychologies emerged there was a compelling historical and personal tendency to formulate theories in the mentalist context. On the other hand, the arguments that must be made to support positivism, operationalism, and behaviorism are arcane and esoteric and not part of the general culture. The relatively new intellectual trends represented by these approaches to the study of human thought and behavior have been largely founded on the assumption on the part of a minority that an objective science depends on consensual agreement on measurements and observations by, as far as possible, unbiased observers. There is a continuing discomfort on the part of many observers of the human scene when psychology is presented as a positivist or operational behaviorism rather than one of the classic mentalisms. This discomfort is not only found among the general public but also among philosophers and psychologists—the two professions historically most concerned with mental processes and actions.

Kimble (1996), in a frank and lucid account of the current status of scientific psychology, points out the vast gulf that lies between the languages of "common sense" and "scientific thinking" in dealing with just the single issue of determinism—a corollary of the accessibility topic. His tabulation effectively illustrates the powerful predisposing forces that are operating when psychologists find it necessary to make that first critical decision in deciding on their respective positions regarding the mentalism–behaviorism controversy.

Determinism	
Common Sense Meaning	Scientific Thinking
Free Will	Determinism
Mental Causes	Physical Causes
Single Causes	Complex Causality
"Tell it like it is"	"More research is needed"
Explanation by naming	Explanation by theory and law
Dispositional explanation	Deductive explanation
"The simple unvarnished truth"	Probabilistic interpretation
"Exceptions prove the law"	Exceptions disprove the law

From Kimble (1996, p. 135).

It must be appreciated that these twin sources of inspiration—the universal intrapersonal self-awareness leading to "common sense" explanations and vocabulary, on the one hand, and objective scientific standards, on the other—have created a controversy of enormous proportions especially in recent years. All too often in the past, decisions about human nature of far reaching importance were not based on rigorous objective arguments, but on common sense and humanist criteria. This was not something that was limited to the protomentalists or their later descendents. As we have seen in Chapter 1, the early behaviorists also were influenced by their scientific, personal, social, theological, and situational backgrounds in forming their personal solutions to the great question on the basis of criteria that were themselves often less than objective.

Indeed, even such a "scientific" principle as parsimony is hardly different from comparable humanistic or theological premises and may not represent anything beyond a desire for elegance or symmetry. It is not, for example, a priori obvious why simplicity or economy should be important in complex systems like the brain; there are quite enough neurons to waste a few, if not many. General guidelines like these, therefore, can set a tone, but cannot convincingly prove in any rigorous sense that behaviorism or mentalism is the preferred scientific approach or even a better approach to understanding what is happening mentally. None of this is said with any pejorative intent toward either our behavioral or mentalist predecessors. It is a historic fact that most of the compelling technical arguments that are able to go beyond philosophical speculation, vague general principles, or social and humanistic criteria were simply not available until very recently.

It is one thesis of this book that times have changed, new knowledge is available, and that it is now time for the debate between behaviorism and mentalism to be reopened. Given new evidence and solid developments in cognate fields, some of the key questions that were posed in the previous chapter can now be reconsidered and, perhaps, even closed once and for all. In particular, the analyzability and accessibility issues are now subject to renewed scrutiny using concepts and data that simply were not available even a few decades ago. It is also possible to now reconsider the role of theory and models in psychological research.

My plan for this chapter is to review the classic and contemporary arguments in this great debate that speak against mentalisms. To be both complete and fair, however, I must also consider some of the criticisms that have been directed at behaviorism. This is done in Chapter 3. As my readers must appreciate, any attempt to develop a taxonomy of arguments is necessarily overlapping and to a degree redundant. Many of the arguments presented in one list are really synonymous or, at least, analogous with those in another. Be that as it may be, hopefully, this exercise clarifies exactly what are the main arguments that have been marshaled on each side. Beyond presentation and discussion, it is also, of course, my expectation that the weight of the various arguments may lead us to a resolution of this continuing controversy in favor of a less prejudiced reconsideration of behaviorism.

2.1 SOME CLASSIC ARGUMENTS AGAINST MENTALISM

Many of the earlier positivists and behaviorists simply made a decision that the gulf between mental activity and observable data was too wide for psychology to accept. Therefore, they rejected the self-reports obtained by the classic introspective techniques as valid indicators of mental processes and actions. They argued on more or less incomplete grounds that there were too many opportunities for subjective states such as feelings, emotions, vested interests, or other mental processes to contaminate or even to dissociate subjective experiences and decisions from the resulting behavior, whether in the form of verbal or motor responses. After all, dissociation of true felt emotions and overt behavior was done professionally all of the time by actors and salespersons, not to speak of the impersonators and sociopaths among us who have prevaricated, dissembled, posed, repressed, or acted out the many scenes of our daily life.

There is, beyond this informal argument, an increasing body of better organized thought suggesting that behavior and mind are regularly disassociated. The scholars discussed in the following sections are among the many who have offered more formal and better articulated (or who have identified) critiques of mentalisms, mental process accessibility, and the technique of introspection.

2.1.1 Rakover's Analysis

Rakover (1990), although rejecting any radical form of behaviorism, raises three arguments against introspectionism in a way that characterizes the classic arguments against any kind of mentalism. He suggested the fundamental issues are:

- Public Availability
- Objectivity
- Repeatability

Using the term private behavior (PB) as a synonym for mental processes, Rakover defined these three pillars of scientific inquiry. Public availability means that "the phenomenon has to be available to everyone" (p. 209). Objectivity means that "neither the observer nor the instruments that he uses should affect the phenomenon being observed" (p. 209). Finally, repeatability is defined as demanding that the "the same phenomenon has to be observed at different times" (p. 210).

Unfortunately, however prevalent throughout the history of this controversy, none of these three criteria can completely satisfy our desire to exclude mentalist concepts from psychological science. The problem encountered when one approaches mentalism with these three weapons is that they are all blunt! Whether mental processes are "available" depends on other issues. A component of mind may or may not be available or accessible depending on the credence one gives to the processes of inference that are used to bridge the behavioral and the mental domains. If we can show that valid inference from behavior to mental states is impossible or constrained (as I think it is now possible to do) then mental processes are not available, however real they may be, in the sense required by a positivist science. On the other hand, if one accepts the argument (on whatever grounds) that it is possible to infer from the observed to the unobserved, then the question of availability is answered in the affirmative without further argument. Thus, unless one goes beyond the bare skeleton of this public availability criterion, it is not useful in helping us resolve the mentalism–behaviorism controversy. It remains an empirical issue that at least some of us still think has yet to be finally resolved.

Similarly, the utility of the criterion of objectivity is equally severely challenged by the existence of widely accepted uncertainty principles in other sciences. Heisenberg's principle did not lead physicists to reject physics, and accepting the facts that subjects can be influenced by instructions or that experimental findings can be distorted by the instruments or methods used in an experiment is not a definitive criterion for rejecting the measurability of mental processes. Other arguments have to be (and can be) invoked to remove mentalist concepts from psychological science.

Repeatability is perhaps the most fragile criterion of the three that Rakover has suggested. For many reasons, all complex systems change over time. Organisms grow and mature, computer programs may adapt to previous inputs, and humans can actually produce new information based on what had been experienced with old information. Thus, behavior is dynamic and, almost by definition, has to change from one moment to the next. This inconstant aspect of complex systems is ubiquitous. It is only in the simplest systems that the conditions are stable enough from one moment to the next to produce even superficially repeatable behavior. Indeed, it is difficult to imagine that even the simplest systems (e.g., a piece of metal used in a test-to-destruction paradigm) are not subject to change (and thus should be classified as nonrepeatable) if given enough time.

Repeatability, therefore, may really be an error of language obscuring the fact that change is universal. It cannot, therefore, be used as a critical criterion for including or excluding any kind of topic from the realm of scientific exploration or in helping us specify the preferred approach. Thus, these three arguments are not very useful. Indeed, Rakover himself proved that point by immediately reversing his field and showing how the same three criteria can be used equally well to support introspective mentalism!

2.1.2 Moore's Theorem

Another argument that has classically been drawn against mentalism is that, in seeking to explain thought processes, psychologists of this persuasion are as likely to invent any plausible internal mechanism as any other. That is, when one is examining a system that is closed to direct observation, there are always many possible and equally plausible internal mechanisms that could produce the same transformation of the stimulus into the response. When a rock falls on your head, in the absence of any other knowledge and criteria, it is not possible to determine if the rock fell because of a malicious spirit that lived in it or because of gravity. Thus, given a state of inadequate information, it is not just possible, but as likely, the theorist will select one that suits some irrelevant need, foundation premise, or a priori hypothesis, as the correct or valid explanation. For pre-Newtonians, the spirit explanation for the rock's behavior would be all too easy to accept and equally difficult to reject.

It is not well known, but there is a formal mathematical proof that there are many, if not infinite plausible solutions to any problem involving unobserved internal mechanisms, processes, and structures. I have discussed this issue extensively in an earlier book (Uttal, 1998), but let me simply restate the theorem now and direct my readers back to that earlier work for a more complete discussion of this important idea. Moore (1956), an early automata theorist, wrote a paper that has all too long been overlooked in the mentalism–behaviorism controversy:

> THEOREM 9: Given any machine S and any multiple experiments performed on S, there exist other machines experimentally indistinguishable from S for which the original experiment would have had the same outcome. (p. 140)

Moore went on to assert:

> This result means that it will never be possible to perform experiments on a completely unknown machine which will suffice to identify it from among a class of all sequential machines. (p. 140)

The implications of Moore's theorem are particularly profound for psychology. It is not only that there are other possible explanations but, because there will always be more possibilities than there are experiments and endless experiments that could be done, the number of alternative possibilities is unlimited. In other words, imagination, not reality, is the only limit to the number of possible explanations of what is going on in a closed system.

To translate this formal statement into an argument that had been traditionally used by many behaviorally oriented psychologists: Given that there are many (perhaps, infinite) possible mental models and explanations that could explain observed behavior, there is no assurance an enthusiastic theoretician would not infer a totally incorrect one. In fact, given there are so many possibilities, many of which are exclusive of each other, it is more likely that you will choose one of the many wrong ones than the rare correct one. The variety of models that could meet the explanatory needs of a science examining closed systems could be molar or elementalist, deterministic or free-willed, or even mechanistic or theological. This antimentalist argument asserts that it is not possible to determine the correct alternative by comparing the stimulus or input with the response or the output. As a preview to my own conclusions, it does not, however, preclude precise and rigorous descriptions of the relation between the two domains in the form of descriptive transformations.

However, it may also be asked: Are there also many alternative *descriptions* of a given behavior just as there are many indistinguishable reductive models? Certainly there are. Although there are many possible models and formulae that can predict the same complex system behavior, the test in the case of a putative description (as opposed to reductive explanation) is only whether or not the predicted behavior is closely enough modeled. The best fitting prediction or reconstruction is without argument the best description. However, this is as far as it should go. No matter how good the description, even the best fitting model has nothing to contribute to the determination of the details of the underlying mechanism. How few of us would accept a polynomial fit of some system behavior as a mechanistic explanation of that behavior even though it provides the best fit. However, we make exactly that kind of logical error when considering other models preferred for some other reason.

Furthermore, superficially distinct models that predict identical behavior usually turn out to be equivalent to each other. It is only when the model that produced the description is accepted as being reductively explanatory that a problem arises. However, this is exactly the situation Moore and others have warned us to avoid. In sum, although many models may produce the same description, they are either mathematical duals of each of other (and, thus, do not discriminate between alternative explanatory mechanisms) or their significance has been stretched to a point where they have become more than descriptions—or both. Clearly, Moore's theorem formalizes the debate over the utility and value of hypothetical constructs in psychology and similar inferences in the biological and physical sciences.

2.1.3 The Homunculus

Another classic argument against the mentalist approach is that it must necessarily invoke some kind of a *homunculus.* The homunculus stands alongside anthropomorphization as one of the major criticisms of mentalist psychology. These are the twin classic sins that mentalists commit when they infer the nature of the mental processes being carried out in the brain–mind interpositioned between the stimulus and the response. According to classical behaviorist, positivist, and operational arguments against mentalisms, homunculi are fallacious theoretical and logical entities that emerge when one assumes accessibility to mental processes is possible. The argument is that some kind of an entity—a homunculus representing some kind of an intervening and independent decision maker—must be invented to carry out the transformations. However, this homunculus would have to be itself explained, probably by its own homunculus. Thus, an infinite regression of such explanations would be required that actually never explains anything.

Behaviorists do not reject the idea that some such kind of an information-transforming mechanism must exist between the stimulus and the response. I have found no instance of any behaviorist totally rejecting the reality of a central transforming mechanism—either a physical brain or a brain process called mind. It is obvious when one considers the enormous adaptability of human behavior that the stimuli do not exactly determine responses and that the brain does more than simply switch stimuli to appropriate responses. Equally obviously, the present state and the past experiences of the intervening organism play an important role in determining behavior. The behaviorist argument, on the other hand, is that because it is impossible to infer specifically what the nature of this hidden level of processing is, we should avoid fanciful inventions of hypothetical constructs just because they may seem to be plausible. The mentalist, the behaviorist contends, attempts to address the issue of the nature of the internal decision-making mechanisms themselves and, thus, inevitably will be led to the creation of a homunculus-type theory.

In recent years, with the increasing general awareness that computers perform input–output transformations without any identifiable "homunculus" but by following a set of precise rules, this argument has come into disrepute. It was not so much that the problem was solved or the argument resolved, but rather that the meaning of the internal processing system could now be conceptualized in a new way. No independent entity need be invoked; the transformations themselves could be instantiated as the decision-making force. In other words, the organism "O" in the S-O-R sequence became a set of processes rather than a object or a homunculus-like entity. The system was able to detect, represent, transform, and select in a manner obviating the need for any sentient decision maker. Like so many other controversies in psychology, in this manner the homunculus simply went extinct.

2.1.4 Mentalism Is Beyond Science

Another classic argument against mentalism has been that it does not fit the basic properties of scientific investigation. That is, it has no dimensions that can be unequivocally measured. As Boring (1933) noted:

> One does not attempt to discover conscious elements, attributes, or dimensions; one makes them up and uses them as phenomenological exigencies require. (p. vii)

The very important point Boring makes here is that, unlike many other sciences, psychology is not a voyage of discovery of real unknown entities, but one whose goal is, at best, the invention of hypothetical constructs to explain behavior. Perhaps there is no other place in which mentalism is challenged so severely by so few words. Furthermore, and perhaps even more important, objective measurement of the amount, the quality, and even the time and place of occurrence of a thought, is difficult if not impossible. For example, there are paradoxical phenomena (such as apparent movement and metacontrast in which the response seems to precede the stimulus) that delink even the temporal dimensions of the stimulus and the response. Given that even such ostensibly straight-forward mental dimensions seem not to be temporally coherent, how then can a system based on measurements of external time (the domain of the physical stimulus) be made compatible with one (the domain of mental phenomena) that is not? Above all else, objective science is based on a common set of agreed on dimensions, metrics, and standards. If these measures are not available, one is confronted with the difficult question—are the methods of normal science that worked so well in physics, chemistry, and astronomy applicable to the study of mental processes?

This physical argument is somewhat archaic in the context of more modern considerations of the nature of measurement and of information processing. It is not that the dimensions of mind are any better understood now then previously, but rather that the nature of dimensions and dimensionality has evolved in the past half century. In the light of Bridgman type operationalism, it is fashionable to define dimensions in terms of the procedures that are executed when we observe and measure rather than some abstract concept of their existence independent of the method of our observations. Distinctions are now drawn between the physical dimensions of the stimulus and the perceptual dimensions of the response that may largely ameliorate the criticism of incongruent time. It is now well appreciated, for example, that the phenomenological dimensions need not be identical or even isomorphic to those of the physical stimulus. Rather the dimensions of the mind and of behavior can be considered to be coded representations of each other and of the messages they convey. To make this point more concrete, one has only to consider the relation between the perceptual dimensions of color and the physical dimensions of light. Hue, saturation, and brightness are not the same as wavelength, purity, and intensity. Nevertheless, the two domains are well correlated and the transformations (if not the actual mechanisms) between them are well understood.

Another form of the same argument arising in many different forms against cognitive or mentalist psychologies is that they are prone to invent internal entities (those problematical hypothetical constructs again) that are not adequately linked to the data. As I have tried to make clear throughout this book, this argument is far more persuasive than many of the others, simply because it is the most technically sound. The engineer's "black box" (Moore's theorem) is a more compelling metaphor in this context than the absence of congruent temporal dimensions or the red herring represented by invocation of the homunculus. It is the integrity or validity, if not the possibility, of the hypothetical construct that is the issue here. The model argument against mentalism in this case is that the invention of any hypothetical construct is the equivalent of committing the Type II error in statistics—failing to reject a false null hypothesis or false hypothetical construct.

2.1.5 The Skinnerian Critique

Next in this review of general criticisms of mentalism, let us consider Skinner's (1963) arguments against mentalism (as opposed to his responses to the criticisms of behaviorism to which he reacts and that I discuss in the next chapter). His thoughts on this matter are spelled out particularly clearly in what has become a classic of psychological writing—the title of which was "Behaviorism at Fifty." In this eloquently written article, which appeared somewhat surprisingly at virtually the birth date of modern cognitive psychology, Skinner spells out his major objections to the mentalist approach.

> 1. *We may object first to the predilection for unfinished causal sequences. (p. 956)*

With this statement, Skinner points out that mentalist explanations are never complete. Putative explanations of behavior may be based on mental events such as pain or pleasure, but only rarely is any attempt made to define what these subjective experiences are or how they can or do affect behavior.

> 2. . . . *a preoccupation with mental way stations [hypothetical constructs used as explanations] burdens a science with all of the problems raised by the limitations and inaccuracies of self descriptive repertoires. (p. 956)*

With this statement, Skinner points out that even without rejecting the value of introspective observations, we are still faced with the problem of unconscious processing and the tenuous link between observers' evaluation of their own mental processes and the actual processes that led to emission of a particular response to both present and previous stimuli.

> 3. *Observations of one's own behavior necessarily follows the behavior. (p. 957)*

Here Skinner alludes to the fact that, even if one could introspect or interpret what one's mental states and processes were when a decision was made to produce some response, these self-interpretations must necessarily be elicited *after* the behavior. The behavior itself would thus become a component of the interpretation, and the original state and causal relations would probably be modified. This is the general "chicken and the egg" problem instantiated in the specifics of mentalist thinking.

Skinner went on to suggest one particularly egregious misinterpretation—the field of psychotherapy. Perhaps he best sums up the discrepancy with the phrase—"I guess I was hungrier than I thought . . ." The dissociation between the presumed prior mental cause and the subsequent behaviorally modified estimate (Gee, I am surprised I ate that much!) of what one's thoughts were earlier, is crystal clear in this context. How, then, could any such highly inconstant self-interpretation be useful as objective data?

> *4. A final objection is that the way stations are so often simply invented. (p. 957)*

This, of course, is the classic argument that has arisen in many different forms in this and the previous chapter. It is another way of expressing the engineer's "Black Box" limitation or the implication of Moore's (1956) second theorem or Boring's (1933) astute insight. It is just too easy to develop post hoc stories or "just so" tales that seem to explain but, in fact, invoke processes and mechanisms that are, at best, just plausible exemplars drawn from a vast number of alternative possibilities.

It is interesting to see what kind of arguments Skinner (1987) raised against mentalism later in the last few years of his career. At this point, his criticisms of mentalism were directed at what he considered to be "three formidable obstacles" (p. 782)—namely, humanistic psychology, psychotherapy, and cognitive psychology.

Skinner first relates the challenges to the humanistic psychologies offered by behaviorism and by evolutionary theory. Both of these scientific endeavors (behaviorism and evolutionism) are threatening to some people because they seem to remove the need for ". . . a creative, mind or plan, or for purpose and goal direction" (p. 783). He suggests that the "disenthronement of a creator seems to some to threaten personal freedom" (p. 783). Thus, his challenge to mentalism is that it is based on a foundation of religious and humanistic beliefs that themselves have no place in science. It is the primitive fear emerging from a perceived threat to some deeply held religious beliefs that Skinner suggests is the foundation of many of the mentalist approaches to psychology—at the expense of a truly objective alternative.

Once again it is interesting to note the important role that religion, as well as some of its secular allies (e.g., humanistic psychology) play in the mentalism–behaviorism controversy. As discussed in Chapter 1, both Watson and Tolman also made explicit antireligious statements. If we were to look back even further for an explanation of this influence, certainly the fear of death and of the resulting loss of consciousness, must lie at the very roots. Skinner's argument, thus, by implication is that this primeval fear is hardly the basis of a science of mind; if any manifestation of this fear is used as an argument against behaviorism, its demonstrated irrelevance is a strong argument against any mentalism.

Skinner then looks at psychotherapy. He points out this kind of therapy *must necessarily assume* mental accessibility to validate itself. The psychotherapeutical interaction requires access to what are assumed to be the interpersonally private mental processes of the client by the practitioner. Thus, the whole profession of psychotherapy has a vested, a priori interest in accepting not only the reality but also the accessibility of mental processes. The compelling forces that direct members of this profession to formulate all of their jargon and theories in mentalist terms are transparently obvious. Skinner considers this force to be a powerful bias against the development of an objective behaviorism and, to the degree that this bias is invalid, a compelling counterargument to any of the many mentalist concepts and theories that have been incorporated in contemporary psychology. In short, the clinical tail is wagging the scientific dog!

If mental activity turns out not to be directly accessible, then psychotherapy loses its very *raison d'être*; it would have to be relegated to the same wastebasket of pseudosciences that include parapsychologies, UFO abductions, fantastic cults, astrology, acupuncture, chiropractic, aroma therapies, macrobiotic food crystals, and the food and other medical fads that have demonized popular thinking in recent years. (My favorite is "harmonic synchronistic attunement," whatever that is.) My readers are referred to the wonderful book by the late Carl Sagan (1995) for a fuller exposition of the wide range of nonsense to which so many of our fellows have committed themselves in recent years. This is not to say that some of these theoretically nonsensical therapies might not occasionally appear to work, but it is usually for reasons far different than those alluded to by these quasi- and full-blown charlatans.

Skinner's third "formidable obstacle" is none other than modern cognitive psychology. The negative forces against behaviorism are computer models and simulations, false neuroreductionist explanations, and the information-processing metaphors that only superficially explain the underlying mechanisms of behavior. But, most of all Skinner laments that the major damage to behaviorism has been the ". . . cognitive restoration of the Royal House of Mind . . ." (p. 784) without a real resolution of some of the fundamental issues concerning the accessibility and analyzability of the mental processes that inhabit that "house."

Skinner continued to describe many other problems that face psychology as a science. However, they are not really germane to this present review of criticisms of mentalism. His discussion of the weaknesses and origins or the three alternative approaches to psychology—psychotherapy, humanism, and cognitivism, however, constitutes a strong general counterargument to mentalisms. Finally, Skinner points out that most of the great problems of psychology have not been solved by any of the mentalist approaches. Because the fundamental question of how the "mind works on the body" has never been answered, Skinner concluded by saying, "Questions of that sort should never have been asked" (p. 785).

2.1.6 The Dualism–Mentalism Link

Next, it must be noted there is an ubiquitous long-term and deep-seated relationship between dualisms and mentalisms. Dualisms simply relegate mental reality to the realm of the unobservable and renege on the scientists responsibility to consider all levels of reality, including mental processes. As Dennett (1991) said: ". . . adopting dualism is really just accepting defeat without admitting it" (p. 41). In making these assertions, it is important for me to reiterate that I, too, emphatically accept the reality of mental processes as processes or actions carried out by the material brain. To say that such events are not directly observable, as is done by behaviorists, is not the same as asserting that they occupy a different kind of reality, as is done by dualists. Although the dualism issue places mind outside of the realm of scientific inquiry for ontological reasons, modern developments in various sciences now allow us to speak more rigorously about the epistemological inaccessibility of mental actions and processes without invoking other kinds of reality or, for that matter, nonreality.

2.1.7 The Fragile Data Argument

There is another empirical issue that I raise with some trepidation because it could be used by antagonists of the entire scientific psychology enterprise. Nevertheless, there is substantial doubt about the validity, even more so than the reliability, of much of the data of cognitive psychology. As I discussed in one of my earlier books (Uttal, 1988), the general validity of the data generated by a wide range of studies of what are now referred to as "high level" cognitive processing is questionable.

My goal when I started to write "On Seeing Forms" (Uttal, 1988) was to search out the solid data and the well confirmed empirical results of visual cognition. I had hoped the book would culminate in a synoptic statement of what we knew and where we were with regard to understanding visual topics that seemed to require effortful attention. This was the general approach I had used in several previous books. That approach had been arguably successful.

As I studied and reviewed the "high level" literature, I came to a rather surprising general conclusion. The reliability, durability, and presumably the validity of the data from the sample of experiments with which I was concerned seemed to evaporate. Data, as well as conclusions, seemed to last only for a few issues of the journal in which they had been published before some criticism of it emerged. Or, when the experiment was repeated, slight differences in the design produced qualitatively distinct, not just marginally different quantitative results. My summary statement on this issue still expresses my conviction that the high level, cognitive aspects of perception and other aspects of mentation are far less accessible than many mentalists would accept simply because the very database is so fragile. It is worthwhile making this summary a part of the present discussion.

> The final source of my concern is that the very empirical data on which we perceptionists base our theories are often embarrassingly transient. We have seen throughout this book many instances in which some observation has drifted away like a smoke ring when attempts are made at replication. I argue that this paucity of reliable data is, at the most fundamental level, a result of the multivariate complexity of most psychological functions and the adaptive power of the cognitive system rather than any deficiency of control in a given experiment's design. Nevertheless, the fragility of even the data base on which we base our theories is a signal of the extreme care that must be taken in such complex situations to guarantee data validity. (p. 282)

I am apparently not alone in this critical evaluation of perceptual findings that require more complicated responses on the part of experimental subjects. One well-known psychophysicist (Lockhead, 1992) speaking of potential interactions between the several dimensions of a stimulus:

> Because of such effects, because there are so many different ones, because so many of them interact, and because judgments also vary from trial to trial because of task and sequence differences, any underlying, true psychophysical scale can only appear in the data as a will-o'-the-wisp with no basis to decide whether the observed scale is the true scale. Except for its esthetic appeal, which is considerable, there seems to be little reason to expect a fixed relation between behavior and the amount of energy in some attribute of a stimulus, and little reason to expect to be able to demonstrate such a function, should one exist. (p. 555)

My concern has now grown that this fragility of the very database obtained from experiments that use "Class B" observations (Brindley, 1960), in particular, or cognitive science, in general, may have strong implications for the mentalism–behaviorism controversy I am considering here. Furthermore, the phenomenon of irreproducible or vanishing findings may have other causal reasons than simple multivariate complexity or the adaptability of the brain. Two additional factors are likely to be involved: the actual inaccessibility of the processes that are being studied, and the sensitivity of the involved cognitive processes to the method used in a given experiment.

These two factors are closely related, of course, because the very inaccessibility of the mental process may degrade the ability of the experimental design—itself a source of situational stimuli—to constrain the outcome of an experiment. If this is actually what is happening, then the results of a given experiment may reflect the design of the experiment rather than the actual psychobiological cognitive processes themselves.

The set of empirical findings discussed later in this chapter (a) dissociating verbal reports from actual mental processes, (b) demonstrating the high sensitivity of cognitive data to methodological influences, (c) displaying the extreme adaptability of humans to play games with our experiments that are other than those we wish them to play, and (d) the interaction of the several separable attributes of a stimulus, all also argue against accessibility, unique measurability, and analyzability of mental processes by the methods available to psychological science. In other words, the interpersonally private barrier to sharing conscious experiences may be much more profound than has, heretofore, been accepted.

2.2 THE PHILOSOPHERS SPEAK AGAINST MENTALISM

The classic psychological arguments against mentalism are many and varied as just demonstrated. Philosophers have also dealt with the issues in several different contexts. Many of their controversies also revolve around the possibility (or impossibility) of bringing mental processes and phenomena into the scientific domain. Very often the debate focuses on consciousness (self-awareness) rather than just the mental information processes, structures, and mechanisms that purport to be assayed by introspective or controlled experimental methods.

Currently, however, the separation between two camps of mentalists has broadened. On the one side are the cognitive scientists who more or less ignore the problem of consciousness and assert that they seek only to unravel the information processes associated with the mental activity lying between the stimulus and the evoked response. On the other side are a group of philosophers and psychologists who are deeply concerned with consciousness itself—that which McGinn (1989) has called "the hard nut of the mind-body problem" (p. 349). For this latter group, consciousness has become the central issue in their discussions. Consciousness has been, according to some modern philosophers, "rediscovered" or even "explained." However eloquent the prose, I find many of these well known works to be very unsatisfying. For example, Dennett (1991) offers up his "multiple draft" model of consciousness. Careful reading of this book suggests, however, that his model is a description or a metaphor that *explains* very little about consciousness. As Dennett himself said:

> I haven't replaced a metaphorical theory, the Cartesian Theater, with a nonmetaphorical ("literal, scientific") theory. All I have done, really is to replace one family of metaphors and images with another, trading in the Theater, the Witness, the Central Meaner, the Figment, for Software, Virtual machines, Multiple Drafts, a Pandemonium of Homunculi. (p. 455)

Dennett went on within the confines of the same page to suggest that "metaphors are not 'just' metaphors: metaphors are the tools of thought" but he has not satisfied me that he had brought us any closer to a valid "explanation" of mind, nor, for that matter, has he done anything else to provide convincing evidence that mental processes are accessible to us.

Perhaps Dennett (1991) was aware of the problems he would face when he suggested at the outset of his book that:

- Human consciousness is just about the last surviving mystery. (p. 21)
- With consciousness, however, we are in a terrible muddle. (p. 22)
- . . . consciousness, like love and money, is a phenomenon that does, indeed, depend on its associated concepts. (p. 24)

Dennett further defined the problems we face when we confront the "Mystery of Consciousness" as well as anyone else when he posed an important scientific question: "How can living physical bodies in the physical world produce such a phenomenon?"

Other writers who have attacked the problems of consciousness have run into the same intellectual obstacles. This is the reason I choose to leave this matter to others. Consciousness has led to a large number of words, some presented as explanations, but usually turning out to be thinly veiled metaphors. Having accepted the existence of mind (or consciousness) as process or function does not automatically mean that it is accessible to scientific inquiry of a kind very different than what Dennett has presented to us.

My choice to finesse this issue is not a solitary one. Others who have dealt with consciousness also suggest that the time is not ripe. For example, Penrose (1989) stated that:

> I do not think that it is wise, at this stage of understanding, to attempt to propose a precise *definition* of consciousness, but we can rely, to good meas-

> ure, on our subjective impressions and intuitive common sense as to what the term means and when the property of consciousness is likely to be present. (p. 406)

Concentrating on the accessibility issue rather than attempting to define the mysterious process of consciousness alleviates many of the difficulties faced in a strictly scientific endeavor. As we see this theme reoccurs throughout the following discussion.

Now let us consider some of the view of others who have challenged one or another of the tenets of historical and modern mentalism.

2.2.1 The New Mysterians

McGinn (1989) is among those presently associated with an emerging philosophical school known as the "new mysterians." His position, and that of others of this mysterian persuasion is encapsulated in the following quotation.

> I do not believe we can ever specify what it is about the brain that is responsible for consciousness, but I am sure that whatever it is it is not inherently miraculous. The problem arises, I want to suggest, because we are cut off by our very cognitive constitution from achieving a conception of the natural property of the brain (or of consciousness) that accounts for the psychophysical link. (p. 350)

McGinn's argument for the mysterian position, so articulated, is that the human mind is simply not capable of "grasping the nature of the property that links them [brain and mind]" (p. 364). It is due to a fundamental limitation of the human mind to conceive of a solution to the problem. But, according to the new mysterians, the mystery is merely one of organization and complexity and not a result of any supernatural influence. The banner of the new mysterians is clearly emblazoned with the motto—*monism without reductionism.*

The nonreductionist ideas behind new mysterianism were enunciated earlier by Nagel (1979, 1986). He summed up his point of view clearly, leaving no doubt of where he stands:

> The reductionist program that dominates current work in the philosophy of mind is completely misguided, because it is based on the groundless assumption that a particular conception of objective reality is exhaustive of what there is. (Nagel, 1986, p. 16)

It is quite obvious that Nagel was dangerously close to a dualism or worse—a pluralism of some kind—in this statement. A nonexhaustive "objective reality" would imply the existence of other kinds of reality. Such a concept has the all-too-familiar tone of entities completely separated from the reality of the physical world that are traditionally invoked by dualists. In spite of this near miss, Nagel rejected such dualisms and turned, instead, to "double aspect theory," the classic view that mental and physical terms are simply different measurements of the same underlying reality.

Nevertheless, the expressed position taken by the mysterians such as Nagel and McGinn includes a firm commitment to a material monism—mind is a function of brain and of brain alone. Both mind and brain are accepted as being real and manifestations of the same kind of reality. What Nagel and the other new mysterians specifically do reject is reductionism—the building of explanatory bridges between the two domains. In this regard, these philosophers come close to some versions of psychological behaviorism in terms of their fundamental assumptions. In other words, regardless of the reality, separate or otherwise, of both mind and brain, they will both have to be dealt with separately in their own languages and using their own methodological approaches.

Boyd (1980), a philosopher who is clearly in the new mysterian camp, also argued strongly for a materialist theory of mental processes, on the one hand, and the impossibility that this physical mind can be reduced to the terms of its constituent components, on the other. He asserted that the operational or functional properties (mind?) that emerge from that physical structure (brain?) are in principle immune to analysis. In Boyd's words:

> Materialists, quite rightly, have been careful to insist that each mental state is identical to, not merely correlated with some physical state. (p. 86)

But also:

> I shall show that the version of materialist psychology best supported by available evidence entails that mental and psychological states are not definable in physical terms. (p. 86)

Boyd, thereby, distinguishes between the acceptable "doctrine that mental phenomena *are* physical phenomena" and the unacceptable one that there necessarily exist "true mind–body identity statements linking rigid designators." His argument was primarily an attack on some earlier anti-materialist philosophies, but his conclusion strongly rejected the idea that mental processes are analyzable at any level. This is also tantamount to a rejection of the mentalist agenda aimed at identification of the underlying processes and mechanisms and strong support for behaviorism, from my point of view.

Putnam (1973) was also among those who argued that psychology cannot be reduced to the terms of physiology, chemistry, or physics. His philosophy can be considered to be close, if not identical, to the mysterian philosophy. Putnam's particular version of the argument was based on considerations of what are the proximal causes of human thought. His main point is familiar—however true it may be that thought is a product of the brain and the brain is a chemical and, thus, physical entity, thought is not directly caused by these low levels of analysis. He said:

> Psychology is as underdetermined by biology as it is by elementary particle physics, and people's psychology is partly a reflection of deeply entrenched societal beliefs.

Putnam's assertion that the most microscopic levels of analysis (including biochemistry and the activity of individual neurons) do not determine behavior is in accord with the idea that it is the complex organization of many neurons that essentially defines mental life.

Needless to say, the "materialism without reductionism" argument is regularly challenged by more neuroscientifically oriented types. Some simply ignore the argument that reduction to neural terms may not be possible and plow ahead with their research. Some more thoughtful neuroscientists have criticized the mysterian's philosophy although acknowledging that behaviorism does not necessarily reject reductionism. For example, Pribram (1979) contends that

> description [as carried out by behaviorists] entails the possibility (though not the necessity) of reduction. By contrast, a phenomenal or existential approach eschews this possibility. (p. 68; brackets added)

Pribram's commitment to neuroreductionism is of long standing and well known. His eclectic willingness to consider at least a potentially reductive behaviorism is admirable, but the outright rejection of any nonreductive approach to mind may be premature.

2.2.2 Eliminativism

A counterpoint to the mysterian philosophy of materialism without reductionism, a view that essentially ignores neural explanations of mental phenomena, has emerged in the form of *eliminativism* or *eliminative materialism.* The main premise of eliminativism is that neurophysiology will not only help us to understand mind but that it will ultimately take the place of psychology. The antithetical difference between the new mysterians and the eliminativists is that the former say that mind is not reducible to brain facts although the latter rejects the objective necessity for any science of mind altogether—mentalism included. The eliminativist view solves the mind–brain problem simply by making mind disappear. Mentalism and mental processes, it says, are simply figments of our scientific primitiveness.

The roots of this philosophical viewpoint are found in the writing of Feyerabend (1963) who proposed that mental processes simply did not exist and, therefore, no science of them is required. (Hopefully, in throwing out mentalist psychologies, he did not also mean that behaviorist psychologies should give up their quest.)

A recurring eliminativist argument against both mentalism and behaviorism is that no subjective psychology can be anything other than a false science. They assert that only true scientific analysis of brain processes such as mind is the study of the neural functions themselves. It is asserted that all of the mental processes with which we now wrestle are nothing more or less than manifestations of neural activity. Therefore, in the light of some future super neuroscience, mind will ultimately be shown to be nothing more complicated than measurable neural phenomena. The psychology of today, it is further asserted by the eliminativists, is only a confused statement produced by our cloudy misinterpretations of our own self-awarenesses. The awarenesses result in a "folk psychology" that makes little sense in the context of modern science, often raising hypotheses and theories that are in direct conflict with "normal science." Paul Churchland (1988), a leading eliminativist, spelled out this argument in the following manner:

> As the eliminative materialists see it, the one-to-one match-ups [between our neuroscientific measures and commonsense mental entities] will not be found, and our commonsense psychological framework will not enjoy an intertheoretic reduction, because our commonsense psychological framework is a false and radically misleading conception of the causes of human behavior and the nature of cognitive activity. On this view, folk psychology is not just an incomplete representation of our inner natures; it is an outright misrepresentation of our internal states and activities. Consequently, we cannot expect a truly adequate neuroscientific account of our inner lives to provide theoretical categories that match up nicely with the categories of our common sense framework. Accordingly, we must expect that the older framework will simply be eliminated, rather than be reduced, by a matured neuroscience. (p. 43; brackets added)

In this manner, eliminative materialism attempts to solve the problem of explaining mental processes not by denying their accessibility or analyzability, but more severely by denying the fact that there is anything there to be made accessible. This is an extreme form of Ryle's (1949) "ghost in the machine" and is in agreement with Rey's (1988) similar suggestion in which the mind was denied any form of real existence.

Churchland (1988) also stated that this extreme antimentalist view is based on three main arguments.

First, conventional, common sense, or folk psychology, simply has not solved any of the most basic questions; for example, we still do not know the how or why of sleep, intelligence, or memory.

Second, it deals with problems that are so complex and difficult (like those just mentioned) that the most likely reason for the persistence of conventional mentalist psychology is the simple fact that nothing (prior to neurophysiology) had come along to take its place.

Third, the hope of a new ultrareductionism in which neurophysiology literally takes the place of psychology is now conceivable. However, as I noted earlier (Uttal, 1998), arguments against such an extreme neuroreductionism are now being raised that suggest this last criticism is not supportable even if it is true that the complexity and scientific failure arguments have merit.

The important general conclusion emerging from this brief review of the mysterians and the eliminativists is that there is a substantial body of contemporary thought that agrees with the argument that mind is not accessible. The logical basis for this conclusion differs—the mysterians conclude that we should all be monistic holists because mental phenomena are unanalyzable. The eliminativists, on the other hand reject mentalist "folk" psychology altogether.

2.2.3 Dennett

Dennett (1988), whose ideas about consciousness we have already encountered, is clearly a cognitive mentalist, as is flagged by his creation of the term "intentional system" as a substitute for cognitive systems. We have also seen in the introduction to this chapter his concern with consciousness as a central object of inquiry. Nevertheless, he helps us to identify some of the arguments against mentalism by what he believes are the errors made by the archvillain of the behaviorist persuasion—B. F. Skinner. Dennett lists what he sees as the main Skinnerian objections to mentalism as follows:

1. Mental events are not physical.
2. Mental events are private.
3. Mental events can only be inferred.
4. Mental events are too easy to invent.
5. The mental language does not explain anything.
6. Mental terms do not reduce to physical terms.

Dennett's attack, as he presents his arguments against each of these positions, was a highly ad hominem one. Skinner's clarity of thought and even intelligence, not to mention his literary skills and logical powers, were unnecessarily, in my opinion, challenged by Dennett in his diatribe. It is obviously not easy being a behaviorist in a predominantly cognitive world.

In his essays, Dennett (1988) attempted to refute these arguments, but mainly by alluding to the inconsistencies in Skinner's presentation of his arguments rather than by dealing with the arguments themselves. Indeed, one is not even sure if Dennett was responding to Skinner's views or creating a non-Skinner pseudoantagonist by requiring that "we must read between the lines" of Skinner's works to fully understand what he is saying (p. 57).

This, then, concludes our review of a few of the classic psychological and philosophical arguments that have been directed against mentalisms. Many of them are logical, philosophical, personal, theological, or humanistic in ways that are very different from those guiding sciences other than those concerned with mind. I appreciate that many philosophers of science argue that such criteria are the necessary fabric of any science, and that values such as these motivated many of the major scientific developments in psychology and other sciences throughout history. Although this is certainly true, it is time to turn to those issues such as accessibility and analyzability that are amenable to empirical research.

It may not be fashionable in today's intellectual environment to dredge up what some consider to be a pre-1960s positivism, but perhaps it is now timely to reconsider some of these fundamental issues that have not yet really been resolved. The history of psychology has been one of dramatic flip-flops in attitudes toward behaviorisms and mentalisms. Perhaps we are at another flip point.

At this point that question arises: Are there more objective arguments that can be brought to bear on the mentalism–behaviorism debate? My answer to this question is an unequivocally affirmative one. I hope the next section convinces my readers that this judgment is correct.

2.3 SOME NEW ARGUMENTS AGAINST MENTALISM

Earlier (Uttal, 1998), I criticized a number of the contemporary paradigms of perceptual science, particularly the goal of reductionism or, in the terminology of the present discussion, analysis. I argued for the acceptance of three major principles governing the use of models, neuroreductionism, and the search for a cognitive architecture, respectively. All three of these principles speak directly to the behaviorism–mentalism controversy. In brief, these principles are:

1. Models can be, at best, descriptions of the course of a process and can never achieve the much stronger role of ontologically reductive ex-

planation. By ontologically reductive, I designate an explanation at one level of measurement that is based on the rules and laws of a lower level of measurement. Thus, a statement in which the behavior of neurons is supposed to provide an explanation of a perceptual phenomenon is ontologically reductive, as well, of course, as neuroreductive. For definitions of different types of Reductionism, see Robinson's (1995) interesting article.

2. Neuroreductionism of this kind, however, is far more difficult and far less well accomplished than many of my colleagues seem to believe. Given the problems of complexity, chaos, and other well accepted physical science principles, it is unlikely that a neuronal network explanation of other than a few peripheral processes will be achieved.

3. Despite the often stated goals of contemporary cognitive psychology, neither behavioral (stimulus–response, input–output) nor cognitive analyses are capable of identifying the components of an internal mental architecture. The methods available are not suitable and, in any event, the task of identifying internal structure from behavioral findings is impossible in principle. The entire approach is based on an interlocking nest of unverifiable assumptions.

In contradiction to these principles, the currently dominant approach of cognitive mentalism—based on formal modeling, reductive cognitivism, and neuroreductionism—assumes that manipulation of experimental findings can reveal the underlying mechanisms. These mechanisms may be either neurophysiological structures presumed to account directly for the generation of the observed responses or cognitive components that participate in processing and transforming internal information, and thus in selecting or shaping external behaviors. The arguments I consider in this section also are presented as critiques of the mentalist philosophy.

Contemporary cognitive psychology is based on the following premises. First, the so far unfulfilled *hope* that mental processes are accessible. Second, the equally undemonstrated *hope* that our research will ultimately permit us to infer *unique* internal explanatory mechanisms given enough experiments and "converging" experimental evidence. Third, neuroreductionist cognitive psychology also adds the *hope* of explanatory neural models just as the computational approach adds the *hope* that our analogs will turn out to be homologs.

Given the detail with which I described the arguments against analyzability and both neuroreductionism and cognitive reductionism in my earlier book (Uttal, 1998) I now present only a summary of the most salient principles and findings that are germane to the issues currently under discussion. The following comments are abstracted and adapted from discussions in that book.

1. The basic ontological premise of the nature of psychobiological reality is known as *material monism.* Even though some professionals in this field reject this premise for personal theological reasons, to do so undermines the entire conceptual basis of the science. Material monism asserts that all mental acts, including conscious awareness, are nothing more or less than one set of the many functions carried out by the nervous system. This is the fundamental principle on which all subsequent ones rest. This is THE answer to the great ontological conundrum—is mind real? It asserts that mind is real in the sense that any function of any machine is real. At the present time, the best estimate of the psychoneural equivalent of mind (the neural equivalent of thought or the essential level of analysis) is the ensemble of detailed interactions among vast networks of neurons in the higher reaches of the cerebral cortex. The ensemble or statistical nature of the information patterns embodied in these nets is what emerges as a unified and molar manner as mental activity and leads to cognitively relevant behavior. Individual neurons are relatively unimportant except to the degree they play a role as constituents in these great neuronal networks. The role of any given neuron may be fleeting without undo instability being introduced in the perceptual experience. This is THE answer to the particular question—what produces mind? It defines the critical level of analysis at which we would have to work to understand how mental processes, such as conscious self-awareness, are generated. Many others have directed us to this same point of view, however. It is what Lashley (1942) meant when he said "It is the pattern and not the element that counts" (p. 306). It is also the message of the distributed neural storage and processing theories of such workers as DeValois and DeValois (1988), Graham (1989), and Pribram (1991) that invoke Fourier or Gabor fundamentals as the primitives of perception. Unfortunately, it also describes a level of complexity of the nervous system that is so enormous that it is likely that the exact relationship between brain structure and mental function may never be fathomable. Indeed, if the distributed models are correct it raises another very difficult problem. How does one study patterns of widely distributed neural networks at the detailed level required without creating a unanalyzable explosion of local measures? It is as if one tried to use a high powered microscope to study the gross anatomy of a specimen. Conversely, if one turns to the low power tool, how does one achieve the detailed information required to understand a neural network at the essential level? This brings us to the next great issue—a confusion of some closely related, but distinguishable, scientific questions.

2. Different questions of perceptual science are often confused. The attempt to answer the *localization question* may possibly be moving ahead under the impetus of new devices capable of examining the macroscopic places in the brain where activity seems to be maximal when some particular

mental activity occurs. The quite separate *representation question* is one of microscopic neuronal network interactions: It remains refractory and intractable. Unfortunately, it is this latter issue that lies at the heart of the effort to build mind–brain bridges. Representation (i.e., psychoneural equivalence) is the essential question. The issue can be restated in the context of the cognitivism–behaviorism controversy—Is it possible for psychology to determine the nature of these representations? In other words—are they accessible?

3. A corollary of 2. is that the mind is an information-processing activity of the brain. The metabolism and chemistry of neurons may set some limits on processing or transmission speeds and are interesting to the degree they define the technology in which mind is instantiated. However, neurochemistry is fundamentally irrelevant to the organizational and informational nature of the process. In principle, any other machine, built on any other technology, but arranged in the same way as the brain (whatever way that might be), would produce the same cognitive and perceptual processes—including conscious awareness. The issue in this case is—does cognitive neuroscience have the ability to determine the neural foundations of a thought?

4. The ideal goal of a science is *ontological reductionism* in which the phenomena at one level of discourse are explained in terms of mechanisms and processes at more microscopic levels. Many arguments, both fundamental and practical, suggest that true ontological reductionism for perception and other cognitive processes, to either neurophysiological or cognitive components, is unobtainable. If this premise is denied or falsified, then the entire mentalist approach including contemporary cognitive science must be ruled out as a valid scientific approach.

5. The arguments suggesting that analysis or reduction of thoughts into neural mechanisms and processes are not possible arise from matters of fundamental scientific principle. Specifically:

- The combinatorial complexity of cognitively relevant neural processes is so great that they are beyond computability or analysis.
- Complex systems can not be analyzed because such an analysis would violate well established physical principles such as the second law of thermodynamics. Mathematics and nature are one way systems and entropy cannot be reversed to order in closed systems like the brain.
- The necessary initial condition information required for an analysis of complex systems like the brain is no longer available when the brain matures according to newly emerging principles of chaos theory.
- Closed systems cannot be uniquely analyzed by examining the transformations that occur between inputs and outputs.

6. The inaccessibility of the higher levels of cognitive processing is due to the complexity of the neural networks. Yet, these regions are indisputatively the locus of the essential representative functions of the brain. It is disappointing to have to acknowledge that we do not know anything about the rules or logic by which neural activity becomes the equivalent of mental activity. It seems likely, although it cannot be proven, that the rules of cerebral logic are not well modeled by either conventional mathematics or current neural network computational models. Contemporary mathematics has evolved from the simple laws of physical science and may not be applicable in the same way to cognitive system analysis. Furthermore, mathematics is highly limited. Contrary to popular and a considerable portion of scientific opinion, mathematical models are neutral with regard to the actual physical nature of the mechanisms they model. At best, mathematical models are only incomplete abstractions of the physical systems they describe. In short, mathematics is descriptive and not ontologically explanatory. It is a means of describing the functional course of a process. The physiological premises of a theory are always distinguishable and separate from the mathematical ones. Mathematics is so powerful that it can introduce irrelevant attributes into our understanding of a system and so fragile that it can ignore critical ones. It shares these limitations with all other forms of modeling. Furthermore, many putatively distinct mathematical theories actually turn out to be duals of each other. That is, the theories are often derivable, one from the other, and may differ only in secondary issues such as their neural premises.

7. Scientific examination of the nature of the relationship between mental activity and neurophysiological activity is so severely constrained and bounded that there exists serious doubt about the possibility of building explanatory bridges from one domain to the other. This conclusion suggests the material monistic ontological metaphysics expressed in 1 may have to be paired with a dualistic epistemology. The major premise of this point of view is the same as "materialism without reductionism" argument of the new mysterians presented earlier in this chapter.

8. One of the most fundamental and most ignored principles opposing reduction of mental processes to brain mechanisms, the Black Box theorem, well known to engineers and automata theorists is usually ignored by cognitive psychologists. To reiterate this important principle, there is no way to deduce the internal structure from input–output (i.e., behavioral) experiments. This holds for all psychophysical and cognitive experiments as well as attempts to infer internal structure of electronic or mechanical hardware. Philosophers have been well aware of the neutrality of models and the limits of stimulus–response methods for years. One of the most eminent of contemporary ontologists, Quine (1969) came to the conclusion that—for each of the models of a theory "there is bound to

be another which is a permutation or perhaps a diminution of the first" (p. 54). The great physicist, mathematician, philosopher of science Henri Poincare (1854-1912) made a similar point when he assured us that any model can be made into many others by adding "gratuitous" parameters.

9. In some cases, attempts are made to circumvent the black box barrier by applying other constraints such as least energy, elegance, parsimony, or economy. Although these criteria may be partially useful in some simple systems, such additional constraints are usually irrelevant in the context of the brain and its produced cognitive processes. The huge number of neurons in the brain obviates the need for parsimony or economy. It is impossible to know what "elegance" represents in a system about which we do not even know the basic logical rules being used.

10. Many proposed neuroreductionist "explanations" or analyses are based on false analogies or spurious correlations between the neural and cognitive domains. Often this misidentification is based on nothing more than a play on words whose similarity is more poetic than real.

11. In other instances it is based on a similarity of functional form or some superficial isomorphism. Isomorphic representation, however, is not a satisfactory criterion for psychoneural equivalence. Some codes cannot be isomorphic (e.g., greenness). Some isomorphic relationships (e.g., retinotopic mapping) may be only indirectly relevant merely characterizing the nature of the transmission codes conveying information to the more symbolic representation of perceptual processes at higher levels rather then the higher level mechanisms themselves.

12. There is such an enormous variety of neurophysiological activities resulting from the vast number of neural responses involved in even the simplest cognitive process that it is usually possible to find virtually anything one needs to support almost any reductionist theory of neural coding or representation by injudicious selection of data.

13. Many proposed neuroreductionist "explanations" of perceptual or cognitive functions are based on dramatic, but misinterpreted, findings from the neurophysiological laboratory. The raw observations can usually be replicated, but their meaning may vary with changes in the current theoretical consensus.

14. Correlation between cognitive processes and neural responses in some region of the brain does not necessarily signify that that location is the site of psychoneural equivalence. Some brain locations or group of locations must be responsible for perceptual experience, but correlation is not tantamount to equivalence. This principle must be kept in mind particularly when one applies the criterion of the first (or lowest) level of explicit correlation between a perceptual experience and a neural response as, for example, a proof of low level vision. Many generally accepted "direct" methods for examining the brain (such as the PET or fMRI scans) may produce results that may later not mean what they seem to initially. Even the "hardest"

and most direct data may not only be difficult to replicate, but even more fundamentally, may prove to be sending different messages at different times because of different theoretical orientations in our scientific history.

15. Psychophysical data take precedence over neurophysiological data. Psychophysical data are the final outcome of the entire perceptual brain–mind system. Any contradictory neural data must, by definition, be incorrect or irrelevant to the information processes that lay between stimuli and perceptions. In other words, the true final path long sought by neuroanatomists is behavior!

16. Reduction of mind to the components of an underlying cognitive architecture is also likely to be an impossible quest. The main reasons behind this assertion are based on the fact that unlikely assumptions have to be made about the nature of thought for such an enterprise to be achieved. Most of these unlikely assumptions are based on an assumed functional rigidity of the putative components that is in conflict with our observations of the actual adaptability of human cognitive processes. The most effective arguments against this kind of cognitive analysis has been provided to us by Pachella (1974).

17. Many dichotomous arguments (e.g., serial vs. parallel processing) that have driven cognitive science throughout its history are extremist "straw men." In almost all cases, the ultimate resolution is in the form of a compromise that adopts neither extreme view. The work of Shaw (1978) and of Townsend and Thomas (1994) is particularly important in making this point. Both showed that the any disagreement concerning whether a cognitive function was carried out in serial or parallel usually was resolved in favor of a compromise system.

18. Psychophysical, behavioral, or cognitive data, the observations of molar psychology, are neutral with regard to the underlying neural or cognitive mechanisms to both the perceptual scientist and the perceiver. Neither the external nor the internal observer can have any insight in the logical processes that lead from a stimulus to a percept. Only the behavioral outcomes are observable or perceivable. Herein is the most fundamental argument separating behaviorists and mentalists. The bald presentation of this statement in an axiomatic form only begins to illuminate what empirical studies such as those of Nisbett and Wilson (1977), which are described fully later in this chapter, document in a more rigorous empirical manner.

19. Our perception of cognitive phenomena—the data and phenomenological observations themselves—is conditioned by the theories that have evolved in our science. We more often than not see what we want to see.

20. Many of the findings of cognitive science reflect the design of our experiments or the instruments and methods used rather than the psychobiological realities of the mind–brain system.

The arguments (in abstract) that I present here are more fully developed in Uttal (1998). They collectively suggest that mental components, even if we can agree they are accessible, are not amenable to analysis or reduction to either cognitive or neural components.

Many of the arguments in the list just presented are close analogs of points made in previous sections that survey arguments against mentalisms. The language and emphases are slightly different but it does not take much effort to see that a wide variety of scholars are now arguing against the foundation arguments supporting cognitive mentalism.

In this section, I have concentrated on principles that are mainly drawn from other fields of science. The next step in our discussion is to examine the literature to determine if there is, in fact, any empirical psychological evidence to support mentalism as an inappropriate approach to understanding whatever it is that mind is. The specific question now confronted is: do verbal or other behavioral responses correlate sufficiently well with independent measures of mental activity to justify both the accessibility and analysis assumptions that are essential to the pursuit of a cognitive mentalism?

2.4 SOME EMPIRICAL ARGUMENTS AGAINST MENTALISMS

2.4.1 Nisbett and Wilson (1977)

Many of the arguments against mentalism that have been described so far are philosophical, logical, semantic, or conceptual. Even the arguments I listed in the previous section are somewhat indirect, mainly using the principles of other sciences to make a case against mental accessibility and analyzability. There are various levels of credibility that adhere to various kinds of arguments, but none should have as much influence as any available direct empirical evidence that speaks to the question of the accessibility of mental processes. The issue now confronted is—what *do* we know about the accessibility our own mental processes from experiments? This is not the same as the related, but much broader, issue—what *can* we know about the accessibility of our mental processes? I am not dealing here with the grand epistemological question of the limits of knowledge at this point, but rather a straightforward analysis of the outcome of specific experiments that compare verbal reports with other indicators of the mental actions that must be going on as people make decisions and solve problems.

Given the long history of the problem of accessibility from the point of view of philosophy and the many uncertainties that accrue to it, it is still somewhat surprising that there is actually a substantial body of empirical data that speaks directly to this question. This research activity is not extensive, and it is found more in the applied fields (such as social psychology) than in the domain of traditional experimental psychology, but it does exist. It is also not well known. Curiously, data showing that subjects are unable to accurately report the causal forces on their behavior seem to have been almost immediately challenged and then to have disappeared from the literature rather quickly.

It turns out that when you ask people under controlled conditions what it is that they "thought" they were doing or why they "felt" the way they did that the correlations between their own self-interpretations, introspections, and reports concerning their behavioral responses, on the one hand, and the implications experimenters may draw from what is known of the actual antecedent stimulus conditions, on the other, are very low indeed. An important pioneering study exploring the ramifications of this issue was reported by Nisbett and Wilson (1977). The work was expanded into an important monograph on the topic by Nisbett and Ross (1980).

The implications of the work of Nisbett and his colleagues are so profound and damning to the mentalist approach of contemporary cognitivism that it virtually had to be attacked and discredited by psychologists of the mentalist bent. The bottom line of both the monograph (Nisbett & Ross, 1980) and their empirical article (Nisbett & Wilson, 1977) is that mental processes of both mundane and sophisticated kinds are not accessible in any valid way to the self-observer!

Let us consider the Nisbett and Wilson (1977) paper in detail. These authors first reviewed a body of relevant scientific literature that dealt with verbal reports of what they refer to as higher mental processes. They subsequently carried out a set of straightforward and well designed experiments to study the correlation between what subjects thought they were doing when they solved problems and what they actually were doing. After their extensive review and laboratory work, Nisbett and Wilson were led to the following main conclusions which I now present in a paraphrased form:

1. Humans subjects cannot, in general, accurately report on (a) the effects of a stimulus; (b) the existence of a stimulus; (c) the existence of a response; or (d) even that any inferential process had occurred.

2. When reporting how they responded when a stimulus was presented, human subjects depend on implicit, a priori theories. If the theory seems to fit the situation, the subject accepts the fact that the stimulus was effective; if not, the stimulus is deemed to be without effect.

3. Sometimes the subjective report seems to be correct, but this is usually not because the subject adequately interpreted his cognitive processes. Rather, the correct judgment was due to the fact that the subject's a priori

theory happened to work in this instance. (Abstracted and paraphrased from Nisbett and Wilson, 1977, p. 233)

Some of the experimental studies they reviewed dealt with the problem of verbal reports of mental processes associated with the well known social psychological concepts of cognitive dissonance and attribution. Nisbett and Wilson reported that subjects were only rarely asked to describe their mental processes in studies of this kind even though the goal of the research was to understand exactly those processes. In those few instances that did include some report of what the subjects thought they were doing, Nisbett and Wilson (1977) concluded that the correlation between self-reported measures of motivation states and of the actual behavior was "nil" (p. 235).

Nisbett and Wilson reviewed five other areas of psychological research that they believed argued against the validity of verbal reports as valid indicators other kinds of thought processes. These include studies of subliminal perception; problem solving; helping behavior; learning without awareness; and complex judgment tasks. It is impractical to review here in detail all of the articles they cite. Suffice it to say that, after this exercise, Nisbett and Wilson reported that the preponderance of data supported their conclusions as paraphrased. The common feature of all of the studies they reviewed was that subjects were "virtually never" (p. 243) able to accurately specify how a stimulus in a complex situation affected their behavior in a way that corresponded to independent evaluations or behavioral measures. As they pointed out, errors in this series of experimental studies varied enormously, but could be summarized as follows:

1. Subjects did not identify the correct stimulus.
2. Subjects were insensitive to the impact of spatial position effects.
3. Subjects were insensitive to the impact of scale anchoring effects.
4. Subjects were insensitive to the effects of their own personalities.
5. Subjects repeatedly reported that some stimuli that had strong effects had none.

Another very compelling finding from this important paper was that Nisbett and Wilson reported that erroneous reports made by subjects were not random. The types of errors were well organized and seemed to derive from the existing conceptual models and "a priori theories" that were a part of the subjects' previous experience but rarely a part of the particular experimental conditions. Cultural traditions, rules of behavior introduced by the family, schools, or the general culture, anecdotal and particular experiences that had been overgeneralized into an explanatory theory, and even the subject's own value systems, seemed to be more important in determining the nature of their reports than the actual situational and stimulus conditions. The question one must ask is: if subjects do so poorly in these simple situations, why should we expect introspective validity in more complex self-interpretations such as those called for in psychotherapy?

Nisbett and Wilson (1977) also reported the results of a number of interesting miniexperiments that they conducted. This collection of demonstration studies was designed, they acknowledge, specifically to deal with stimuli intended to produce wrong responses. Nevertheless, in spite of some subsequent criticism of this strategy, the generality of their conclusions is not diminished because so many of these miniexperiments were close to real-life situations. For example, they found that subjects did not appreciate being given word cues that were essential for the solution of a presented problem. They also found that subjects did not realize how compelling the position of a set of items in a series was to their subsequent qualitative evaluations. Furthermore, they found that subjects were incapable of appreciating that their evaluations of other people were determined by a previously viewed videotape; that the experimentally manipulated warmth or coldness of personality strongly affected their evaluations of that person in other situations. They reported further that what subjects read prior to an experiment affected their evaluations and decisions and that distractions affected their ratings of the artistic quality of film clips.

The specific details of these experiments are not terribly important to our present discussion, but they all carried a common message—what humans verbally reported in experiments in which they were required to make statements about their own thought processes seemed to have little to do with their actual cognitive processes. The general result was that in the quasi-real life situations set up in the Nisbett and Wilson miniexperiments, their subjects were incapable of discriminating between the stimuli that affected their logical processes and the irrelevant ones or accurately reporting their actual decision-making processes. Supplemented by the more formal earlier experiments that Nisbett and Wilson reviewed, the case against valid introspective self-reports became increasingly strong. If it is finally concluded that they were correct, Watson's intuitive repugnance for introspective reports would be placed on a much more solid foundation and the case against mentalism of all kinds would be substantially strengthened.

To summarize, Nisbett and Wilson (1977) described a situation in which introspective verbal reports must be considered to be a failed and flawed tool for accessing higher mental processes. Problem solving and decision making certainly does go on more or less successfully, and in some rare cases subjects may correctly report the logical processes when asked to report on how these cognitive actions were carried out. But, in many, if not most cases, the introspective interpretations reflected in the verbal responses of their subjects were terribly inaccurate. Indeed, based on their review and studies, it seems impossible for any experimenter to determine whether these subjective reports were correct or incorrect. This is hardly a basis for a solid scientific approach to the nature of human nature. It is, however, another strong empirical argument that mental processes are generally inaccessible.

Nisbett and Wilson are social psychologists and deal with complex high-level cognitive processes. Perhaps, it might be argued, the spectrum of studies with which they were concerned produced a valid but ungeneralizable conclusion. Social psychologists deal with very different stimuli and response categories than with the more microscopic elements used by more traditional experimental psychologists. Perhaps their choice of experiments can explain why subjects may not have understood their own cognitive processes. It is, however, remarkable that their vigorous argument against introspective reports should have come from the domain of social psychology—a field in which subjective reports are so central to almost all of that field's theoretical and empirical activities. If Nisbett and Wilson were correct, it should have made a shambles of many of the more applied fields of psychology that depend on subjective reports, verbal responses, and introspective probes into cognitive processing. As discussed later, it did not have that impact.

Because of the putative importance of their work we must ask: How general are the conclusions that can be drawn from the Nisbett and Wilson paper? It may be argued, as a counterexample, that in well controlled laboratory situations dealing with the precisely defined mental processes typical of other fields of scientific psychology, it should be possible to use the subject's behavioral responses to infer something about the nature of the underlying mental processes. Continuation of this line of logic might lead some to suggest that the Nisbett and Wilson's work, although interesting, is not relevant to studies in sensory processing, learning, or other topics of more circumscribed and formal types carried out in other psychological laboratories.

Although there may be some merit to such a counterargument, Nisbett and Wilson's findings are classic examples of *dissociation arguments.* By this term, I mean that a general principle can be validly falsified by simply showing a single counterexample. If one were to assert, that "all people are taller than 6 feet," falsification would be mandatory if only a single example of a person who was 5 foot, 6 inches could be identified. Similarly, the general presumption that it is possible to derive valid statements about intrapersonal thought processes by means of introspective reports is falsified by showing that in many situations the process leads to ambiguous or false inferences. Nisbett and Wilson have provided just such evidence. They have accumulated enough contradictory evidence to the premise that verbal reports accurately portray actual cognitive processes to do more than just simply suggest that verbal reports will always be problematical. Their work suggests that one would *never* be able to trust responses of this kind.

Nisbett and Ross (1980) employed these ideas to applied problems of human daily life. The topics considered in the 1980 monograph range further afield than those covered in the Nisbett and Wilson (1977) article but the argument is essentially the same. People can solve problems and reason, but all too frequently they are incorrect in their insights into how they arrived at the solution to the posed problem. It is, as many psychologists have appreciated over the years, the end product of cognition of which we are aware, not the procedures, processes, or mechanisms that led to those end products. This fundamental concept, however, is virtually always ignored in mentalist psychologies. At the very worst, direct introspective access to mental, no less than physiological, mechanisms is just not possible. Once this fact is accepted, then many of the other controversies become much easier to resolve. To coin a phrase, when a person solves a problem, what they think they are thinking may be totally unrelated to what they are actually thinking!

The significant general conclusion that can be drawn from this important body of work is that introspection, in particular, and self-evaluation reported in the form of verbal reports, in general, cannot serve as a solid basis for an objective psychological science. This is a strong argument for behaviorism. The most striking thing about Nisbett and his colleagues' work is that it is based on empirical evidence rather than the value judgments and speculations that seemed to be typical of the early behaviorists. However prescient the pioneers may have been, it must be acknowledged that the decision of those early behaviorists to reject introspection was based on far less compelling arguments. Perhaps this is one of the reasons that the controversy has continued for so long.

It is not surprising that not all experts in the field agreed with their conclusions. Indeed, the work was severely criticized almost immediately following its publication on both methodological and what were called "theoretical" grounds by Smith and Miller (1978). Their methodological argument can be summed up by noting that:

> To take the fact that this methodology succeeds in hoaxing subjects and then to generate a general perceptual rule from it carries this point [people are generally unsuccessful in self-reporting the mental processes] too far. (p. 356; brackets added)

Smith and Miller raised three specific arguments in their rebuttal article. First, they argued the hypothesis put forward by Nisbett and Smith cannot be falsified. By invoking both the failed correspondences and the successful ones between verbal reports and the "independent" measures, they contend there is no way critics can show that Nisbett and Smith are not correct. Thus, they reject the argument on the falsibility grounds suggested by the distinguished philosopher of science, Popper (1959).

Second, they reiterated the argument already quoted from their article—the experiments were intentionally designed to mislead and thus this experimental approach confounds the true issue—the validity of the introspective method.

Third, the experiments involved the manipulation of certain variables but did not control others that may well have been salient. Therefore, the question of how could either the subjects or the experimenters have been able to determine what reality (i.e., the actual cognitive process) was in this case. The subjects may have been more correct than was thought by the experimenters. Other methodological arguments were also raised about the way in which the statistical analyses were carried out, but they seem to me inconsequential in the context of Smith and Miller's main counterarguments.

In their final comments, Smith and Miller (1978) concluded that Nisbett and Wilson are probably right in many cases in denying subjects the ability to validly report the logic of their thoughts. However, they argued "their [Nisbett & Wilson's] claim that access is almost never possible is overstated" (p. 361). Furthermore, they asserted that (as is usual when scientists cross swords) "more research is needed."

My conclusion, however, is that they greatly underestimated the compelling force of Nisbett and Wilson's (1977) research because they misunderstood the main point made by this important study. That point was that access to our mental processes is inaccurate *enough of the time* so that any attempt to use it as a *reliable* source of valid data, particularly in the highly multivariate areas of psychology concerned with higher level cognitive processes, must lead to absurdities *at least some of the time.* Indeed, there is ample evidence that this is just what has happened throughout the entire programmatic history of psychotherapy—a topic I leave to more knowledgeable critics such as Dawes (1994).

More germane to this anti-introspective argument is the following set of metaphors: The use of verbal reports as data in the development of cognitive theories is as worthless as trying to discern the fine structure of an image through a low pass filter; as worthless as trying to determine whether the properties of an automobile in which you are interested are as communicated by the salesperson; as worthless as trying to reconstruct the evolution of a species for which there is no fossil history; as worthless as trying to predict a stock market driven by what are essentially random forces. No! I should correct myself; none of these examples is as challenging as the problems faced by psychologists when they attempt to infer thought processes by means of verbal reports from an entity that does not even have access to its own cognitive mechanisms.

Shortly after the Smith and Miller (1978) critique, Ericsson and Simon (1980) also challenged Nisbett's and Wilson's (1977) findings and conclusions and attempted to rebut their main conclusion that "people often cannot report accurately on the effects of particular stimuli." Ericsson and Simon argued that although verbal reports are often inconsistent or inaccurate when compared with independent behavioral or situational estimates, they are acceptable as data (i.e., they represent the cognitive processes of the subject in a valid manner) in many other situations. In particular, when the verbal reports are collected concurrently with the experimental task, they argued that they were solid indicators of the underlying cognitive processes.

In their critique of Nisbett and Wilson's (1978) report, Ericsson and Simon (1980) attempted to identify the sources of the observed inconsistencies between verbal reports and behavior. They identified two main causes: Failures of retrieval from long-term memory so that related but inaccurate material is reported, and the filling in or completion of a memory to make a cognitively consistent story. Fair enough! However, there are probably many other sources of bias that pollute our memories. Indeed, the list of possible sources of cognitive bias can grow so large as to make Nisbett and Wilson's point even more forcibly than they originally did.

Ericsson and Simon went on to suggest that several other reports of dissociation of the verbal report from what apparently was actually occurring in the cognitive machinery were confounded for one reason or another. The brunt of Ericsson and Simon's criticism of the Nisbett and Wilson paper can be summarized as follows:

1. The language used by Nisbett and Wilson is equivocal. Phrases such as "often" and "sometimes" were used and this attenuates the value of their conclusions.
2. No explanatory model of their findings was presented.
3. Subjects in many of the cited studies based their answers on a priori theories rather than on their actual memories.
4. The experiments that served as the basis for Nisbett and Wilson's conclusions were examples of situations in which the false verbal responses were forced.

Ericsson and Simon suggested that whenever inconsistencies occur, in many instances they can be explained, at least *ex post facto.* They then proposed an explanatory model and some methods for overcoming what they accepted as real dissociations between the verbal reports and behavioral or situational indicators.

The essence of their argument was that verbal reports *are* satisfactory indicators of underlying cognitive processes when they are collected concurrently, but can be polluted when they are processed *ex post facto* by means of memories. It is in those situations that subjects will resort to recall of specific programs, reconstruct partial memories, or infer from prior or ad hoc theories of what they should have done, or fall back on general procedures that might have processed the data. In this latter context, they did agree with Nisbett and Wilson's conclusion.

Ericsson and Simon (1980) were, it must be emphasized, not accepting the classic procedure of introspection. Rather, they argued against the "unjustified extrapolation of a justified challenge to a particular mode of verbal reporting (introspection)" (p. 247) to valid uses of verbal reports as data concerning cognition.

Finally, Ericsson and Simon specifically rejected the claim made by anonymous psychologists who are obviously antagonistic toward the validity of verbal reports that

> . . . the premise that if one could produce a single case of a clearly inaccurate or inconsistent verbal report, then verbal reports are wholly inadmissible as data. (p. 243)

As I noted earlier, this is at least an arguable point. But, more important is the fact that whether or not their rejection of this point is logically sound (and I think it is not), the mere presence of a single contradictory example to the validity of verbal reports means that we would never be able to fully assure ourselves of the validity of any other without exhaustive identification and subsequent testing of all possible sources of inconsistency. Obviously, this is not possible and, however inconvenient it may be to mentalist psychologies of many different kinds, the specter of a dissociation of verbal reports and cognitive processes remains. In sum, its utility in some other context does not justify the postulation of a nontruth.

It is further interesting to note that people do almost as poorly in interpreting the world around them as they do in reporting on their own internal thought processes. Gilovich (1991) provided a wonderful account of why people have such peculiar beliefs about the world. Many of the reasons he cites as sources of people's incorrect conclusions about their environment are also applicable to the problem of why people misinterpret their own thought processes. For example, according to Gilovich, most of our fellow human beings:

1. See what they want or expect to see
2. Misperceive random data
3. Overgeneralize from incomplete data
4. Love a "good" story
5. Accept what is plausible rather than what is real

6. Are strongly influenced by authority, the printed word, or what others around them think

among many other strong psychological and social forces at work to distort our judgment.

Discussions among psychologists of the sources of erroneous beliefs in both popular and scientific thought occur frequently. The interested reader is directed to Kahneman, Slovic, and Tversky's (1982) very important book. However, it is not just the naïve subject in an experiment who is influenced in these manners. It is certainly also true that the experimenter–theoretician, being human, is also subject to many of these same sources of misperception. (I refer my readers to Hanson's [1958] insightful book on the way in observations and data are controlled by theories and methods.)

What, then, can we say about some of the more narrowly defined areas of psychology, for example sensory psychophysics. Verbal reports are a major part of the methodology of even these sciences which are well anchored to the stimulus. It is here that the thoughts of Brindley (1960) in a long forgotten book on the visual pathways may be relevant. Brindley was a physiologist who was primarily concerned with the anatomy, physiology, and chemistry of the visual pathway rather than the perceptual phenomena that we are manly concerned with in psychological studies. However, he was also concerned with what he called "sensory experiments, that is, experiments in which an essential part of the result is a subject's report of his own sensations" (p. 144). Brindley distinguished between two kinds of observations—Class A and Class B. Class A observations are those that are essentially pure discriminations of identity or equality. In other words, the Class A experiment is based simply on the question: Are two stimuli identical or different? Or the subject might be asked and equally valid Class A question of the form—is there anything there or not? Class A observations of this kind require only the simplest kind of discriminative mental processing on the part of the observer. Like all other psychophysical judgments, they may be susceptible to biases emerging from conservative or loose criteria, but these bias are either controllable (e.g., by the use of a forced choice psychophysical procedure) or measurable (e.g., by the application of the Signal Detection Theory method). To whatever degree they are not so controllable, at least they represent the simplest possible and perhaps the least cognitively affected kind of verbal report.

Class B observations, on the other hand, are those that require something more than this basic judgment of identity or difference or presence or absence. In visual experiments, subjects are required to go beyond a simple discrimination to apply some metric of quantity, quality, time, or space or even more intricate judgment or interpretation. Brindley believed that, in general, Class B observations "have mostly been used unsatisfactorily . . ." (p. 145) as data for the justification of what he called "psychophysical linking hypotheses."

Brindley's point was that only the simplest Class A judgments are acceptable as scientific data. Virtually all other types of responses that require much more complex cognitive processes are affected and modulated in such a way that the report of the perceptual experience is distorted. Experiments that seem to initially require Class B observations are useful only, Brindley asserted, when they can be converted to Class A responses by appropriate redesign of the method. The classic psychophysical techniques, for example, were all designed to require only Class A responses in order to minimize the mental transformations required of the subject. The examination of the effects of a wide-ranging parameter was accomplished by repeated trials in which the experimenter may have manipulated the conditions of the experiment in a complex manner, but the subject's task was never more complicated than a simple Class A response. As discussed in Chapter 3, response simplicity of this kind must be one of main characteristics of a revitalized behaviorism.

Brindley's main point was that Class A observations are the only ones that at least modestly assured the theoretician that the verbal report is validly describing or measuring the true mental (i. e., perceptual) processes that account for the stimulus–response relations. If it is difficult enough to ask a subject to answer a question such as—how bright is that light? How much less confidence should we have in the answer to the question, "On what basis did you solve that problem?" When attention, social factors, expectancies, relationships, motives, and individual differences are involved, the situation is simply too heavily polluted by the many factors active at these "higher levels" to trust what is being reported as representing anything specific about the underlying mental mechanisms. Unfortunately, all-too-many psychological studies are confounded by such biasing forces. One must decide whether the confusion is of sufficient interest itself to change the goal of the work from *what people think* to *what people think they think*. The more applied fields of social and clinical psychology may well have some hope of determining what are the normative ways that people think they are thinking. However, if the barriers to valid verbal reports reviewed in this section are real, then what people are actually thinking may be far less accessible.

2.4.2 Bargh On Automaticity

Many of the findings discussed in the preceding section speak against the validity of using verbal reports as data for the explication of models and theories of mind. This argument can be extrapolated to the inference of relations between the elicited responses themselves and the subject's awareness of the causes for that behavior. If, for example, our behavior is elicited by influences of which we were only vaguely "aware," the verbal reports of what was "going on inside our minds" could hardly be expected to be of much use. What may seem to the experimenter to be intentional and a result of conscious choice may, to the contrary, turn out to be automatic, even thoughtless, responses far removed from the actual mental transformations. Our behavior may be much more the result of previous stimulation that elicited a more or less automatic response when an appropriate trigger stimulus was presented. In other words, *automaticity* is another example of a dissociation between the actual causes of observed behavior and what the subject may introspectively believe was the source of that behavior.

Bargh and his colleagues (Bargh, Chen, & Burrows, 1996; Bargh, 1997) have been among the most active and productive students of automatic behavior in recent years. Their summary point, like that of Nisbett and Wilson, is that although the influence of cognitive mechanisms cannot be excluded in the determination of behavioral responses, subjects are so unaware of the actual sources and mechanisms of their behavior that verbal reports cannot be depended on in any attempt to describe or explain those mental processes. Indeed, according to Bargh and his colleagues, it is likely that subjects will as often as not attribute their behavior to totally irrelevant external causes rather than to their actual cognitive goals and processes.

Clearly, Bargh and his colleagues are weaving a behaviorist logical thread into the fabric of social psychological theory. Their approach points out that active "conscious" decision making by the individual may play a much smaller part in the determination of many different kinds of behavior than had been previously believed. A much more influential determinant, according to them, is the ensemble of previous experiences and the ways in which these experiences are modified by the feelings, goals, and sets of the individual. Bargh and his colleagues, like many other more explicitly behaviorist psychologists, do not reject either the reality or the efficacy of mental activity. However, they are very clear in their assertion that what we perceive and how we respond—in other words, the ways in which the stimulus will be incorporated into our mental states—is going to be as strongly influenced by these preexisting feelings and goals as by current stimuli.

The important point in evaluating the work of Bargh and his colleagues in the present context is that it represents another compelling example of the dissociation of introspective verbal reports and actual behavior. Evidence for automaticity of responses is additional proof that people are disconnected from their actual cognitive mechanisms in a way that makes any hope of accessing the components of their cognitive system virtually hopeless.

The empirical studies that Bargh and his colleagues carried out are from a field that is fairly remote from the arena of traditional experimental psychology. Nevertheless, their work adds to the other arguments against the mentalist approach that are collected in this book. They challenge the ability of psychologists to access directly or infer indirectly the nature of those mental processes. I now review some of their more important findings and conclusions.

An exemplar study from the Bargh laboratory is reported in Bargh, Chen, and Burrows (1996). The goal of this experiment was to show that a subject's subsequent behavior could be strongly modified by what had seemed to be an unrelated previous experience. They showed that previous experience had a powerful *priming* effect on a subsequent behavior that was undetected and unappreciated by the subject. In this case the priming experience was a word game in which three groups of subjects were given a collection of scrambled words and asked to arrange them into a grammatically correct sentence. The independent variable in the experiment was the tone of the vocabulary items used in the word games. The tone could be either polite, neutral, or rude. Thus, for example, "considerate" was a "polite" word, "occasionally" was a "neutral" word, and "brazen" was a "rude" word.

After playing this word game, subjects were unknowingly introduced into a frustrating situation in the hall outside the experimental chamber. As the subject exited from the room in which they had played the "word game," the experimenter carried on a prolonged conversation with a third person—a confederate—and persistently ignored the subject's presence. The dependent variable in the experiment was the proportion of subjects who ultimately interrupted this frustrating and delaying conversation. The results were highly significant. The *polite*, *neutral*, and *rude* word games led to 18%, 37%, and 65% interruption rates respectively. The important specific point in the context of the present discussion was that in later briefings none of the subjects ever indicated any awareness their behavior had been influenced by the priming conditions produced by the selection of vocabulary items in the word game.

The general importance of the Bargh, Chen, and Burrows (1996) study is that complex patterns of behavior can be modified by stimuli without conscious awareness on the part of the subject. The subjects were totally unaware these stimuli played any part in determining their behavior. Once again, as in the Nisbett and Wilson study 2 decades earlier, there was a dissociation between the subject's verbal reports of their cognitive processing and the actual chain of causal cognitive factors.

Bargh (1997) summarized many of his ideas about other kinds of "automatic" behavior in a extensive review of the literature. He made an important additional and very germane point concerning serial and parallel models of mental activity—models that have played such an important role in the cognitive movement. Noting that historically the idea of a series of steps was the normative model, he suggested that this led to the idea that the several serial steps (e.g., perception, decision making, response selection) were all cognitive processes not consciously accessible to the introspecting subject. With the emerging realization that many of these steps could be carried out in parallel, it became even more difficult to associate conscious mentation with any one of the stages—one would have to be conscious of several of the involved steps simultaneously. This line of reasoning, Bargh asserted, leads to a diminution of the theoretical role that consciousness plays and an enhancement of the role of automatic processing. Consciousness, he said, "can no longer be viewed as *necessary* for behavior and judgments and evaluations to be made in a given situation . . ." (p. 37). If this line of logic is correct, how could any kind of psychology that depends on verbal reports have access to the real underlying cognitive processes and mechanisms?

It is important to appreciate that neither Bargh's (1997) nor Bargh, Chen, and Burrows' (1996) empirical results, nor those of Nisbett and Wilson (1977) deny the importance or the existence of mental processes or of any form of consciousness. Rather, all this work simply emphasizes that introspection and verbal reports by subjects of their own cognitive processes are, in many cases, completely disjoint from the actual mental processes.

These results, therefore, add to my argument that mental processes are, for all serious research purposes, inaccessible. They do so, however, without denying that there are massive transforms carried out by our brains between an incident stimulus and the resulting response. What these transforms are, however, is not apparent to the subject. To the degree that any kind of verbal report is used to achieve the stated goals of mentalist psychologies, the obtained data may be misleading. Direct determination of mental states and processes by means of verbal reports, therefore, would be impossible.

2.4.3 Loftus' Work on Memory

In the preceding sections we have been concerned with the degree of correlation between what a subject verbally reported as the perceived reasons for and causes of their immediate behavior, on the one hand, and independent estimates of the reasons and causes made by an experimenter, on the other. The verbal reports made by the subjects were based on their immediate recall of the experimental situation immediately after it happened. Throughout the history of psychology, and particularly since the introduction of Freudian psychoanalysis as a therapeutic method, the idea has persisted that there is a high correlation between what happened early in a child's life and later adult behavior. The basic concept was that even if an individual was not "consciously aware" of or could not remember early experiences, those experiences could have a powerful causal effect on subsequent behavior. Unlike the Nisbett and Wilson (1977) or the

Bargh et al. (1996; Bargh, 1997) studies, which explored short-term effects, these influences could persist, it was asserted, over many years if not the entire lifetime of an individual.

In recent years, such a hypothesis has led to one of the most irresponsible episodes in the history of psychotherapy. On the basis of the premise that long-term memories could be repressed and then influence subsequent behavior, a cottage industry of "repressed memory" therapists has grown up. The professed strategy of these charlatans was to open the door to the repressed memories and thus permit them to be both remembered and reported in a way that could expose perpetrators of childhood abuse, solve current personal problems, and, in general, enhance human existence.

However, there is an increasingly formidable literature suggesting that not only can we not understand our own current cognitive processes, but the failures of long-term memory can be substantial. Specifically, Loftus (1979, 1994, 1996) and a number of others have repeatedly shown that our long-term memories are not only fallible with regard to how much is forgotten or distorted, but can also be completely fictitious. Loftus argued that the ability to implant memories of events that never occurred is so strong that completely fallacious memories can be constructed in the laboratory that are both compellingly real to the subject and highly significant in determining experimental results. This is not an exotic and minor effect; these memories are extremely susceptible to the suggestions of an experimenter or, much more seriously, a therapist with a hidden social agenda.

It is not necessary for me to recapitulate the specific experimental techniques that Loftus and the others used to demonstrate this process of inserting false memories. For the purposes of the technical argument made in this book, the demonstration of the ease with which false memories can be injected into the memory store of a subject represents another strong piece of evidence that cognitive reality and verbal reports or observed nonverbal behavior may be completely uncorrelated and dissociated from the mental events that actually occurred. Once again, the main premise of mentalist psychologies—that mental processes can be accurately accessed—is challenged.

2.4.4 Implicit Learning

Given the difficulties in linking verbal behavior and the underlying mental processes, some psychologists have sought to develop a model of mind that ameliorates the problem by incorporating such findings into an alternative theoretical construction. One such palliative theoretical concept is *implicit learning*—a matter of such interest to psychologists that it has been the topic of a special issue of the journal *Psychonomic Bulletin and Review* (Roedinger, 1997). Implicit learning is defined as "the acquisition of abstract knowledge regarding the statistical regularities within a learning environment, that it occurs outside of awareness, and that it is insensitive to volitional control" (Neal & Hesketh, 1997, p. 24). Other workers in the field have pointed out that we must also account for the concept of *implicit behavior.* For example, Dienes and Berry (1997) argue that when we speak, we use rules acquired during implicit learning to create sentences that are both semantically meaningful and syntactically lawful. Both language learning and speech production have been studied extensively in this regard.

The distinguishing aspect of implicit learning and behaving is that both the experiences and the behavior occur without any awareness of what the specific rules were that were learned or that are being used when we construct behavioral sequences. In other words, the cognitive processes involved in what is obviously a major part of our behavior are unavailable to introspecting subjects—they are unable to explain, interpret, understand, or report the underlying mental processes that led to the behavior.

Implicit learning, even according to these experts in this field of psychological inquiry, is an extremely controversial topic. Some researchers (e.g., Perruchet & Pacteau, 1990) doubt its very existence. However, another part of this controversy is fought over whether this kind of learning is "implicit" purely as a result of our inability to verbally express an existing awareness of the underlying processes or, to the contrary, whether it is the result of being below a *subjective threshold* of awareness. Dienes and Berry (1997) have argued that the processes are subthreshold. In other words, they suggest the learning is more or less normal, but the process is actually unavailable to introspecting subjects, not just verbally inexpressible.

In either case, the phenomenon of implicit learning represents another situation in which there is a profound barrier between the external world of observable behavior and the internal world of mental processes. The details of the mental process, according to the implications of this point of view, are impenetrable and inaccessible. Implicit learning and the resulting behavior, therefore, represent other examples of a large set of accumulating data that suggests an inability on the part of humans to evaluate their own mental processing and thus of psychologists to accurately access the components of that processing. Implicit learning, therefore, provides another argument to support the contention that mental processes are generally inaccessible.

2.4.5 Wegner's Ironic Processes

The failure of an introspective link between consciousness awareness and behavior is perhaps no more compellingly demonstrated than in the work of Wegner (1994). His studies, however, were aimed at a slightly different relationship of mind and behavior than we have considered so far. Wegner was particularly interested in the discrepancy between what we want to do and what we actually do. Humans, he argues, simply do not have the ability to control their behavior or their thoughts to the degree desired by both society and the behaving individual. Rather, in his words:

> It is not just that we make errors, . . . but that a large portion of them fall into an especially aggravating category: the precisely counter intentional error. (p. 34)

Wegner provides many examples of this phenomenon, which he calls "ironic" because the end result is counter to our intentions and expectations. He also points out that ironic processes have been a part of psychology throughout its history. He lists three classic examples of behaviors demonstrating that conscious intent does not always lead to corresponding behavior: The kinesthetic illusion that produces Ouija board or dousing behavior; the Freudian concept of the *counterwill*; and the Baudoin suggestion of the *countereffect*. All were suggested as situations in which people behaved counter to their own intentions.

Counterintentional error is a further example of the delinking of thought processes and behavior. Like the several other examples of behavior and mental process dissociation discussed so far, it argues against the ability of behavior to provide information that validly allows us to infer what is going on in the mind. It adds another component to the argument that mind, however real, is essentially private and not accessible to any stimulus–response or introspective procedure.

2.5 SUMMARY

In the preceding sections I have been concerned with the dissociation of verbal behavior and mental processes. This is an important part of the antimentalist position that I have taken. Clearly, however, the arguments presented here are only modern expressions of the original anti-introspective conclusion at which Watson and the other early behaviorists arrived on more intuitive grounds.

However, because most of the arguments have been concerned with verbal behavior, other issues remain unanswered. For example: Is it possible to infer from behaviors such as reaction times what mental processes are being executed? Perhaps, we ask too much for people to introspect, but can other nonverbal behavioral responses provide a pathway into the mental processes? Unfortunately, the answer to this query must also be a negative one. The argument that this is so is made best by Pachella's (1974) discussion of the many difficulties introduced when even experiments utilizing narrowly defined motor responses are carried out in an attempt to achieve that goal. The main problem is the assumptions that have to be made to go from such simple behaviors as reaction times to mental components are so numerous as to make the whole task impossible.

Given what we have said about the engineer's Black Box and Moore's (1956) automata theorems, chaos, and the general difficulty imposed by unreasonable assumptions concerning the nature of the internal cognitive structure, indirect inferences about the nature of these mental processes drawn from simpler responses are precluded. The tortuous hypothetical routes leading from the stimulus to the cognitive states that are actually significant in determining behavior must raise serious questions about how far we can backtrack from behavior to mind. These arguments against direct and indirect methods for accessing mental states beg for a new look at a behavioral, rather than a cognitive, approach to psychology.

Chapter 3

Some Arguments Against Behaviorism

In Chapter 2, I concentrated on arguments against mentalism and, in particular, its instantiation in the form of contemporary cognitive psychology. However, this exercise would be incomplete and inadequate, not to say unfair, if I did not make an equivalent effort to consider the many criticisms that have been made against behaviorism. There has been a long-term outpouring of extremely abrasive, in part unprincipled, and certainly unscientific criticism against behaviorism in all of its varieties. The reason for this antagonism is not hard to discern. Behaviorism strikes hard at many of the most deeply held features of human culture, religion, and history, as well as our individual self-esteem. It is perceived by many, if not most, people as a hostile and threatening enterprise attacking things that are very important to us. It challenges some of the most deeply held concepts concerning the meaning of our lives and our ultimate destinies. Within the scientific psychology community, behaviorism is also threatening in view of the huge commitment that has been made to the yet-to-be proven or disproven assumptions of the accessibility and analyzability of human mental processes. To contradict the basic premises of that enormous effort is to strike at not only an enormous scientific enterprise but also, nowadays, a vast economic empire.

Hostile responses from mentalists hardly waited for the ink to dry on Watson's earliest publications and, as we see in this book, Skinner's intelligence, as well as his vocabulary, have regularly come under what can only be considered to be ad hominem attacks. Nevertheless, a study of the nature of these criticisms can be extremely useful in helping us both to understand the history of scientific psychology and to make the case for a revised and renewed behaviorism. It is the purpose of this chapter to as dispassionately as possible examine the antibehaviorist arguments. I say "as possible" because from my own point of view, I am more likely to respond to these critiques than to those presented in Chapter 2.

Criticisms against behaviorism come in many varieties. They vary from the most esoteric philosophical arguments to the most intimate emotional reactions. The immediate problem at a personal level is that behaviorism in many of its forms, according to some critics, is nothing less than a rejection of the very existence of our minds. However, in spite of these repeated criticisms, it is hard to find even the most radical behaviorists making any such claim. The argument made by behaviorists is, as we saw in Chapter 1, an epistemological one and not an ontological one. The great debate is not between the extremes of "mindless behaviorism" and "metaphysical cognitivism." The scientific kernel of this debate is over the accessibility and the analyzability of mental processes, not their reality. The eliminativists and a few other extreme reductionists and philosophers would have it otherwise, but this is the expression of a very small minority, mainly from outside psychology. No matter how mysterious or nonreducible mind may be, it would be difficult for any sentient human being to reject the immediate personal evidence of their own conscious experience.

Given the criticism that behaviorism is "mindless" is simply a straw man, it is instructive to probe the deeper meaning of some of the other critical attacks on behaviorism. Although some are sophisticated, many of them turn out to be synonyms for vague longings, dreamy hopes, or unfulfilled satisfactions. Others are simply misdirected attacks at presumed, but mythical, characteristics of nonexistent behaviorisms. In other instances the behaviorist philosophy is all-too-often confused with other philosophical issues such as dualism, materialism, reductionism, societal impact, aesthetics, and ethics, all of which are subjects worthy of deep consideration, but none of which are synonymous with the real core concepts of the behaviorism–mentalism controversy.

To clarify this fog of confusion (a goal that I appreciate is hardly likely to be consummated given the strong emotional and vested interest aspects of the controversy) I now briefly review the major criticisms against behaviorism. This review is not intended to be comprehensive or deep, but is presented merely to highlight the main antibehaviorist arguments.

3.1 THE ARGUMENTS

3.1.1 Marx and Hillix' Analysis of Criticisms of Behaviorism

Marx and Hillix (1973), in one of the most influential histories of psychological science, reviewed many of the philosophical and psychological arguments leveled specifically against Watson's version of behaviorism. Some of the most salient of these include:

1. Behaviorism hindered the development of research in sensory and perceptual processes.
2. Behaviorism cannot give adequate accounts of consciousness or the accuracy or meaningfulness of verbal reports.
3. Behaviorism accepts verbal reports in much the same way as structuralists accepted introspection and, therefore, is not a step forward.
4. Behaviorism rejected inner feelings or mind ("the chief distinction [of] human nature") and therefore is incomplete.
5. Behaviorism, by adhering to a strict S–R methodology was too mechanical and deterministic and does not take into account either variability or free will. (Abstracted and adapted from Marx and Hillix, 1973)

All of these arguments seem to either misinterpret the fundamental tenets of behaviorism or to be secondary to the fundamental issues of accessibility or analyzability. "Too mechanical," "chief distinction of human nature," or "not a step forward" are comments that convey wishes, hopes, and prejudgments, not engagement with the central issues of the real debate. Certainly it would be wonderful if any psychologist could directly study perception, but it is not behaviorism that denies such an approach. It is something much more fundamental about the private nature of perceived experiences as well as all other cognitive processes. To blame behaviorism for the intrapersonal privacy of individual minds is to blame the messenger for the "bad" news about the nature of human nature. To criticize behaviorism for being incomplete is hardly a sufficient justification for an alternative theory that is complete only by virtue of extreme interpretations of and extrapolations from the observed facts of human existence.

To argue against behaviorism by asserting that it, too, accepts verbal reports and, therefore, is really a crypto-mentalism little different from its predecessors, is also an unsatisfactory argument; it does not help to resolve the fundamental issues. Modern behaviorisms, like other scientific psychologies, offer a variety of other means of measuring performance and only rarely ask for verbal reports. Even then, the issue is only superficially about what can be measured but, rather, what the measurements mean and how valid they are.

The argument against behaviorism based on a supposed requirement that we "must" study inner feelings simply finesses the fundamental scientific issue of the accessibility of mind. It uncritically accepts as a premise, that which is personally satisfying to the observing intellect, but that which really should be answered by empirical research.

Finally the criticism that behaviorism is too "mechanical" simply reifies the mysterious concept of free will and presumes the existence of something that should also be an object of objective inquiry. The fundamental issue remains—however much it may be a manifestation of the brain, and however we may desire it to be the case, the accessibility of mind is yet to be established by the methods of psychological science.

3.1.2 Zuriff's Analysis of Criticisms of Behaviorism

Zuriff (1985), in what I believe is one of the most thoughtful, nonpolemic, and best organized books on the topic of behaviorism, astutely locates and precisely characterizes some of the antibehaviorist arguments. One of his most succinct discussions considers a classic version of the antibehaviorist argument by taking us through the following logical sequence:

1. Behavior is typically not in one-to-one correspondence with the environment.
2. Therefore, there must be something else to which behavior corresponds, namely an internal representation of the world.
3. Therefore, there must be internal operations by which the organism transforms its input from the external world to the internal representation.
4. Therefore, an adequate theory of behavior must postulate internal representations and processing operations. (p. 161)

First, it should be noted that Zuriff is a behaviorist. So this argument is likely to be intended by him to be a caricature of what he sees as the logical processes of others with whom he does not agree. Seriously meant or not, I believe he has captured the essence of many antibehaviorist arguments that go beyond inconsequential statements of "wouldn't it be nice if we could . . ." Furthermore, no psychologist, behaviorist or otherwise, can or should argue with the first three steps in this sequence. Irrefutably, there is something going on inside the organism that must have some sort of physical representation and that does execute some kinds of transforming operations. The response from an organism is never strictly determined by the stimulus environment and, therefore, ipso facto, the organism must transform the stimulus into what hopefully is an appropriate and adaptive response.

It is only with Step 4 that the chain of logic characterized by Zuriff leads to a non sequitur. It is here that we confront the essence of the arguments of those who assume, without full consideration, the de facto accessibility of mental processes. This fourth step leaps to, what I believe, is the spurious conclusion that because these mental states do exist, that they are also accessible to empirical examination.

In fact, however, there is no a priori reason that an "adequate theory of behavior" *must* be able to postulate, invent, measure, or analyze any of these internal states or representations. To assume *ab initio* that we can, subverts consideration of what is clearly a scientific problem in its own right—as must be repeatedly emphasized if this message is to get through. The logical chain of argument characterized (but not intended to be supported) by Zuriff, accepts the final step purely on the basis of the desirability of the action, rather than on its plausibility, possibility, or scientific credibility. It is the *human* thing to do given our own personal self-awareness; it is the *natural* thing to do; it is the *commonsense* thing to do. However, it may not be the *scientific* thing to do. Logical leaps of this sort reflect our commonsense desires and wishes, not our objective analyses. Unfortunately, "common sense" in this context may be the greased slide to the hell of false theories, mythical explanations in the form of unjustifiable hypothetical constructs, and gross misunderstanding about the capabilities and limits of an empirical psychological science.

3.1.3 Koch and Mackenzie's Critique of the Behaviorism–Logical Positivism Conjunction

One of the most vigorous challenges to behaviorism came from a psychologist who was perhaps best known for his encyclopedic six-volume *Psychology: Study of a Science* (e.g., Koch, 1959, 1962). Koch, however, was much interested in the philosophy of psychological science and published a number of articles (e.g., Koch, 1964) severely criticizing the behaviorist movement as discussed in Chapter 1. Above and beyond his criticism of operationalism I considered there, he saw behaviorism as a combination of an overemphasis on a simplistic kind of empirical psychology combined with a flawed methodological philosophy—logical positivism. The mix, he argued, was inappropriate for psychology because, at its outset, the logical positivists had mainly been concerned about the physical sciences and their ideas and methods just did not fit the needs of psychology. Koch further argued that logical positivism itself had fallen into disrepute and, therefore, any psychological science based on it (or equivalent to it) also had to be rejected.

A similar, but mirror, view was expressed by MacKenzie (1977). He also believed that logical positivism and behaviorism were closely linked, but instead attributed the failure of the combination to the failure of behaviorism. Logical positivism did not drag down behaviorism, but rather the psychological approach, emphasizing so strongly their common methodology, dragged down the philosophical school.

The relationship among logical positivism, behaviorism, and, to a more controversial degree, operationalism (see pp. 53–54 in chap. 1) has been discussed in detail by Smith (1986) and Leahey (1997). It is a complex relationship but throughout all of these discussions there is a kind of a priori assumption that all three of these movements grew and declined together. It is assumed that there were adequate reasons for the decline. It seems to me, however, that these authors mainly reported the decline or discussed the philosophical arguments, but did not consider the possible scientific reasons that should have been invoked to explain the decline. Smith, himself, makes clear the fragility of such a purely philosophical critique when he said:

> The foregoing considerations do make clear that behaviorism cannot simply be dismissed with purely philosophical arguments or ridicule based on preferences for alternative underlying metaphysics. (p. 315)

Nowhere in Smith's (1986) book, for example, do we find a consideration of the fundamental scientific issues of accessibility and analyzability that are highlighted in this present work. The identification of those key issues makes it much easier to reconsider whether or not both behaviorisms and logical positivism (or some revised version of them) may now be in order.

3.1.4 Skinner's Analysis of Criticisms of Behaviorism

Let us continue our review of antibehaviorist criticisms by looking at the work of Skinner, the arch behaviorist and the most frequently denounced theorist of this genre since Watson himself. The slings and arrows directed at him have been ad hominem as well as intellectual. Based on a long and continued (even after his death) series of repeated challenges, Skinner (1974) was perhaps in the best position to help in this quest for a tabulation of antibehaviorist arguments. In the following paragraphs, I quote verbatim his list of such criticisms as presented on pages 4 and 5 of his 1974 book. Each item is then immediately followed by a brief paraphrase of Skinner's subsequent counterargument in italics.

> 1. It [Behaviorism] ignores consciousness, feelings, and states of mind.

A science of subjective experience is independent of a science of behavior. Behaviorism does not ignore the existence of mental states, but they may be someone else's business.

> 2. It neglects innate endowment and argues that all behavior is acquired during the lifetime of the individual.

This is simply incorrect. Virtually all behaviorists accept the fact that both heredity and environment affect behavior. The contributory role of each must be determined through experimental methods.

> 3. It formulates behavior simply as a set of responses to stimuli, thus representing a person as an automaton, robot, puppet, or machine.

Skinnerian behaviorism is not a reflexology. Far from it, it is well appreciated that stimuli do not drive or determine all of behavior. For example, behaviorists appreciate that although stimuli play a major role in the probabilities of operant responses, they do not determine the response.

4. It does not attempt to account for cognitive processes.

Higher mental processes occur and behaviorism is studying the contingencies under which they occur. It does not, however, accept the "unwarranted and dangerous metaphor" that they occur in the "mysterious world of the mind."

5. It has no place for intention or purpose.

Modern evolution theory replaces "antecedent design" with "subsequent selection." Behavior therapy similarly replaces free will with reinforcement. "Felt purpose" can have no causal effect.

6. It cannot explain creative achievements—in art, for example, or in music, literature, science, or mathematics.

"Contingencies of reinforcement" may be a more powerful tool to explain such creativity than individual differences.

7. It assigns no role to a self or sense of self.

Nothing in behaviorism denies the existence of self-awareness, but science has yet to determine if the self is an initiator of action.

8. It is necessarily superficial and cannot deal with the depths of the mind or personality.

This is primarily a matter of the semantic meaning of the words "superficial" and "deep." Genetics, the environment, and current stimuli may provide a more appropriate vocabulary with which to search for the meaning of concepts such as "mind" or "personality."

9. It limits itself to the prediction and control of behavior and misses the essential nature or being of man.

Understanding is useless unless it leads to action. The more we can determine the relation between behavior and its antecedents, the more we understand human nature.

10. It works with animals, particularly with white rats, but not with people, and its picture of human behavior is therefore confined to those features that human beings share with animals.

The same basic processes are at work in animals and humans. The use of a simple model organisms, like other kinds of controls in experiments, helps us to unravel the very complex mysteries of human nature.

11. Its achievements under laboratory control cannot be duplicated in daily life, and what it has to say about human behavior in the world at large is, therefore, unsupported metascience.

This is a limitation of all sciences. But, people who say that science does not help "in daily life" assume that there are better ways to solve problems. Those alternatives are less capable of answering the most important questions about human nature than behaviorism. Science at least allows us to define relevant variables.

12. It is oversimplified and naïve and its facts are either trivial or already well known.

Behaviorism is less naïve than is mentalism. To criticize behavior in this way is naïve. Simple causes can cause complex effects.

13. It is scientistic rather than scientific. It merely emulates the sciences.

All social and behavioral sciences are subject to this criticism. However, the use of measurements and mathematics, the goal of prediction, and the analysis of behavior by controlled experimentation are as useful in these fields as elsewhere. Wishes and intentions cannot substitute for careful study in controlled situations.

14. Its technological achievements could have come about through the use of common sense.

Common sense has sometimes produced useful practices, but just as often has resulted in social catastrophes (e.g., the use of punishment as a means of modifying behavior.) In the long run, objective science is more likely to provide the best practices.

15. If its contentions are valid, they must apply to the behavioral scientist himself, and what he says is therefore only what he has been conditioned to say and cannot be *true.*

Scientists, of course, are also behaving organisms. However, the scientific method helps control the scientist's behavior, which itself may become an object of scientific investigation.

16. It dehumanizes man; it is reductionistic and destroys man *qua* man.

To say that laws govern human behavior is not to say that they are the same laws that govern an automobile. This argument usually ends up discussing mental concepts that are beyond scientific inquiry. Behaviorism is hardly reductionist.

17. It is concerned only with general principles and therefore neglects the uniqueness of the individual.

Science will always be unable to map out the full richness of whatever it is that it studies. But, general principles, are, in fact, the ultimate goal of science. Although case histories are interesting, there is more to be learned from universals than from particulars.

18. It is necessarily antidemocratic because the relation between experimenter and subject is manipulative, and its results can therefore be used by dictators but not by men of good will.

Conspicuous control (such as that used in experiments) should not be confused with inconspicuous control (such as that used by political dictators). But, both are possible. Control without exploitation is desirable; not all control is negative.

19. It regards abstract ideas such as morality or justice as fictions.

Morality and justice can be and usually are the result of behavioral controls exerted from social agencies. There is no inherent inconsistency or competition between such values and the science of behaviorism. This statement is simply wrong.

20. It is indifferent to the warmth and richness of human life, and it is incompatible with the creation and enjoyment of art, music, and literature and with love for one's fellow men.

Here too, the premise is simply wrong. Science does not interfere with these pleasures. These pleasures in no way interfere with understanding. (Tabulated and Abstracted from Skinner, 1974)

Skinner has done us a major service in tabulating the many attacks that were directed at the behaviorist approach to psychology over the years and in providing a response to each of them. Given the vigor of the way in which these antibehaviorist arguments are often presented (see, e.g., Dennett, 1988) and his (Skinner's) radical approach, he was certainly one of the best qualified to gather these ideas together simply by virtue of his being the most conspicuous target for the cognitive attacks of the last few decades.

Let us now consider the criticisms and Skinner's responses to them to see if there are any common features that can be abstracted. Several clusters can be discerned in this list. First, of course, is a group of simple misunderstandings or misstatements concerning behaviorist writings. It is difficult to find any place in the literature of behaviorism that suggests that proponents of this view reject the existence of mental states, ignore the influence of environment, treat organisms as robots, or that it is reductionist. These statements, among others, are a priori incorrect assertions about behaviorist theory and simply represent false characterizations of the science.

Second, there is a group of statements that are based on otherwise noble humanistic value judgments. These criticisms represent the views of humans who wish to explore some other aspects of human life in a manner that transcends scientific thinking. The "dehumanization," the "antidemocratic," the "morality and justice," the "warmth and richness," the "naïveté," the "essential nature" arguments are all members of this cluster. Behaviorists, who as humans are as interested in these topics as anybody else, do not believe that their science interacts with these matters in any way that would be a fundamental impediment to human joy, happiness, or any other "inalienable right." However, these are issues of aesthetics and not of theoretical and empirical science. Although they may represent psychobiological activity originally arising from the same physiological mechanisms and processes as, for example, operant behavior, all of these "higher order" topics are most likely matters for methods other than those of science. It is hard to find a behaviorist who would disagree with this point and would reject the need for human moral and ethical caveats and constraints that cannot be easily studied in the laboratory.

A third group of the criticisms against behaviorism that Skinner listed are also value judgments, but of the nature of science rather than of the more distantly related humanistic issues. The high value put on cognitive processes, purpose, and self and their putative effect on our behavior; the denigration of prediction and control; judgments about behaviorism's level of "oversimplification"; the charge that it merely emulates science; and the value placed on anecdotal and case histories are highly controversial issues concerning the debatable nature of what constitutes "proper" science. Arbitrary intellectual positions, value judgments, and hopes and wishes are often presented as "rigorous" arguments against the tenets of behaviorism. Such scientific malfeasance is without merit in a serious discussion of the role of this or any other science.

Why do these misdirections and fallacious arguments occur so frequently in scientific psychology? The answer to this question lies in the nature of the same fundamental argument that has erroneously been used to support mentalisms throughout history—our own personal self-awareness is so compelling and so real to each of us that we abhor the idea that these mental processes are not accessible to inquiry. It is only in the context of new scientific developments and new ideas that we can even begin to consider this matter in an objective fashion. The arguments against reductionism and analysis presented in Chapter 2 are designed to help us toward a more rigorous and objective evaluation of these value judgments.

3.1.5 Kimble's Analysis of Criticisms of Behaviorism

Kimble (1996) carried out an extremely interesting survey asking for endorsements or rejections of a set of statements he felt were often used to criticize behaviorism. The results of his survey were surprising—a substantial number of contemporary psychologists endorsed these admitted caricatures of behaviorism. It is, however, the nature of the criticisms, rather than some kind of a popularity contest that I wish to emphasize here. Kimble's list includes the following statements about behaviorism.

1. Behaviorism sacrifices mind, purpose, thought, and human experience at the altar of stimuli and responses. It rejects everything that is mentalistic, thus everything that psychology is supposed to be about.
2. Behaviorism's stimulus–response approach is atomistic. By its very nature, behaviorism cannot deal with complete individuals or total situations.
3. Behaviorist explanations are reductionistic: Human behavior is either materialistic biology or abstract mathematical equations.
4. The laws that behaviorism seeks are mechanistic laws of passive adaptation. There is no place for human beings conceived as self-directed coping, causal agents.
5. The behaviorist approach is nomophetic. It deals with averages and promotes the concept of "standard man." It neglects the variance in behavior and fails to recognize that every human being is a unique individual.
6. Behaviorism is "scientistic" not scientific. It presumes to measure human attributes that are not quantitative. Its laboratory methods are artificial. They dissect behavior from its natural context and yield results that have no useful application.
7. Behaviorism is simplistic. It lacks the complexity required to capture the subtle nuances and the richness of its subject matter.
8. Behaviorism's contributions to the understanding of the human condition are trivial. They are a catalog of small effects produced by insignificant causes.
9. Behaviorism turns human beings into lower animals. It is insensitive to the scope of human potential and blind to the essential human quality in all of us.

10. Behaviorism is without human values, without a conscience, without morality or ethics. (Kimble, 1996, p. xi)

Many of the items on Kimble's list are synonymous with equivalent items on Skinner's list and the same counterarguments hold. However, there is a special and more emphatic tone to several of these criticisms that suggests something increasingly specific happened over the 2 decades since Skinner's (1974) work originally appeared. A much larger proportion (in Kimble's list than in Skinner's list) of these comments is aimed at the idea that behaviorism is too reductionist and atomic.

It is hard to comprehend why this particular target has become such an issue when it is so transparently wrong headed. Behaviorism, in its modern form, is quintessentially molar (and, I feel, properly so) rather than elementalist, to a degree that belies any such reductionist criticism. Every aspect of the operant methodology, as well as its philosophy, is based on the idea that it is the overall form of the behavior that is the basic datum. If there is any elementalist or reductionist thinking lurking about, it is only to the degree that the details of stimuli and responses are precisely measured. Although some of the early behaviorists (e.g., Watson) suggested that there was an underlying level at which the basic elements of sensation were combined or associated, the modern behaviorist enterprise is aimed at examining the organism's response as a unified whole. Perhaps this misunderstanding arose because the responses studied by behaviorists are often relatively discrete, but reduction to underlying components or analysis into components are the exact antitheses of the behaviorist approach.

Rather, it is the contemporary cognitive mentalists who are much more reductionist, even in the face of continued evidence that input–output methods cannot fathom the structure of underlying mechanisms and processes. It is the cognitive mentalists who seek out analytical models such as the neural network or the flow chart or the system model of cognitive processes, not the behaviorists. The argument that behaviorists are hyperreductionists seems particularly ill-construed in this context.

3.1.6 Amsel's Analysis of Criticisms of Behaviorism

Another behaviorist who has taken up the task of analyzing the nature of the critical attacks made on the behaviorism is Amsel (1989). Though primarily interested in the impact of the cognitive revolution on the empirical foundations of learning theory, Amsel felt it necessary to consider the roots of the apparent antagonism exhibited by the new cognitivists toward what they considered to be an archetypical behaviorism. The initial point made by Amsel is that it is not clear that the word *behaviorism* is really able to include all of the different versions of the ideology that have been collected under that rubric. Thus, he contends that there really have been a number of different directions that the antibehaviorists have taken and that not all of their criticisms are relevant to all of the behaviorisms.

Amsel considers the following kind of criticisms to be prototypical of those marshaled against particular aspects of behaviorism. First, he notes some of the most extreme statements made by both Skinner and Watson in which they suggested that the environment was virtually the sole force in the determination of subsequent behavior. For example, the hyperempiricism exhibited by the following quotation from the latter day Watson (1930) was certain to raise the hackles of anyone (including most other behaviorists) who accepted the important contribution made by both the genetic heritage and normal development in shaping at least some behaviors.

> Give me a dozen healthy infants, well-formed and my own special world to bring them up in and I'll guarantee to take any one at random and train him to become any type of specialist I might select. . . . (p. 104)

It should be noted that this and other equally extreme environmentalist and empiricist statements by Skinner were made late in their respective careers. Such comments may be less characteristic of the core tenets of the behaviorism of either psychologist than of some intentionally provocative statements made by these two giants to make some point other than a scientific one. Nevertheless, statements like this did provoke and, whatever their intent, became targets for critical comments about behaviorism in general.

The antibehaviorist argument expressed here was that by expressing the idea that little or nothing was innate and most everything learned, much of the accumulated knowledge of behavior genetics was ignored. The same argument, stressing the importance of innate evolved forces in determining behavior, has been brought forward by a number of psycholinguists including Chomsky (1959) in a slightly different guise. The disagreement in this case depended on one's position on the nativism–empiricism controversy with specific regard to the problem of language acquisition.

Amsel also pointed out that many criticisms of behaviorism were actually aimed at any kind of scientific approach to studying human psychology. He cited Rogers' (1964) challenge to behaviorism noting that it really was a attack against an "impersonal" scientific psychology in all of its different manifestations. This same argument emerged from observers outside the scientific establishment in the form of an unabashedly antiscientific humanism.

Amsel (1989) saw many of the criticisms of behaviorism as being the result of "stirrings in some quarters of a return to introspective methods" (p. 25). This, at least, returned the discussion to the empirical arena.

However, other critics attacked the positivist and operationalist philosophies that provided the foundation premises for the behaviorist culture. Even other criticisms, Amsel suggested, were not directed at behaviorism itself, but rather at such unrelated, but controversial, topics as the use of animals in research or the extrapolation from animal findings to conclusions about humans.

Finally, Amsel highlighted one of the great issues that permeates this entire discussion—the role of theory. Here, once again, are raised the countervailing issues of description and explanation, of intervening variables and hypothetical constructs, and of the power and utility of reductive analyses. Reasonable differences between reasonable scientists regarding these fundamental issues, many of which are still unresolved, are still matters of active discussion.

3.1.7 Searle's Criticism of Behaviorism

The philosopher Searle (1992) is an interesting source in our search for the arguments and criticisms that have been made against behaviorism. He is well known for his criticism of the computer metaphor as it is used in contemporary cognitive psychology. His argument in this context is that, in committing itself so heavily to this analogy for mind and brain, cognitive mentalistic psychology has actually ignored consciousness. In its stead, Searle argued, the computer metaphor substitutes programs, processes, and transformations (which may or may not be equally accessible to the external observer) for what the proper object of the science of psychology should be, namely consciousness. Thus, Searle argued, computers that are purely syntactical machines just do not adequately represent or model the semantic properties of brain and mind.

In his discussion of what is wrong with cognitive psychology from the point of view of an extreme mentalism that even outdoes contemporary cognitivism, Searle does present, almost casually in passing, some illuminating comments on what he feels is wrong with behaviorism. It is interesting, therefore, to see what kind of criticism is made by someone from this ultramentalist point of view.

Searle (1992) first mentioned (and quickly rejected) the "commonsense" argument that, by just ignoring the mental in constructing its science, behaviorism fails to deal with an essential part of our own awareness. He then described three of what he calls "technical" counterarguments to behaviorism. In abstract, these arguments are:

1. . . . behaviorists never succeeded in making the notion of a "disposition" fully clear.
2. There is a problem about a certain form of circularity in the behaviorist analysis:

3. . . . it (behaviorism) left out the causal relation between mental states and behavior.

By "disposition" Searle is referring to the tendency or proclivity to perform some behavior that is proposed by behaviorists as an alternative to willful control. The circularity issue deals with the necessity to invoke conscious constructs to explain behavioral ones. The third criticism simply says that the nonveridicalities—the transformations—between the stimulus and the elicited response are not explained in any way by behaviorists.

It can be counterargued that, in fact, dispositions are treated adequately by behaviorists. I believe Skinner's use of the word "contingency" comes closest to the mentalist ideas of dispositions. By a contingency of reinforcement, Skinner (1974) referred to the weighting or loading of the probability of a behavior being emitted by a particular stimulus. In his words:

> Operant theory moved the purpose which seemed to be displayed by human action from antecedent intention or plan to subsequent selection by contingencies of reinforcement. (p. 224)

The circularity issue is more difficult to counter because of the nature of psychological research in general. As we saw in Chapter 1, the basic act of defining mental and behavioral terms is so difficult that a certain degree of circularity is almost inevitable regardless of one's school of thought. However, by eschewing consideration of mental constructs, it seems to me that behaviorism is intrinsically less susceptible to this criticism than are any of the mentalisms.

Finally, Searle's third argument—the omission of the causal relationship between mental states and behavior—once again strikes at the heart of the matter. This is another version of a fundamental question: Do mental processes influence behavior? The answer to this question is extremely important, but as I said in Chapter 1, it is not yet clear that it can be answered in the affirmative. Searle obviously assumes that this is possible, but our mental responses may be nothing more than epiphenomena that *appear* to have influence but, in fact, do not. Nevertheless, it is obvious how one's personal resolution of the mentalism–behaviorism controversy can be strongly influenced by how this single essential question is answered. In any event, if mental processes are not accessible, the question of mental influence is moot.

Searle also suggests that identity theory (mind IS a brain function) or any other mechanistic monism implies at least a property dualism. That is, there are both mental properties and brain properties. He argued that this segregation leads to logical fallacies and inconsistencies in the behaviorist point of view. It appears to me that this argument confuses the ontological issue of materialism and the epistemological goals of the behaviorist methodology. If this distinction is made, then the inconsistency in the logic targeted by Searle does not exist.

In other parts of his book, Searle (1992) retreated to the commonsense argument and asserted that:

> The view of the world as completely objective has a very powerful hold on us, though it is inconsistent with the most obvious facts of our experiences. (p. 65)

This is, as we have seen, a recurring theme throughout the entire history of the ongoing war between mentalism and behaviorism. From some points of view, it is all too close to a statement that there are nonobjective and (perhaps even) nonphysical aspects of existence. This stretches the anti-materialist philosophy to an uncomfortable degree. This comment by Searle also characterizes the highly mentalist position that he so obviously holds. Unfortunately, it also reifies the role of consciousness and self-awareness without considering the fundamental scientific questions of accessibility and analyzability—questions that are subject to empirical attack—and the ones with which this book is concerned.

3.1.8 Pylyshyn's Criticisms of Behaviorism

One of the most vigorous proponents of the computer as a cognitive theory engine has been Pylyshyn (1986). True to his position as a supporter of cognitive psychology, he argued that behaviorism is a failed science and that although they purport to eschew mental terms, all behaviorists have done is to introduce a new vocabulary for concepts that are actually quite mentalistic. For example, he asserted:

> Instead of a physical vocabulary, they [behaviorists] use a "behavioral" vocabulary in which things are described as *stimuli, responses, reinforcers* and so on. The reason this works is that, in practice, such categories are cognitive. (p. 9)

Pylyshyn further stated the usual cognitive argument that there is no strict relationship between stimulus and response—therefore, there must be some kind of an intervening mechanism that accounts for the lack of simple transformations between the two. He noted that with the exception of things like tripping and reflexes most human responses would have to be considered random if attempts were made to link them to stimuli. It is only by invoking mental terms, he suggested, that human behavior becomes meaningful.

Although it certainly may be convenient (i.e., easy) to think in terms of a mentalist vocabulary, this constraint does not resolve the question of how the basically *intra*personal can be made *inter*personally verifiable. The reality of human variability and adaptability, an empirical fact that is shared by mentalists and behaviorists alike, should not be confused with any in-principle limits to understanding that exist because of fundamental complexity or inescapable privacy. It is this controversial point that separates the two schools of thought.

Another point made by Pylyshyn is that a major criticism of mentalism made by behaviorists is simply not true. Behaviorists, according to Pylyshyn, assert that mentalisms offer unlimited and uncontrolled opportunities for theorists to all-too-easily generate any wild kind of a hypothetical construct. Quite to the contrary, he argued that anyone who has tried to develop an operational or computer program model of some mental state is faced with a challenge of what often can be heroic proportions. This is a strange kind of counterargument to be expressed by a cognitivist who depends so much on the description and invention of explanatory mechanisms by means of computer models and metaphors. Indeed, computer programs, although sometimes difficult to construct, do act as important constraining influences on theory. This is one of the strongest arguments made by those who use them. Classic precomputer mentalisms, which invoked a priori, ad hoc, and post hoc verbal explanations and models, were far more susceptible to this criticism of limitless varieties of internal models. From another point of view, the act of developing a computer program or model is identical in principle to the invention of a hypothetical verbal construct. The degree of difficulty or ease of generating either one of them neither confirms nor denies their validity.

The tight link between modern cognitive mentalism and computers is, however, seen by others as a weakness itself. For example, Pribram (1985) suggested that both the dominant computer metaphor—the serial, Von Neuman computer and its attendant information processing model—with which we are so familiar is a poor model of the parallel processing that goes on in real brain. He suggests that a deeper consideration of modern parallel processing computers could ameliorate this difficulty. In my opinion, by so doing, Pribram was simply providing another crutch to prop up the essential weakness of the computer metaphor in cognitive psychology. The difficulty is that a descriptive and metaphorical model (e.g., a computer program) is all too often misinterpreted as an ontologically valid explanatory model. This challenge to the computer metaphor was effectively represented by Pribram himself when he noted the association between the Artificial Intelligence (AI) movement and cognitive science also may be hindering progress toward a valid psychology. His very important point in this context was that many very successful, and some not so successful, computer programs have been written that mimic some kind of human intelligence. However, these programs may do so by means of algorithms and routines that are very different than the processes used in the human system. To equate mimicry with true reductive explanation subverts the goals of both sciences. Certainly, the list processing or production rule metaphors (e.g., Anderson & Lebiere, 1998) should not be interpreted as exact explanations of human thought. However analogous or however successful their simulations and descriptions of human thought may be, it is not likely that either programming language or system represents the actual logical processes of the human brain.

3.1.9 Chomsky and Verbal Behavior

Behaviorism comes in many kinds and, yet, a consistent theme throughout all kinds is that behavior can be modified, indeed, programmed by a series of learning experiences. Watson and Skinner both argued at one time or another that behavior was generated as a composite effect of the sum of all of the relevant previous experiences of the organism. Sometimes, as we saw on page 122, this emphasis on previous experience was carried to extremes. In making such statements, both these pioneers exposed themselves to an enormous amount of criticism because of this overly strong empiricist stance. Both became closely associated with what was perceived by many psychologists and educators to be a rigid and simplistic reflexology in which stimuli led to responses on the basis of contingencies and probabilities determined solely by those previous experiences. This extreme empiricism, however, was anathema not only to professional mentalistic psychologists, but to anyone interested in child rearing, development, or even intercultural comparisons. The offensive idea that an infant was insensitive to its genetic heritage stoked the fires of what came to be an exceptionally virulent form of antibehaviorism.

The extreme empiricist, or nurture, approach taken by some behaviorists some of the time raised strong antagonistic feelings, particularly among those who more strongly supported heredity-based theories that suggested there were innate tendencies to respond in certain ways. This point of view culminated in the sociobiological movement (Wilson, 1975), arguing that most of behavior was genetically determined. Among the areas in which the concern with this controversy was the greatest was the study of language. Skinner's (1957) excursion into this arena created consternation and a swift reaction by linguists. The most vigorous of the critics of Skinner's stimulus–response approach to language was Chomsky (1959). In brief, Chomsky's argument was that the limited variability and complexity of language is completely inexplicable in terms of acquired stimulus–response relationships of the kind that he believed underlay the extreme empiricist theories championed by behaviorists. Chomsky (1959), however, had much more to say about behaviorism in general in what has become a classic of the literature of this genre. Indeed, in an extremely critical review of Skinner's book he asserted that:

> [t]he insights that have been achieved in the laboratories of the reinforcement theorists, though quite genuine, can be applied to complex human behavior in only the most superficial way. . . . (p. 28)

and then added the following:

> [w]e must attribute an overwhelming influence on actual behavior to ill-defined factors of attention, set, volition, and caprice. (p. 30)

Elsewhere, Chomsky (1972) made clear that his antagonism was not directed only toward behaviorism but, more generally, toward psychological theory:

> It seems to me that the essential weakness in the structuralist and behaviorist approaches to these topics is the faith in the shallowness of explanations, the belief that mind must be simpler in its structure than any known physical organ and that the most primitive of assumptions must be adequate to explain whatever phenomena can be observed. (pp. 25–26)

It is, however, in his role as a linguist that Chomsky's specific criticism's of the behaviorist views of verbal behavior and language became most acerbic. One of Chomsky's (1972) main criticisms of Skinner's theories of verbal behavior was that he (Skinner) jumps from his highly constrained laboratory experiments to "analogic" guesses (p. 30) in a way that is as mentalist as are the concepts of any other psychologist. Indeed, throughout this article, he (Chomsky) suggested that Skinner's vocabulary (including such terms as "stimulus control" and "reinforcement") are examples of a "complete retreat to mentalistic psychology" (p. 32). It is this weakness of definition, this absence of well-defined content, that Chomsky feels is the weakness of the entire behaviorist approach to language.

Another specific criticism made by Chomsky of Skinner's approach to verbal behavior is that the concept of reinforcement leads to ill-defined areas of discussion. Alluding to the fact that what was then called *latent* learning (learning a task without any identifiable reinforcement) creates a need on the part of behaviorists to invoke "curiosity and exploration" drives and problem solving itself as a reinforcement, Chomsky asserted that these ideas are much more mentalist than behaviorist.

At the time Chomsky's (1959) well-remembered paper was written, he was willing to accept the fact that no one knew how language was acquired. What were involved were such characteristics as casual "observation and natural inquisitiveness" as well as reinforcement. He felt that, to the contrary, the former two properties are either innate or ". . . may develop through some sort of learning or through maturation of the nervous system" (p. 43). It was his feeling that because the processes were still not known, the task ahead was to answer these questions rather than depend on the "dogmatic and perfectly arbitrary claims . . ." (p. 43) of behaviorism. Elsewhere, Chomsky rejected Skinner's verbal behaviorism as being "hopelessly premature" (p. 55).

Much of the rest of Chomsky's review was then aimed at the idiosyncratic aspects of the Skinnerian terminology. He argued against the introduction of neologisms such as "mands," "tacts," and "autoclitics"—some of the conceptual elements of Skinner's verbal behaviorism—as well as against the term *verbal behavior* itself. He criticized all of these terms as either being too specific to adequately represent language or as being so general they offered nothing new or were actually mentalistic terms in disguise.

In summary, Chomsky (1959) was obviously not a happy camper concerning Skinner's (1957) book however much he seemed to enjoy the debate itself. His arguments can be summarized as:

1. Skinner's vocabulary is empty or crypto-mentalist.
2. Skinner's theories on language are extreme extrapolations from a narrow experimental paradigm.
3. In any case, it is too early to say we understand language acquisition.
4. The behaviorist tendency to remove the speaker (i.e., the organism) from the process ignores the importance of innate influences on language and "permits only a superficial account of language acquisition." (p. 58)

Obviously, some of Chomsky's arguments were well taken. Not enough is yet known about some of the issues with which both psychologists and linguists are jointly concerned and theory building from inadequate empirical data is always treacherous. However, implicit in his criticism are some conclusions that create more serious problems than his explicit statements solve. The antithesis of the behaviorist attempt to remove the speaker cum organism from the discussion is the danger of injecting empirically and logically unsupportable mentalist concepts. Going from a sparse database to a hypothetical mental construct would be a far greater extrapolative leap than going from a sparse database to an objective and operational behaviorist description.

3.2 SUMMARY AND CONCLUSIONS

Mentalistic cognitivism and behaviorism, in one derivative form or another, have contended for preeminence in psychological science for most of the 20th century. Arguments varying from the unbelievably naïve to rigorous mathematical proofs have been invoked on both sides. The intellectual pendulum that is a metaphor for the various historical outcomes of this controversy has swung from one extreme to the other even if it has never moved back to exactly the original conceptualization. In essence, the debate often boils down to the question: What are we going to do about consciousness? If it were not for our own personal self-awareness, the issue would probably not exist. We could be considered as extremely complex and well-designed automata by an external observer. The problem is, thus, further complicated by the fact that, because consciousness is private, the actual observer in any psychological experiment or observation ultimately must be one's conscious self. We can communicate only by means of verbal reports or other equally heavily encoded and biased forms of behavior. Although some philosophers solve the problem by denying the existence of consciousness, others have made it a very hot topic, indeed, these days.

There are powerful forces supporting the assumption that there is nothing inaccessible about such mental processes and that they have to be explained. Both conscious and unconscious mental activities have played a role in the human experience since our species arose. However, a priori acceptance of the accessibility of mind and the necessity to explain consciousness can lead uncritically to mentalist psychologies with inadequate consideration of the scientific questions that should be raised. As I noted earlier, it is not only possible, but desirable, to accept the reality of our mental processes and yet also to question their accessibility and analyzability. To reiterate, the ontological argument is not the same as the epistemological one. There may well be constraints and limits on what we can know about something that is itself very real indeed.

There are still, however, many remaining obstacles to be overcome before closure on the accessibility issue is achieved. The very words that are used in this discussion have always been sources of disagreement and contention. In this book and in my earlier ones on this topic I have repeatedly pointed out how difficult it is to arrive at definitions for any word that had mental implications. Many others including Skinner (1975) have made the same point. In site of this difficulty, debate over these ill-defined entities continues. It is notoriously difficult to resolve a controversy when there is no consensus on the salient terms.

The accessibility issue comes in many alternative shapes and forms. It has been made more specific by many authors by focusing in on the word "infer." An alternative form of the question then becomes: Is it possible to accurately infer the nature of mental processes from the observed behavior? Nevertheless, however metamorphosed, the question remains the same fundamental one asked whenever the consciousness or self-awareness issue is raised. However casually or seriously used, inference implies accessibility. To fully explore this issue, we must necessarily probe deeper into even the revised meaning of this question. Of course, anyone can draw inferences from anything, but in this exceedingly important case, it is absolutely necessary to be sure that the implications of the behavior support the inferences about the underlying mental processes drawn by the psychologist.

In particular, the process of inferring always raises the specter of incorrect inferences—of creating entities because they fit in with some other aspect of our experience or point of view, not because the data compels their emergence. Make no mistake about it, science is filled with such false inferences and manufactured concepts as is any other component of human intellectual activity. Psychology, perhaps more than any other science, must face this question in a completely open and frank way.

In pursuing our discussion in this direction we necessarily come to the problem of the potential truth or validity of the inductive inference process. Needless to say, philosophers have argued this matter for centuries. Black (1967), in an extensive encyclopedia article, outlined the history of the problem in a comprehensive manner. The difficulties encountered in any inductive argument are not going to be resolved in this present discussion, but Black has done a good job of enumerating them. His list of fundamental questions encountered when one attempts to carry out the kind of inference that psychologists regularly, and usually uncritically, pursue are:

1. The general problem of justification: Why, if at all, is it reasonable to accept the conclusions of certain inductive arguments as true—or at least as probably true?
2. The comparative problem: Why is one inductive conclusion preferable to another as better supported?
3. The analytical problem: What is it that renders some inductive arguments rationally acceptable? (p. 170)

Though couched in the terminology of formal logic, it is clear that these problems are analogs of the problems faced by any mentalistic psychology that attempts to infer from a body of observed data that which is presumed to be going on in the privacy of our thoughts. Therefore, it would be useful to consider the validity of the general method even before we consider the validity of the particular application of the method.

The satisfactory use of inductive logic in psychological research depends at its most fundamental level on the hypothetical connections between behavioral observations and mental states being demonstrable, repeatable, and valid. Clearly the work on verbal behavior reviewed in this book suggests that these connections are frail, variable, and problematical at best. Therefore, even if the inductive method were not fraught with its own difficulties, the equivocal nature of the processes on which it is brought to bear should raise serious questions about any program of psychological research that seeks to determine the nature of the private responses we call mind. It is distressing that the as-yet-unsolved problems raised by the inductive method are so often ignored by its practitioners these days.

A cleaner, neater, more compelling approach would be to use logical deduction—a step-by-step progression from premises to conclusions by means of strict rules. Such an approach has the advantage of clear starting points—its premises and axioms. I include in this rubric not only formal logic, but any other formal modeling procedure that operates on the basis of strict rules of transformation. This category includes mathematics and computer modeling.

The problem with formal deduction in the case of mental states and actions, of course, is that the necessary premises are rarely sufficiently well substantiated or clarified to justify the drawing of strong conclusions, however impeccable are the rules. Defective premises can be operated on by the most correct logic or mathematics to produce the most absurd conclusions. Many defective syllogistic fallacies are well known. Deductive logic in psychology all too often results in a myth-making process in which a priori, but false, assumptions are given substance and credibility.

The problems confronted by psychological science become even more focused now. When we create hypothetical constructs to explain our data, can they really be substantiated? Can a *valid* deductive bridge be built between that which can be externally observed and that which is internal and private? What convincing evidence is there that such hypothetical constructs are more than the ingenious and convenient inventions of psychologists or the results of fallacious deduction or induction? Psychological inference does not usually enjoy the luxury of sharply honed rules of either transformation or proof.

The problem is further complicated because behaviorists themselves disagree on the capabilities and limits of the inferential approach. The most radical behaviorists eschew it to a greater or lesser degree, feeling it will inevitably lead to the creation of a false pantheon of hypothetical constructs that can not be justified.

Behaviorism sometimes has surprising allies in its rejection of inference as a means of identifying underlying constructs. The philosopher Wittgenstein (1953, 1958), for example, also argued strongly that it was not possible to infer anything about internal processes; regardless of the experiments that one may carry out, they may or may not exist. There are two points embedded in this brief sentence of enormous import. The first is that Wittgenstein is arguing that trying to explain some kind of an internal state such as consciousness is futile. Reductive explanations must have an end and the terms and rules at one level of discussion do not necessarily bear within them the traces of lower levels. There are fundamental, nonreductive concepts (perhaps including behavior) that should not be reductively explained, however well they may be described. Furthermore, there is nothing unusual about the difficulty that psychology faces. Most of physics also ends at a level that is not reductive. Forces such as gravity and the strong force that hold nuclei together are well described; however, their exact mechanism or nature remains unknown.

The second point made by Wittgenstein is even more germane to the present discussion. Perhaps, he suggested, there are no internal states or processes to be explained! Wittgenstein looked on psychology as less than serious science because its logic seemed to him to be so flawed in the most fundamental ways. Psychologists examined behavior using very specific methods. They then invented entities that might plausibly produce that behavior. Unscientifically, these invented constructs were later reified and became targets for explanation even though they did not actually exist. Extrapolations from behavioral observations to such entities as memory or perception or even consciousness may be artifactual, according to Wittgenstein. Nevertheless, they have become the realities of a psychological science searching for a reductive ontology. This idea is closely related to the concept that the "things" of psychology are really dependent on the nature of the methods used more than on their underlying reality. Wittgenstein's analysis, as interpreted by some philosophers (e.g., Hanfling, 1989), suggests that there are such profound limits on our use of language and that word meanings are so private that it would never be possible for the very private sensations of one person to be communicated to another. This is certainly the stuff of a very extreme behaviorism.

As we have seen in this review of critical comments, the decision underlying one's personal or scientific stand on the mentalism–behaviorism issue is often based on much less solid foundations than those required by even a fallible logical system. In the past the decision has often been made on the basis of some kind of ill-defined plausibility, on one's personal beliefs and convictions, on specialized definitions of critical terms, or even on one's a priori estimate of what would be interesting, worthwhile, or exciting.

Now, however, the scientific milieu is changing. As I hope I have convincingly argued in this book (particularly in chap. 2) and in my earlier book (Uttal, 1998), there are new empirical and theoretical arguments that deal directly with the accessibility and analyzability questions posed earlier. It is my opinion that these new arguments taken collectively are extremely compelling and should force us toward a more behaviorist than mentalist approach to understanding human nature.

Finally, as we saw in the tabulations by Skinner, Kimble, and others, all too many of the arguments against behaviorism have been based on a priori, humanistic, or aesthetic judgments that transcend the limits of normal science. It was often an initial commitment to the premise that there is something special about human consciousness, in particular, that prejudged the scientific issue. These a priori decisions were sometimes made as a substitute for a critical consideration of the extremely difficult logical, scientific, and conceptual challenges that must be solved before we can determine the plausibility of inferring mental processes from behavioral data. In their most extreme statements, the behaviorists seem to some to threaten some basic humanistic or theological ideals about the dearest parts of our personal existence. This fear, however, is usually unwarranted. Behaviorism is a scientific epistemology using a particular methodology to study one special aspect of human existence, not an effort to diminish others that are of value and worth in their own right. If this fact is accepted, then mental processes need not be rejected and those psychologists who do study what people think they are thinking can go about their business. There are many ways in which all sides in this controversy can be satisfied without doing damage to either scientific or humanistic ideals. It depends on our ability to segregate goals and methods that are suitable for one side of the debate from those that are appropriate for the other.

Chapter **4**

Toward a Renewed and Revitalized Psychophysical Behaviorism

In this chapter, my goal is to summarize the arguments presented so far and to draw from them what for me (and I hope for some others) is the best possible resolution of the mentalism–behaviorism controversy in the context of our time and of what we now know. I also extract from the material so far presented what I believe are the best possible answers to the questions posed in Chapter 1. My aim is to offer a renewed and revitalized version of a behaviorist psychology that is more consistent with scientific and logical standards than is any existing system. Finally, I briefly review some of the contemporary versions of behaviorism to see how well they meet the criteria I have expressed here. In accomplishing these goals I am also expanding on comments made about many of these same issues in my earlier book (Uttal, 1998).

4.1 AN ANALYSIS OF THE CRITICISMS

The behaviorism–mentalism controversy is of such fundamental importance that it seems appropriate to step back for a minute and ask—can it be resolved? Is there any way to seek, if I may further abuse the word, an *objective* solution to an issue that has created such turmoil and instability in the psychological sciences for a century or more. My answer is that I believe there is a possible solution, and that the solution is already available to us. It is embedded in the discussion presented so far and a clarification of what the essential, as opposed to secondary or irrelevant, arguments are on each side.

In the previous two chapters, I reviewed the most germane and central of the arguments made by proponents of the mentalist and behaviorist schools respectively. The following two lists summarize what I believe are the main arguments against mentalism and behaviorism respectively.

The Essential Arguments Against Mentalism

1. The absence of public availability, objectivity, and repeatability for mental processes.
2. Mentalism leads to the Homunculus or infinite regress arguments.
3. Mentalism produces unprovable hypothetical constructs.
4. The empirical data argue against the accessibility of mental processes.
5. Mentalism requires complex experimental designs and unprovable assumptions that produce fragile data.
6. Mentalism arises because of the vested interests of its humanist, theological, and personal protagonists or from the professional needs of psychotherapists.

The Essential Arguments Against Behaviorism

1. The limited range of behaviorist psychology.
2. Behaviorism dehumanizes humans.
3. Behaviorism is too "mechanical" or is "not sufficiently mechanical."
4. Behaviorism is not a step forward.
5. Behaviorism overemphasizes the environment and underemphasizes heredity as sources of behavior.
6. Behaviorism is nothing more than common sense.
7. Behaviorism is antidemocratic.
8. Behaviorism is antireligious.

As I reviewed these arguments, it became increasingly clear that a science of mental life in the manner proposed by the mentalist traditions (up to and including the contemporary cognitive version) is driven more by extrascientific interests than scientific principles or logic or, even more important, empirical data. Several common features can be discerned in these arguments.

First, it seems to me that few of the antibehaviorist arguments in any of their forms really speak to a seriously objective scientific issue. Most argue against the "dehumanization" of humans by what is perceived as a "sterile, mechanistic, and incomplete" approach to the study of human nature. Nowhere in any of the arguments that I have surveyed in this book is there any foundation established for a scientific evaluation of the issue at hand. "Incompleteness," "antidemocratic" or "antireligious," and "mechanical" are issues for philosophers and sociologists of science, not hypotheses amenable to experimental test and analysis. The most compelling argument made by the antibehaviorists is their challenge to what is obviously an overstated and extreme empiricism at the expense of the genetic and maturational influences—statements made by behaviorists such as Watson and Skinner in what many would agree were injudicious excursions into pop psychology late in their careers.

As for the behaviorists, it should be stipulated that many of their arguments also fall into the same category of untestable yearnings as opposed to testable hypotheses. However, there are two kinds of arguments from among the many presented that do have a much greater impact: First, the empirical tests that have been carried out to determine how well verbal reports concur with other independent estimates of the causes of behavior, and second, the logical, if not mathematical, arguments emerging from other natural sciences made against the uniqueness of any mental hypothetical construct developed by behavioral or input–output methods.

With regard to the empirical tests of the links between verbal behavior and mental states, there appears to be an overwhelming preponderance of evidence—when experiments are designed specifically to test this linkage—that the two are dissociated or at least dissociatable. Nisbett and Wilson (1977), among others, suggest that association is almost fortuitous when it does occur. Certainly, a firm correlation between verbal reports and mental states is absent sufficiently often that a question arises concerning how much credence can be given to those instances in which the two domains do seem to be related.

Does this invalidate all experimental approaches that are designed to determine the relations and transforms between verbal reports and mental states? Of course, not! In a practical sense, people can report mental states such as pain or hunger and their subsequent behavior can determine that much of what they were saying is reasonably close to some kind of cognitive truth. Wittgenstein's cryptic philosophy aside, some validity in human intercommunication must be assumed or everything behavioral would become chaos. Similarly, in psychophysical experiments, with sufficient regard given to the control of biases and other confounding influences, simple verbal responses (Class A-type "yes, I see it" responses) can be used to precisely track out the threshold of the visual system as a function of some variable of the physical stimulus. However, whenever verbal reports beyond the complexity of Brindley's (1960) Class A responses are used to describe one's thought processes, the glass through which we are observing the mind becomes not just passively murky or opaque, but transformationally active. This is the undeniable tale told by the experimental evidence specifically directed at answering the question of the accessibility of mental processes—as opposed to research that finesses this issue and simply assumes that accessibility as a premise.

The other class of exceptionally influential arguments against mentalism asserts that, in terms of the most fundamental principles, the analysis of a closed system into its internal components is not possible. These arguments from cognate sciences are rarely considered by mentalist psychologists. Rather, like their a priori commitment to accessibility, analyzability is usually taken as a premise rather than as a researchable issue.

In conclusion, the facts are (a) that there seems to be no hard evidence supporting the validity of cognitive analysis as practiced by mentalisms, and (b) that there is a substantial weight of empirical and formal evidence that the mentalist agenda cannot be achieved. Therefore, I am now convinced that the accessibility controversy must ultimately be resolved in favor of some kind of a renewed and revised behaviorism. The behaviorism of the next century, however, must operate within the confines of the other natural sciences, without violating the great principles of logic, mathematics, and rigorous and critical inquiry in general, but still be responsible to the specific needs of its own content.

I next consider what should be some of the distinguishing characteristics of a 21st-century behaviorism.

4.2 THE CHARACTERISTICS OF A REVITALIZED PSYCHOPHYSICAL BEHAVIORISM

In this book and its predecessors, I have been building the case for reconsidering behaviorism as the appropriate paradigm for scientific psychology in the next century. It is now time to specify exactly what are the characteristics of this revised behaviorism. Based on the discussions presented earlier in this book, I am convinced that the next swing of the psychological pendulum should take us toward a behaviorism that is:

- Psychophysical
- Mathematically descriptive
- Neuronally Nonreductive
- Experimental
- Molar
- Empiricist_1 and Nativist
- Empiricist_2 and Rationalist
- Antipragmatic

The following sections elaborate on this skeletal list.

4.2.1 Psychophysical

Throughout the history of scientific psychology, sensory processes have been studied by means of a highly standardized methodology called psychophysics. Psychophysical methods were developed to measure, as objectively as possible, the functional relationships between the properties of the physical stimulus and measures of the responses produced by biological organisms. Psychophysical studies of sensory processes, such as those summarized in Weber's, Fechner's, and Stevens' laws provided the intellectual foundation for much of modern psychological science. Others associated with human performance, such as Fitts' and Hick–Hyman's laws, are among the most important contributions of our science in recent years. These principles are among the jewels of psychological research and remain significant milestones for four fundamental reasons.

First, and perhaps most important, there existed in each case an anchor to the physical reality of the external world. The measures of physical science (such as the wavelength or luminance of a stimulating light—units of quality and quantity respectively—or length and velocity) served as precisely defined standards against which the perceptual response could be calibrated.

Second, in traditional psychophysical experiments, the subject was permitted only the simplest possible discriminative response. The concept of a threshold—the boundary between the perceivable and the imperceivable—was used as a criterion for tracking the functional relationship between some dimension of the stimulus and some dimension of the response. In other cases, in which, for example, the magnitudes of suprathreshold functions were to be estimated, the subject's response had to be more complex and required more complex processing. Even in that context, however, the preferred approach was to require only the simplest possible discrimination (e.g., the paired-comparison procedure in which the subject was required to simply say whether Stimulus A was greater than Stimulus B, or vice versa). When absolute judgments were used, for example in the magnitude-estimation procedure (Stevens, 1961), it was always the case that there was much greater response variability than in those experiments where only a simple discriminative response was permitted.

As the psychophysical methodology matured, protocols become increasingly constrained to control, regulate, and even measure that most basic kind of cognitive penetration—variation of the criterion level. Initially, forced-choice procedures that prevented the criterion level from biasing responses replaced yes–no judgments. Ultimately, signal detection methods (Tanner & Swets, 1954) allowed the experimenter to separately measure subjective criterion and physiological discrimination factors. In all of these cases, however, the goal was to minimize the information-processing load on the part of the subject. No introspective judgments, no interpretative self-analyses, just the simplest possible response to a well-defined stimulus.

Whether it was a yes–no procedure or a multialternative forced-choice one, the subject was permitted only a simple, Class A, discriminative response.

The third factor leading to the success of classical psychophysics was the procedure itself. Precisely measured values of well-defined stimulus parameters were systematically scanned according to sharply defined rules. The experimenter, as well as the subject, was limited by such procedural rules and constraints in order to avoid any biasing effects.

The forth and final factor that inoculated psychophysics against overly imaginative and fragile explanations was that the obtained functional relationships were usually intended to be the final outcome of the investigative process—the answer to the posed question. No hypothetical mental constructs or pseudophysiological explanations were a necessary part of the traditional psychophysical agenda. The results of an experiment were plotted on a graph on which one dimension was that of the physical stimulus and the other the trajectory of the perceived response according to some criterion of detectability, equality, or nonequality. In a few special cases, of course, the mechanisms underlying the transform were sought in some fortuitously related physiological or anatomical knowledge. However, even for the simplest, most elemental psychophysical graphs, there was little that could be used to reductively explain the underlying processes. Wherever such attempts were made, they usually resulted in ambiguous and unverifiable theories. It took a whole new technology—neurophysiological recording from single neurons—to even begin to suggest some explanatory causes and that approach only worked with relatively simple peripheral structures.

I have gone into detail to spell out the logic of the psychophysical methods because it seems to me that given what we now know about the barriers and obstacles to accessibility and analysis of other kinds of cognitive processing, the highly structured and inherently nonreductionist psychophysical methodology represents a much more plausible approach to other problems in scientific psychology than does any approach that aims at identifying and measuring hypothetical constructs. The psychophysical model, it must be appreciated, is basically a behavioral one—controlled stimulation and subsequent observation, typically using some very simple criterion and, to the maximum extent possible, equally simple responses. Indeed, the classic psychophysical method is exactly the prototype of Brindley's (1960) Class A response category. A simple forced choice "yes—I see it" (in the first or second presentation) is probably the closest possible approximation to an uncontaminated ideal response. It is innocent of the obfuscating cognitive cloud that affects so many other types of experimental paradigms.

The psychophysical behaviorism proposed here would ideally constrain its empirical methodologies to such Class A-type psychophysical responses. The motivation for this constraint is simple—to minimize cognitive penetration and confusion. As we have seen, judgments of complexity beyond simple psychophysical responses are always confounded, clouded, obscured, modified, and rationalized by actions and criteria other than the one intended to be measured. Even in the simplest case involving criterion level shifts, quantitative errors can be introduced. In more complex experimental designs in which the subject's responses are not adequately constrained, subjects can introduce qualitative errors into the process that can lead to totally erroneous conclusions. It is this qualitative misreporting that obstructs so much of psychology's agenda. The only hope for reducing this kind of bias in psychology is to retreat to the much more direct methods that psychophysicists have traditionally used.

A corollary issue then arises: Can the simple well-structured experimental design that is prototypical of a psychophysical experiment be applied to psychological processes that are considered to be higher level or cognitive? The answer to this question is that to a substantial degree these techniques are already being used. Averaged reaction times and the percentage of the total number of correct responses, simple indicators of decisions and judgments, are often used in cognitive level experiments. In many other situations, however, the subject is required to make much more complex judgments and to respond with behaviors that are far from Brindley's ideal Class A responses. The recommendation I make here is that there should be an effort to simplify experimental designs to more closely approximate the psychophysical ideal of the simplest possible judgment.

4.2.2 Mathematically and Behaviorally Descriptive

One of the most important characteristics of the proposed new psychophysical behaviorism concerns the role that theories and models should play. The argument I now make is that, where hitherto we have tended to look at our models and data as permitting us to infer the details of internal mechanisms and structures, we should reconfigure our thinking to acknowledge only their descriptive role. I believe this reorientation is the heart of any successful behaviorist approach.

There is abroad in mentalisms of all kinds the implicit premise that behavioral measures, in some extralogical manner, allow us to validly infer the nature of the underlying mental processes. This notion is, from the point of view of the arguments made so far in this book, erroneous. It ignores the fundamental nature of what are essentially descriptive and nonreductive techniques for the study of mental processes—mathematics and behavior. To reiterate, mathematics is a descriptive tool that is completely neutral with regard to the mechanisms it describes. This powerful system of thought can work in situations in which the premises that govern the physical or biological reality are totally distinct and separable from those governing the mathematical manipulations. Indeed, mathematics works perfectly even when there are no physiological or mechanical assumptions.

Psychological research methods are, likewise, descriptive techniques constrained in exactly the same way. Being a molar (i.e., an ensemble) measure, the behavior that psychologists measure is also inherently neutral with regard to the underlying mechanisms. The descriptions provided by both mathematics and behavior are, thus, subject to this same limitation. Both can be accounted for by a host of different internal mechanisms. Neither provides the means for distinguishing between the real and the merely plausible.

The use of either mathematics or behavior creates another potential danger. Each may add superfluous meaning to any putative explanation; mathematics does so by introducing its own properties even when they are not actually present in the system under study; behavior does so by encouraging the invention of hypothetical constructs that are, at best, functional analogs of the underlying mechanism but not valid manifestations of what are really inaccessible cognitive realities.

The advantages and disadvantages of analogical reasoning are all too often misunderstood or unappreciated. It is, for example, overlooked by enthusiasts that Fourier-type analyses, although providing a powerful means of describing a system, are not truly analytic in a process or mechanism sense. Fourier analysis can succeed in representing a function *even though there is nothing that corresponds to the sinusoidal basis functions in the physical system being analyzed.* Indeed, there is nothing unique about the sinusoidal functions that are most often used. There are innumerable other sets of orthogonal basis functions that work as well including square waves, Gabor Functions, Wavelets, normal curves, and even sawtooth waves.

To make the same point, consider that there is no reason to assume that a polynomial equation (to pick a trivial example) that fits some process is actually physically instantiated as a sum of a series in the physical system. One has only to work briefly with analog computers to appreciate the fact that assumptions about process and mechanism, respectively, are separable and distinct, and that the relation between analogs (functionally similar entities) is not the same as that between homologs (mechanically or embryologically similar entities). The message is that mathematics works well in doing what it does and what is does superbly is to describe. However, neither mathematics nor behavioral research can pass through the *in principle* barrier between description and reductive explanation.

In other words, no descriptive procedure based on the final outcome of a series of complex processes, however powerful, can peer deeply into the workings of an unopened black box. It must also be noted that such a system may be closed either because the system is truly closed or because it is functionally closed by virtue of complexity of interaction or numerosity of its components. No formulation can create truth about internal structure from studies of the transformations that occur between inputs and outputs. In short, both mathematics and behavioral (including all psychological) research are operating at such a molar level that they are constrained in a fundamental way. Unfortunately, psychologists, in particular, rarely appreciate this limitation and tend to infer more than those methods can validly imply.

It is important to emphasize that what I say in the present context for mathematical and behavioral theories of mental processes is also true of all other forms of theory that aspire to play an ontologically explanatory, rather than a descriptive, role in science. All statistical models can also be challenged as being spurious if they are presented as reductive explanations. However, their fit and predictions are not spurious if description is all that is being claimed. Then, the fit is either satisfactory or it is not. In this case, a precise criterion for choosing among the various alternative descriptions exists—*goodness of fit*. Assumptions about internal mechanisms must be handled separately.

I hope it is understood that mathematics is an absolutely indispensable part of modern science. Killeen (1995) put it very well when he stated that "Mathematics puts a fine point on the dull pencil of metaphor" (p. 425). The problem is that even as it sharpens our language and makes precise the relationships, it is still a form of metaphor or, more precisely, of analogy. No matter how "fine a point" may have been added to the "dull pencil" it is still a pencil!

In conclusion, both mathematics and behavior are useful means of describing the functional relationships or transforms that are observed to exist when one probes a complex system. They may do in a highly powerful and accurate manner, but no matter how good the process description, neither essentially descriptive technique is capable of peering into the internal mechanisms and processes of even a relatively simple system. (Consider the intractability of the three body problem!) Both are neutral, both are intrinsically nonreductive, and both must be appreciated within the context of their own limitations and utilities. Given this argument, and what we know about the complexity and inaccessibility of underlying mental processes, a new behaviorist psychology must strive for description and eschew any false or illusory extrapolation of these limits to the unredeemable hope that ontological explanation can emerge from any conceivable kind of behavioral analysis. Misleading ourselves that our ad hoc mentalist theories are anything more than myths is the price that has been in the past and must be paid in the future for ignoring this admonition.

4.2.3 Neuronally Nonreductive

The revised and revitalized behaviorism for the 21st century must also be neuronally nonreductive. There are many neurophysiological findings shown to be associated with some behavioral attribute. The relationship between color vision and the biochemistry of the absorbing molecules in the cones is an extraordinary intellectual achievement. The identification of places in the brain that are more likely than others to be involved in some particular, if poorly defined, mental function is also an active and interesting area of modern neuroscience. As admirable as these accomplishments are, however, there is another goal far less likely to be achieved. That unobtainable goal is the unraveling of the neuronal nets—the details of the vast numbers of neurons—that are the actual psychoneural equivalents of all mental actions—including conscious self-awareness.

There are two ways in which such goals have been pursued at the neuronal level and each is equal to the other in terms of the myths that it has stimulated. First is the idea that individual neurons encode or represent complex ideas. The second is that the vast networks of neurons, which must, in some ontological sense, be the equivalent of mental processes, can be disentangled to "explain" how they give rise to mental actions. Two key points must be reiterated here:

1. Any hope of finding the psychoneural equivalent of any mental process is unlikely given the sheer complexity (and, thus, the computational difficulty) of the responsible neural nets.
2. Single neurons are unlikely candidates to encode complex cognitive functions. In the past, we have turned to such unicellular models for mind because of the difficulties suggested in point 1.

Existing single neuron theories of cognitive representation are based primarily on correlative associations between the response of a fortuitously impaled neuron and a phenomenal report from an observer, usually in totally different experiments. There never has been a well controlled experiment that shows that any single neuron is uniquely and solely associated with any mental process. In fact everything that we know about the nervous system tells us that a more likely explanation is that widely distributed nets of neurons are the true equivalents of mental processes. Novel procedures like the fMRI, of course, do not operate at this level. They only answer the question "where?"

Looking back at its history, it becomes obvious that the entire single neuron hypothesis cum theory was stimulated by the prevalent technology of the time—the single cell recording microelectrode—as well as by the sheer combinatorial hopelessness of a comprehensive network analysis. Because of these twin factors, technology drove theory building to a degree that greatly distorted the most fundamental appreciation of the ways in which brains give rise to minds.

Neuronal reductionism based on the role of very large networks of redundant, adaptive, and cooperating neurons is also a poor candidate for a reductive psychology. The reason in this case is not that such an idea is not correct in some ontological sense. Rather, it is founded on the plain fact that there is no hope of analyzing these networks because of their enormous complexity and numerosity. The number of neurons that must be involved in even the simplest plausible psychologically significant network makes it impossible to consider using any electrophysiological recording technique that attempts to measure or simulate the activity of all of the relevant and necessary neurons. Indeed, this practical consideration may be further buttressed because some modern fields of analysis (e.g., thermodynamics and chaos theory) suggest that even if such a neurophysiological tour de force was achievable, the information necessary to explain the relationship between the neural net and mental activity would simply not be available.

It is reasons such as these that speak against the romantic longing for bridge building between neurophysiology and psychology. Proponents of any revitalized behaviorism must act realistically and strive for a psychology that is not neuronally reductive. Attempts to stretch analogies to cross the insurmountable gulf between the two domains ultimately lead to misleading theories and, thus, to perversions of a true understanding of both mind and brain.

4.2.4 Experimental

Any renewed version of behaviorism must be an empirical science in terms of its most fundamental axiomatic foundations. Although firm in eschewing false theorizing, fantastic hypothetical constructs, cognitive- and neuroreductionism, and unrealistic extrapolation from behavior and mathematics to internal processes and structures, it must never abandon the direct contact with nature that experimentation provides. To do so would remove psychology from the scientific arena altogether. Given the special difficulties faced by a science like psychology, a nonempirical approach would be a disaster. Clearly, it is only to a degree that a science stays in touch with objective measures of the phenomena of interest that it can earn a place at the scientific roundtable. For a time period that literally must be measured in millennia, the subject matter to which scientific psychology now claims ownership was the property of speculative philosophers and theologians. The creation of the psychological laboratory in the 19th century, following close on the intellectual revolution of preceding centuries created a new objective approach that must be preserved. To the degree that speculation is allowed to replace experimentation, scientific psychology will not only be diminished, but destroyed.

Psychological experimentation must be guided by the same principles as any other science. The design of psychological experiments must be in accord with good statistical practice that prevents artifacts and confounds from inadvertently biasing the results. Because the number of variables involved in all psychological experiments is quite large, it is to be expected that variability will also be large. Because it is unlikely that a psychological experimenter will ever be able to control all of the salient variables, experimental design will have to incorporate repeated measures and cumulative summaries. Even more important, is the need to examine extended ranges of the critical variables. All too often in the history of this science, misleading results have occurred because the experimenter has not extended the range of the independent variable to values at which there are substantial, but totally unexpected, discontinuities.

A related issue often arising in experimental design is whether or not the data obtained from one subject should be combined with those from others. One side of the problem is that individual variability can sometime produce idiosyncratic but meaningful results that are lost when data are pooled. The other side is that noise and individual variability can sometimes obscure general trends and population norms. Obviously, different experimental goals will require different solutions.

4.2.5 Molar

The antithesis to a reductionist approach is one that emphasizes the whole, the molar, or the holistic[1] properties of the observed aggregate of the components, processes, and transformations of the stimulus, organism, and response. Because I argue that neither cognitive reductionism nor neuroreductionism is likely to be achieved in psychology, a major characteristic of the renewed behaviorism must be its commitment to a molar or holist approach. This is hardly a revolutionary suggestion. From the very beginning, behaviorism has been explicitly a molar science. It has been concerned with the specific measurable actions of the subject, not the components of that action. This is contrary to the elementalism of the structuralisms or associationisms that preceded the behaviorist revolution, an approach that proclaimed analysis was possible. Along with the methodological issue of introspection, support of the flawed hypothesis that mental processes could be analyzed into components was the main stimulus to behaviorist revolution.

This fundamental adherence to the desirability of a molar approach does not deny that from Watson's time on many behaviorists had some

---

[1]Unfortunately. The word "holistic" has been appropriated by other less-than-scientific fields of discussion. I do not use the word in the sense that some therapy should involve the whole body and/or the mind. Rather I use it in the same sense that a physicist would assert that the individual particles that make up a gas can be collectively characterized by the holistic term "pressure." The analogy is between molar behavior (pressure), on the one hand, and the cognitive or neural components, on the other.

analytic concepts built into their theories. Watson, as discussed in Chapter 1, was an associationist in the abstract if not in terms of his concrete behavioral methodology. Tolman certainly also was searching for the cognitive components that he assumed underlay observed behavioral responses. Nevertheless, if one is to accept the evidence so far presented that analysis of cognitive processes is as limited as is their accessibility, then the logical conclusion must be that an emphasis on the overall, molar response should be a mandatory feature of 21st-century behaviorism.

A molar behavioral approach dictates an emphasis on the overall configuration of the stimuli as well as the response. All too often in current research, the local attributes of the stimulus—the features—are emphasized to the exclusion of their arrangement or organization. From the viewpoint of a modern behaviorist, the Gestalt psychologists were absolutely correct in emphasizing the overall configuration of the stimuli with which they dealt to the exclusion of its details. A satisfactory modern behaviorism should, likewise, concentrate on the organization of the parts of a stimulus rather than the nature of the parts. As such it would encompass and incorporate many of the holistic and phenomenological aspects of Gestaltism.

A revitalized behaviorism should also emphasize the study of the transformations made by the cognitive system as a whole rather than making any effort to dissect the mind or its processes into components. Attempts to do so are probably the major source of nonsense in the science, as was so eloquently argued by Pachella (1974).

Finally the new version of behaviorism must deal with the emitted behavioral responses in their entirety. Exercise scientists and others from the allied field of kinesthesis may gain some advantage from analyzing responses into the contributing muscle groups, but such information is rarely useful to psychologists interested in studying mental activity. Indeed, it is often the case that it really does not even matter what is the response mode—the left arm, the right arm, or the foot. It is the adaptive *effect* of the response, not which muscle group exerted the force, that tells us the most. Similarly, it is the sum total of the behavior, not how it was arrived at, that may be all that a psychology can expect.

4.2.6 Empiricist$_1$ and Nativist

Throughout its history, psychology has been the legatee of a heavy conceptual burden from the speculative philosophy that preceded it. Among the most contentious issues in that legacy have been the nature–nurture and the direct–mediated controversies. In an earlier work (Uttal, 1981), I denoted the first of these as the Nativism–Empiricism$_1$ dimension or axis and the second as the Rationalism–Empiricism$_2$ dimension or axis. The reasons for characterizing these controversies as continua rather than dichotomies was that it was historically never the case that any system of psychology exclusively took one or the other of the extreme conditions. Rather, there were always intermediate positions that could vary from one end of the dimension to the other.

The first dimension (Nativism–Empiricism$_1$) characterizes many theories of perception in particular and cognition in general along an axis running from a total commitment to the innate nature of thought (Nativism) to the other extreme (Empiricism$_1$) at which it is asserted that everything is learned. The second dimension (Rationalism–Empiricism$_2$) characterizes many theories along an axis running from the extreme of humans as mechanical robots whose behavior is totally determined by the stimulus (Empiricism$_2$) to the other extreme (Rationalism) at which behavior is determined by logical, symbolic, adaptive, and active cognitive mechanisms that are only distantly related to the stimuli. The main point being made here is that none of these extreme positions is any longer tenable given what we now know. An eclectic, intermediate position must inevitably be chosen to be the proper resolution.

The controversy between empiricism$_1$ and nativism is beyond contention at this point in the history of psychology. No respectable psychological science, behaviorist or mentalist, can ignore either the genetic and maturational or the experiential aspects of our behavior. The outrageous statements by Watson and Skinner that given appropriate training patterns, a human could be made into anything are certainly outdated given what we know today about the powerful role that genetics plays in behavior. But, then, so too is the equally arguable assertion that our psychological life is totally defined by our genetic heritage. A modern behaviorism must accept the interplay of both maturation and experience in determining our responses.

4.2.7 Empiricist$_2$ and Rationalist

Just as the nature–nurture controversy has to be resolved in the form of an eclectic compromise, so too must the direct–mediated debate. Regardless of whether or not one is a mentalist, there is no question that the brain–mind, the "O" in the "S-O-R" is not a passive transformer of stimuli into responses in the strict empiricist$_2$ sense. Behavioral outcomes are clearly not directly and solely determined by stimulus conditions, but rather are modulated and modified by a host of factors internal to the responding organism. This conclusion is not just a matter of satisfying traditional humanistic philosophies or meeting some deep need for free will. Rather, it is now a matter of empirical fact. From the most primitive geometrical illusions to the experiments on the limited validity of verbal reports discussed in Chapter 2, there is ample evidence to support a new rationalism as well as a new empiricism$_2$.

Both behaviorism and mentalism have been justifiably criticized for extreme positions on both these dimensions. Few psychologists currently take any of the extreme positions I have highlighted here. So each is more or less a red herring in this discussion. There is, however, a more general issue that should not be overlooked—that is, a general eclecticism may be among the most important criteria of any new psychological position. Eclecticism requires any science to keep an open mind toward new developments as well as ancient controversies. Behavioral extremism is as bad as mentalist extremism.

4.2.8 Antipragmatic

Throughout the history of American psychology, there has been a continuous pressure from all kinds of frontiers and other practical considerations to solve the immediate problems of the world. This intellectual force came to be referred to as pragmatism—the philosophy asserting that practical considerations should dominate and qualify the way we approach our sciences. Such a point of view was a fundamental part of the philosophies of Charles S. Peirce (1839–1914) and William James (1842–1910). Pragmatism has had and continues to have profound effects on psychological thinking, particularly in the United States. I argue here that this otherwise worthwhile point-of-view may have actually inhibited the development of the science of psychology by establishing criteria for decision making that were misleading if not demonstrably wrong. In our quest to solve human problems and to make our science useful, we have all too frequently lost sight of a more fundamental criterion than utility—the quest for truth and understanding.

The revitalized behaviorism that I hope will emerge should emphasize the much longer term goals of understanding and knowledge for their own sake. If mind is inaccessible and unanalyzable, so be it. We should not attempt to build a façade of false knowledge simply to achieve practical goals for human factors engineering, education, psychotherapy, or for some wistful humanistic longing, no matter how worthwhile they may otherwise be. When a question of such fundamental importance as the one of accessibility is asked, we should not be misled by the need or desire to solve some important extra-scientific problem to impute or infer that which is unobtainable. No question should be asked with the presumption that it would be useful or practical to answer it affirmatively. Rather it should be approached with the intent of objectively and independently (of other reasonable and respectable human needs) determining an answer that is rigorously true.

Unfortunately, psychology is so intimately related to so many other aspects of human existence that it is all too easily confounded by extrascientific considerations. Certainly, many of the criticisms of behaviorism are contaminated with what may be considered to be extra-scientific pragmatic criteria. Some sociologists of science, more imbued with the pragmatic view or the point of view that science is just another human activity will probably disagree with this assertion. Nevertheless, any revitalized behaviorism must be based on an antipragmatic and proscientific foundation.

4.3 SOME ANSWERS TO THE CRITICAL QUESTIONS

Now that a framework for an updated, revised, and revitalized behaviorism has been presented, we are in a position to provide some answers to the questions posed in Chapter 1. In the following discussion, I am particularly interested in determining whether or not the question posed is also a "good one." That is, although some of these questions are serious scientific issues, some are really irrelevant to the basic matter at hand: Are mental processes accessible to empirical inquiry?

4.3.1 Are Mental Processes Real?

One of the greatest misunderstandings about behaviorism, *any* behaviorism, is its position with regard to the reality of mental processes. I recall from my graduate school days (during the heyday of behaviorist thinking) that any mention of the word "mind" was greeted with, if not contempt, humorous derision. However, a reading of the behaviorist literature, from the most mentalistic words of Tolman to the most radical antimentalist writings of Watson and Skinner makes it clear that there have never been any psychologists who denied the firsthand evidence of their own awareness. Skinner (1974), for example, repeatedly raised varied issues of mind and of mental processes in virtually every one of his published works. For a psychologist or, for that matter, any other human being, how could it be otherwise?

Perhaps nowhere is Skinner clearer about his acceptance of the reality of mind than in his oft quoted remark

> The objection to mental states is not that they do not exist, but that they are not relevant to a functional analysis. (Skinner, 1953, p. 35)

To Skinner, as to most other normal human beings, people think and emote and feel and perceive; that is not the issue. Whether we can tap into those mental states with objective, scientific methods, however, is at the heart of the great controversy between mentalism and behaviorism.

In other contexts, however, it must be acknowledged that Skinner (1953) was somewhat more equivocal and has suggested that the word *mind* may be nothing more than a lexical error. That is, the word is seemingly used by him, at least sometimes, as an expedient and as a surrogate or metaphor for unobservable "hypothetical constructs" that describe the causal inner forces at work. Elsewhere in this same book Skinner joined the epiphenomenalists in pointing out that it is difficult to understand how the immaterial mind could "cause" (p. 10) physical events.

Skinner (1953) further suggested that the very use of the word *mind* raises the issue of dualism, something that is only partially ameliorated by substituting the word *brain* for the word *mind.* He stated that

> Thinking has the dimensions of behavior, not of a fancied inner process which finds expression in behavior. (pp. 117–118)

And, thus, identifies mind (inner process) with behavior.

Perhaps, he would be more comfortable with the distinction of mind as *process* and brain as *material mechanism* now popular among many psychologists and neuroscientists. It is possible that he would also be comfortable with the term *information state* as a better term for the mind. However, it is clear that all of these terms also founder on the conceptual shoals of any attempt to specifically define mind or consciousness.

Be that as it may be, Skinner was perfectly willing to accept the fact that some future physiology might ultimately take the place of mentalistic analyses. He was not willing, however, to allow the inadequate neural models of his time—the so-called "conceptual nervous systems"—to substitute for behavior even temporarily. It was, to him, a futurist fantasy that someday such a full neuroreductionism would evolve. As argued in my earlier book (Uttal, 1998), and as discussed in Chapter 2, such a "full neuroreductionism" is probably a chimera, extremely unlikely ever to be achieved regardless of the fervent dreams, wishes, and hopes of the eliminativists.

Given that virtually all behaviorists and all mentalists accept the reality of mind (at least as a brain process), it is clear that a criterion based on the resolution of the question of the reality of mind cannot be used to distinguish between mentalist and behaviorist psychologies. We must look elsewhere for key identifiers and distinguishing characteristics; this brings us to the next question.

4.3.2 Even If the Mind Is Real, Is It Accessible?

I have repeatedly asserted in this book that the most fundamental scientific issue on which mentalisms and behaviorisms do diverge concerns whether or not mental processes and mechanisms are accessible. This, perhaps, is the most salient distinguishing criterion of the two kinds of psychologies discussed in this work. Logically, this question must follow the issue of reality and precede the question of analyzability. It is in answering this question that I believe the single most important judgment is usually made by a protobehaviorist or a protomentalist. If one accepts the idea that the intrapersonal self-awarenesses can be communicated interpersonally or that verbal reports or other behaviors validly carry with them signs and indicators of the true nature of the underlying mental processes, then one is logically driven to become a mentalist.

If, on the other hand, an examination of the history and findings of psychological science and other sciences leads one to believe that *inter*personal observations are neutral or even misleading with regard to the *intra*personal mental actions, and if one wishes to be logically consistent, then one must necessarily become a behaviorist in the empirical, positivist, operationalist tradition.

All the evidence and argument presented so far in this book leads me to the inescapable conclusion that behavior is, in fact, neutral with regard to the underlying mental and neural processes and mechanisms. By behavioral neutrality, I mean that there is no way to infer anything specific or unique about internal mechanisms from behavior—many internal mechanisms can account for any externally observed behavior. We are therefore led to the further conclusion that mental processes are fundamentally inaccessible and private. From there it is hardly a long logical leap to some kind of a revitalized behaviorism.

4.3.3 Are Mental Processes Analyzable?

If inaccessibility is the answer of choice to the previous question, then by definition, the analyzability question is also answered: No accessibility—no analyzability! If, on the other hand, one does affirm, rather than deny, the accessibility of mental processes, then the logical next question has to be asked: Are the measurable mental processes made up of separable components in a way that permits them to be disentangled or analyzed into their component parts? A corollary question is: Can the interrelationships of the component parts be understood?

These issues have been concretized in the debate between the two protagonists designated respectively as holists and elementalists. The holists, led by the remnants of the Gestalt tradition, argue that it is the overall or molar pattern into which the components are arranged rather than the nature of the parts that is essential. In other words, they argue that the nature of the components is less important than their arrangement. Holists argue, furthermore, that the configuration cannot be broken up without the loss of the essence of the processes under investigation.

The alternative elementalist view is that psychology has experimental tools available to it that can analyze complex mental processes into simple ones in much the same way that a chemist analyzes chemical compounds into their elements. Not only are the techniques available, proponents of this viewpoint assert, but the analysis is possible in fundamental principle. The analysis may be carried out in the form of a reduction to cognitive elements such as a "short-term memory" or to neurophysiological elements such as a "face encoding neuron." Such an analytic point of view was central to Titchenerian structuralism as well as implicit in Watsonian and Hullian behaviorism. Elementalist reductionism of this kind is, of course, also the prevailing mainstream tradition in contemporary cognitive and neuroscientific psychology.

There are two main arguments why the contrary configurational or holistic argument should be considered to be the correct one. First, the very act of concatenation, combination, or aggregation may introduce new and essential attributes that would be lost if one tried to tease the components apart. Second, the mental components are themselves not constant, but highly adaptable, and, by adapting to each new mental task, they lose any fundamental and simple identity that would allow them to be used as analogs of the more constant basic particles in physics or elements of chemistry. Furthermore, the configurationist, Gestalt, or holistic position contends that because of this indivisibility, it follows immediately that there can be no effective technique for peering at "mind" in any other way than as a molar, indivisible entity even if we accepted its accessibility. To the extent they are correct, the elementalist metaphor provided by physics and chemistry may have led us terribly astray for centuries. The process continues. Faculty psychologies and phrenology are ancestral to the current trend to break up psychological processes into components that some psychologists believe can localized by a fMRI system.

4.3.4 What Is the Role of Theory in Psychology?

Another question that is purported to help us characterize the variety of approaches to psychological inquiry concerns the position taken by each concerning the nature and role of theory. The answer to this question depends very much on the meaning of the word *theory* in each school of thought. Obviously theories come in many varieties and the term means vastly different things to different theoreticians. Some merely wish to use a kind of descriptive or nominalistic vocabulary to simply name that which has been observed. Psychological theories that are merely verbal restatements of the data proliferate. Similarly, psychiatrists and psychotherapists all too often merely name and describe a disorder and then mistakenly assume that a theory has been enunciated (or, worse, that a pathology has been identified.) So, too, do theoreticians who develop mathematical and computational simulations that produce functional outcomes that follow the same course as some observed phenomenon often mistake ever more precise *description* for theoretical *explanation.* Other reductively oriented theoreticians seek to infer from their data by processes of induction or deduction facts about the mental activity that is not accessible by any means. Some seek to express the relationships between input and output in the form of a transformation without delving deeper into the underlying relationships. On the other hand, some eschew any kind of reductive or interpretive theorizing and argue that the data should speak for itself. To decide if the attitude toward theory is a criterion for distinguishing between behaviorism and mentalism, one must first specify what it is that is meant by theory in each case.

The main distinction I draw in this book between different types of theories is between explanatory reductionism and description. *Explanatory reductionism* includes any theory that strives to explain by converting the discussion at one level (e.g., psychology) to the terms and language of another (e.g., neurophysiology). *Description* includes any metaphor or model that describes the course of some process, but in the neutral language of mathematics, computer programs, flowcharts, or even word stories. Of course, not all modelers agree that their metaphors are not reductive. Usually, however, it can be shown that any reductive assumptions can be completely separated from the descriptive ones.

Furthermore, attitudes toward acceptable kinds of theorizing change from time to time and these changes have often reflected the prevailing Zeitgeist with regard to behaviorism or mentalism. There has, for example, been a substantial change in recent years in what has been acceptable to the referees of scientific psychology journals. A few decades ago it was anathema to go much beyond descriptive statistical analyses of the data into what was considered to be "inappropriate speculation." More recently, it has been almost de rigeur that some kind of an explanatory (either mathematically or neurally reductive) explanation (i.e., theory) of one's findings accompany the empirical report. In fact, there has been a major effort on the part of many federal granting agencies to specifically demand some kind of a neurophysiological explanation of even the most complex psychophysical results. Even accepting the fact that the major reason for this has been to justify psychology to the general public and the legislatures as a quasi-medical activity, there is still at the core of all of this activity a more profound scientific issue being raised. It is our old friend—analyzability.

Thus, the role and expectations of what is acceptable theory change drastically from time to time. However, there remains a constant continuum along which the various psychological theories can be arranged. It varies from one end at which theory development is minimized to the other where enormous efforts are made to build conceptual bridges between different scientific domains or to develop comprehensive formal models of some set of psychological findings. Certainly, Hull (1943) and a plethora of contemporary computer oriented cognitive psychologists are closer to the latter end than to the former. The most radical behaviorists anchor the other end.

The juxtaposition of Hull and cognitive psychologists on the theory dimension suggests that this, like the ontological issue of the reality of mind, is not a good criterion for distinguishing between cognitive and behaviorist psychologies. The reason for the lack of utility of the theory issue as a criterion for classifying the various schools of thought is that no psychology is truly and completely atheoretical. Even the most radical behaviorist at the other end of the spectrum does not completely reject theory. Skinner, perhaps the most extreme antitheoretical behaviorist of all did not completely eschew all levels of explanation. Like most other antitheoreticians, it was a very specific target at which he aimed his criticism—the speculative or even fantastic hypothetical construct. Given that the ultimate goals of science are to seek some general understanding and some degree of control over our world, a completely "bare-footed" empiricism would be hard to sustain and would not be very interesting. It is certainly the case that all recent neo-behaviorists (new in terms of chronology rather than fundamental conceptual foundations) regularly invoke theories of some kind as well as continuing to champion objective experimentation.

This then brings us to the question of the nature of the theoretical entities that are produced by psychological theory. Although I have repeatedly used them in earlier parts of this book, there are two terms that are extremely helpful in our understanding what theories really are and what they can actually do for us. In what has become one of the classic papers of psychology's history, MacCorquodale and Meehl (1948) drew the distinction between *intervening variables* and *hypothetical constructs.* Intervening variables were considered to be simply possible stages in the measured transformation from a stimulus to a response. They were equivalent to steps in a mathematical derivation describing a transformation, but they did not necessarily imply any particular structural entities or processes. Intervening variables are tightly linked to the measured observations and phenomena and, therefore, essentially descriptive concepts. Therefore, like all other models and mathematical descriptions, intervening variables are essentially neutral with regard to the internal mechanisms.

Many current mathematical theories of human perception incorporate what are best considered to be intervening variables. For example, Sperling and Lu (1998) developed a comprehensive control system model of the motion perception system. This model invokes concepts such as lag, gain, feed-back, and "texture-grabbers." The model is illustrated with flowcharts that show the flow of information in the system. Although this kind of model is often presented as an analytic one with each box representing some actual internal mechanism, a little further consideration suggests that many of the boxes are actually doing nothing more than describing some derived aspect of function of the system as a whole. For example, the lag "mechanism" is not a place or a thing but a property of the entire visual system constructed on the basis of behavioral observations. In other words, although cloaked in mechanical language and metaphors, these boxes are really just intervening variables in a mathematical description of the visual system.

Just as any other theory based on behavioral data is incapable of peering into the mechanisms, the boxes and lines of this type of model are also incapable of uniquely defining independent processes within the complex system. The mathematical entities invoked by Sperling and Lu in their model can represent any one of a number of physically different instantiations.

Nothing I say here attenuates the enormous value of Sperling's theory. It does provide a description of the visual system that is sufficiently powerful to predict future outcomes. In the final analysis, however, even such powerful models essentially turn out to be behavioral models populated with intervening variables rather than reductive theories involving actual internal mechanisms. Although more complex in a formal sense than the additive factors model developed by Sternberg (1969) or the even older subtractive methods of Donders, 1868/1969), in principle all these models share the same descriptive nature.

In their now classic paper MacCorquodale and Meehl (1948) suggested that hypothetical constructs were, unlike the intervening variable, actual entities that were assumed to be inferable from empirical outcomes. Hypothetical constructs go far beyond the data to literally embody processes and mechanisms that are not just process descriptions of the transformations between the stimulus and the response but, rather, real mechanisms that can be inferred from the data. Hypothetical constructs were deemed to be essentially process and mechanism "inventions" that transcended the data in contrast to the descriptive formalities of the intervening variable. They represented entities that were invoked to reductively *explain* the transformations rather than to only *describe* the course of the observed action. Of course, it is not always obvious whether something is a process description (i.e., an intervening variable) or a reductive explanation (i.e., a hypothetical construct). Nevertheless, behaviorists and logical positivists argued that the invention of hypothetical constructs was an unacceptable procedure that was all-too-prevalent in all-too-much mentalistic psychology (as well, of course, as in many others areas of human activity.) For behaviorists, this was a violation of the basic laws that should govern science. The fundamental difficulty is that it is too easy to invent hypothetical constructs that cannot be validated or refuted. There is literally an infinity of alternative possibilities waiting to be invented or inferred. Furthermore, there is no way to distinguish between them on the basis of molar behavioral observations.

MacCorquodale and Meehl (1948) helped psychology enormously by clarifying the nature of different kinds of theoretical constructs and concepts. By doing so they also helped to clarify the role of theory in psychology. They left us a legacy in which it was appreciated that, however much it may have been minimized, spuriously reductive theory was ubiquitous in this science. Therefore, any attempt to distinguish between mentalisms and behaviorisms on the basis of which was more or less theoretical was (and probably still is) pointless.

It should not go unremarked that the general attitudes toward theories of all kinds in psychology have continuously been subject to criticism. Watkins (1990) caustically speaking of learning theories, in particular, but with direct relevance to psychological theories, in general, said:

> Once formulated, a theory has several safeguards, First, it is unlikely to draw much criticism from other researchers, for other researchers are primarily concerned with their own theories. Second, when a theory does attract criticism, the critic almost always has to have misunderstood, and the theory stands as originally proposed. Third, on the rare occasion a criticism demands action, fine tuning will almost always suffice. Thus, the chances of a theory having to be abandoned or even appreciably revised as a consequence of criticism are vanishingly small, and hence researchers can be confident that their theories will stay alive just as long as they continue to nourish them. (p. 328)

In a similar vein, McFall and Townsend (1998) speaking of psychological theories asserted:

> . . . theories rarely, if ever, are tossed out on the basis of definitive experimental tests. One might question whether any of our current psychological theories even are capable of being falsified. Indeed, cynics might argue that no psychological theory has ever been discarded for any sound reason whatsoever. Psychological theories seldom fade away, let alone die. (p. 324)

Both these comments ring true. However, it is also important to appreciate that these criticisms are directed at theories that purport to explain and reduce, not to those that only provide a concise description of the data. For the latter class, all one can ask of the "best" theory is that it fits the data best with the fewest free parameters.

4.3.5 What Is the Role of Experimentation in Psychology?

Another seemingly useless criterion for distinguishing between the various kinds of mentalisms and behaviorisms is based on a selected school's use or nonuse of the experimental method. The reason for this is that every scientific psychologist accepts the classic tenet of postmedieval science that controlled observation producing data that can be interpersonally shared by all interested observers is the *sine qua non* of any science. There is no evidence in any of the psychologies we have discussed so far that the empirical methodology that characterizes the other sciences is not applicable to this science. The controversy is not over slight variations in scientific methodology, but rather over the nature and accessibility of whatever it is we do purport to be studying.

One has to be troubled, however, by an ubiquitous rejection of the validity of any kind of psychological research by many from outside the field of psychology. It is often asserted that human nature is not amenable to experimental research or, more metaphysically, that there are mysteries concerning the human spirit (mind) that cannot be resolved by empirical science. Assertions of this genre come from many sources—from theologians in efforts to preserve the validity of some of their own untestable hypothetical constructs, from humanists and ethicists who feel that morality is in some incomprehensible way incompatible with science, or even from otherwise sophisticated engineers and scientists who are unfamiliar with progress in the measurement of human performance. From any of these sources, one is likely to hear assertions such as, "Psychology cannot be a science!" or "Thought is intangible and cannot be measured since it has no dimensions." Considerable time is wasted in many elementary psychology textbooks trying to refute these spurious ideas.

It is important for me, as a critic and an iconoclast of mentalism, to point out that asserting that there are limits to what can be known by psychology does not support the argument that the experimental method is not applicable to our science any more than do limits on time travel or perpetual motion support the parallel argument that physics should not be an empirical science. Psychology has problems with accessibility and analyzability, but these problems are not different in kind from those faced by macrosciences like cosmology and astronomy or by microsciences such as basic particle physics and molecular biochemistry. The main difference is that the problems faced by psychology are far more complex and multivariate than those faced by the physical and biochemical sciences. It would be wonderful, indeed, if neural interactions were as simple as electrostatic or gravitational attractions; but they are not. Therefore, especially careful attention has to be paid to the design of experiments in psychology, just as it does in agriculture and medicine—other multivariate topics of general interest to humans. Because of multiple causal factors and the resultant high degree of variability, all kinds of scientific psychology are even more dependent on careful experimental design than are many other sciences. This is so regardless of the particular school of psychology or approach to which one is committed. The experimental criterion alluded to in this question, therefore, is another contentious issue of little real consequence in discriminating between a mentalism and a behaviorism.

4.3.6 Is the Goal of Psychology Understanding or Control?

Another one of the profound, yet useless, questions that has frequently been raised in an effort to differentiate between behaviorisms and mentalisms concerns the ultimate goals of a scientific psychology. Is the purpose of this science to understand or is it simply to control? Given the barriers between theories and models on the one hand and conscious awareness on the other, it seems likely that true reductive and explanatory understanding is likely to be a will-of-the-wisp, a chimera—an unobtainable goal for any kind of psychology. However, even without understanding, more or less complete control may be possible in many cases. Some, of course, would argue that control is tantamount to understanding. However, there cannot be a true equivalence between the two. Almost anyone can drive a car or word process on a computer without any appreciation (i.e., understanding) of what is going on in the mechanics or electronics of these complex systems.

The purported linkage between control and behaviorism, particularly as carried to the extreme by Skinner, became set in conceptual concrete to a degree that has led some psychologists to suggest that behaviorists had little interest in achieving understanding of human mental processes and mechanisms. This is patently an extreme view that has little justification in the behavioral literature.

Although it is possible to extrapolate from the scientific study of behavior to its control, the main theme of behaviorism, like all other scientific psychologies, has always been to understand—to the limits of the possible. Without a continuing and consciously intended effort to achieve some kind of deeply valid understanding, the whole scientific psychology enterprise would be futile and meaningless. The noblest of human activities would be reduced to a kind of mindless social or personal engineering or, even worse, a medium for providing dictatorial control. The point is that behaviorism is a reasonable scientific endeavor and it offers a powerful route to the understanding of human nature—even in light of the fact that it rejects the accessibility and analyzability of mental processes. In other words, a false, but presumably full, understanding is of less value to science in the long run than a limited but valid one. At the worst, a false impression of understanding can mislead and delay science in its quest for that true understanding. History is replete with such examples.

Accepting that there are limits to understanding, all scientists would prefer to understand as much as possible about human mentation or whatever else is the subject matter of their science. A realistic appreciation of the limits of a science should not lead either its practitioners or its critics to suggest that nothing of value can be obtained through its pursuit.

4.3.7 Can Consciousness Influence Behavior?

One question that repeatedly arises when one is concerned with mental processes is the role they play in the interaction between organisms and their environment. There is little doubt that mental processes are affected by the environment. All findings and observations from sensory and perceptual science as well as abundant evidence from our own personal experience make it clear that what we perceive and to a large part what we think is driven by patterns of physical stimuli from our environment playing on the momentary state of our nervous system. It would make our very existence nonsensical to deny that the communication of information from the physical world to ourselves or between ourselves and other organisms does not influence both mental activity and behavior.

Materialistic monism also asserts that if we feel or see or hear something (mental responses all), there must have existed in our nervous system some pattern of neural (i.e., physical) activity that is equivalent to the perceived experience. It should be an axiom of any science that one must have some mechanism to execute some process. Otherwise, we are talking about metaphysical (i.e., supernatural) matters that are beyond science as we know it.

It cannot be overemphasized that one of the most difficult of all questions in science is how consciousness emerges from that neural activity. However it may ultimately be accounted for, few would deny that mental experience exists, that it is strongly influenced by both internal and external environmental forces, and in some fundamental ontological sense, it is totally and fully accounted for by neural activity. Anything else would be a mystical dualism.

It is not always appreciated, however, that the converse issue is much more logically, if not philosophically, complex. That is—can conscious experience control (a) the nervous system, and (b) the behavior of the organism? The complexities of this question have usually been ignored by laypersons and psychologists alike for an obvious reason—associated with it are the closely related issues of free will, psychosomatic influences in medical treatment, and other currently popular ideas of "mind over matter." Such parascientific issues inevitably rise up to becloud and confuse any discussion of the relationship between brain and mind, in general, and the efficacy of mental events on behavior, in particular.

I do not expect that my discussion here will produce a final answer to the fundamental question of mind's effect on the brain and behavior. Nevertheless, it is necessary to make one important point here that may at least reformulate the issue in a more tractable form. That point is that mind (i.e., conscious self-awareness) may be nothing but an *epiphenomenon,* that exists *as a result of neural activity* but *without the ability to exert any physical or informational force* on the outside world.

Philosophers and logicians can easily see the difficulties generated by the formulation of the issue in this way. If mind is brain activity and brain is the neuromechanical system on which this activity is played, then what does it matter if we use the words interchangeably? On the other hand, if mind is but an ineffective epiphenomenon unable to exert any physical or chemical force, then it is the actions and interactions of the nervous system (to cause speech, motor movements, glandular secretions, or even other forms of nervous activity) that are behaviorally influential and not the manifestations of those neural activities that we designate as mental. Perhaps this problem can be best illustrated by considering Fig. 4.1.

This conceptualization of the interactions in the sensory–perceptual system distinguishes between information and energy communication pathways that are unarguable and irrefutable and those that are questionable. The pathways (solid lines) from the stimulus to the neural mechanisms and their responses (I) and from the neural activity to behavior (III) simply have to exist. It would be necessary to deny most of the rest of physical and biological science if these pathways were not functional. Similarly, if neural responses are the equivalent of perceptual (or, in general, mental) responses then there must be something that is the equivalent of the unidirectional causal connection (II) between the two. Furthermore, it is clear that behavior can change the stimulus; turn your head and you will not see the same scene. Therefore, IV must exist.

However, the three dotted lines (V) indicate a much less certain flow of either effective information or physical energy. Mind, itself, may not be

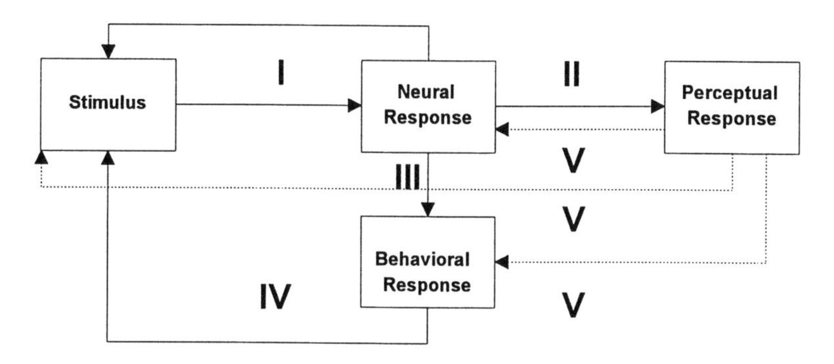

FIG. 4.1. A chart of the relationships between the external world, the nervous system, and mental activity. The question is—which of the links can exert effective forces and which are epiphenomenal and ineffective in creating subsequent actions?

influential in causing behavior, changing the stimulus scene, or modulating neural activity; it simply may be something that the nervous system produces, en passant so to speak, as it goes about its biophysical business. To us, the self-aware, self-observer, it would appear that our mental activity (consisting of decisions, choices, will, and so on) is directing and guiding our behavior. However, it may be it is our physical brain producing the effective forces, not the epiphenomenological illusion of self-awareness.

To clarify this point, let me suggest a simple metaphor—a steam engine equipped with a pressure gauge. The gauge is an accurate indicator of the internal steam pressure of the engine. However, should the engine explode from some unmonitored overpressure, can the blame (if not the force) be placed on the pressure gauge? In an analogous manner, can the forces driving human behavior be attributed to the indicating gauge we call mind? Or, to put it more directly, is it the neural activity that produces mental activity or the mental activity itself the source of behavioral events? Obviously this is a very tender issue: It strikes deeply at the heart of what many believe to be among the most important ideas of human existence, especially those that involve freedom and values. In short, the behaviorist position on this question may be interpreted as threatening the very existence of whatever it is that is the essential "me."

The question of free will thus raised is an extraordinarily complex one and competing forces join the debate from far outside the scientific arena. Advocates of one persuasion or another constantly raise this issue in order to support their own favorite solutions to human problems as well as their own pet social theories. Students of ethics are deeply concerned with the issue vis-à-vis the putative sources of our responsibility for leading a moral and humane life. Clearly, the side of the issue that one chooses may determine whether one prefers to support the death penalty or early childhood education. Nevertheless, many scholars feel the issue may not be resolvable in a scientific manner. For example, Skinner (1975) said:

> The extent to which a person is free or responsible for his achievements is not an issue to be decided by rigorous proof, but I submit that what we call the behavior of the human organism is no more free than its digestion, gestation, immunization, or any other physiological process. Because it involves the environment in many subtle ways it is much more complex, and its lawfulness is, therefore, much harder to demonstrate. (p. 47)

I expect that nothing said here is likely to satisfactorily resolve this issue. However, it is clear that behaviorisms and mentalisms often implicitly take opposite positions on the potential influence of mental actions although it may not be so explicitly acknowledged by proponents on either side. Mentalisms are much more likely to support the actual influence of mental activity and behaviorisms are much more likely to consider mental activity epiphenomenal. My judgment is that this is probably one of those issues that will always be unresolvable because of the tight correlation between the neural measurements and the mental responses, if not their total identity.

4.3.8 Can Neurophysiology Replace Psychology?

The eliminativist neurophilosophers suggested it is possible to completely ignore "folk" and other kinds of scientific psychology (including both mentalisms and behaviorisms) in favor of what may ultimately be a purely neurophysiological explanation of human thought and behavior. My readers must be completely aware by now that I have drawn from my analysis of the question, "Can mental states be reduced to their neural states?" the conclusion that such a reduction is not practically possible, even if neural states *are* mental states. If I am correct in this conclusion, then any hope that the language and technical details of neurophysiology can ever completely supplant psychological terms and technical details would have to be without merit. Molar psychological terms and concepts will always be necessary in the absence of any hope of a completely reductive science just as gas dynamics will never be replaced by tabulations of the individual momenta of molecules. The eliminativist fantasy is simply unobtainable for reasons of numerosity and complexity.

4.3.9 What Is Behavior?

Next, in this quest for understanding the fundamental controversies that distinguish between mentalisms and behaviorisms, we must consider a fundamental question that sometimes is ignored in attempts to distinguish between mentalisms and behaviorisms. Given that behaviorists are students of behavior, what then is behavior? To Watson (1924), the founder, behavior was simply "what an organism says or does" (p. 6). Tolman (1932) defined behavior in the context of his molar approach, as:

> *Behavior qua molar.* Behavior . . . is any organic activity the occurrence of which can be characterized as docile (q.v.) relative to its consequences. Behavior in this sense is to be distinguished from such other organic activities as are neither a result of past learning or capable of future learning. (p. 438)

The term "docile" as used by Tolman was not intended to connote obedient, but rather amenable to being taught. The defining aspect of behavior to Tolman, therefore, was that it could be modified as a result of experience. This criterion, as mentioned earlier, was part of the major movement that led psychology toward an almost exclusionary emphasis on learning studies in the decades following Tolman's work. This definition, unfortunately, is conceptually sterile ignoring the innate and maturational influences on the repertoire of responses available to the organism.

Skinner's (1938) definition of behavior is also quite molar, but somewhat more specific:

> Behavior is what an organism is doing—or more accurately what it is observed by another organism to be doing. (p. 6)

and

> behavior is that part of the functioning of an organism which is engaged or acting on or having commerce with the outside world. (p. 6)

and

> By behavior, then, I mean simply that movement of an organism or of its parts in a frame of reference provided by the organism itself or by various external objects or fields of force. (p. 6)

Pribram (1979) offered another pair of definitions of this elusive term:

> When a behaviorist ordinarily analyzes "behavior" he is studying a record of responses emitted by an organism in a specified situation. The record can be studied in any location; it could have been produced in any of a number of ways by any number of different "response systems"—arms, legs, beaks, etc. The behavior under study is an environmental consequence of any of these response systems. At other times, however, "behavior" is understood to mean the pattern of the organism's movements, or of his endocrine or neural responses in a situation. (pp. 66–67)

Clearly, any attempt to specifically define behavior is fraught with many of the same kind of difficulties faced when one tries to define consciousness. Definitions proposed by different psychologists vary enormously. Some behaviorists have despaired of any solution to this problem finding the term as difficult to define as the mentalistic concepts they seek to avoid. Certainly, the confounding introduced by definitions such as those proposed by Watson (1924): ". . . (thinking) is just as objective a type of behavior as baseball" (p. 6), only helps to totally muddy the waters of what is presumed to be behavior by even the most confident contemporary behaviorists.

It is probably the case that there will always be as many difficulties in defining behavior as there are in defining more blatantly mentalistic terms. The one great commonality shared by most proposed definitions and presumably by all behaviorists is that, whatever behavior is, it is (or should be) observable and interpersonally comparable and directly measurable. It is this objective approach to a psychological science that joins psychology to all other biological sciences and separates it from metaphysical and speculative vagueness. Perhaps, then, the best way to define behavior is simply to consider it to be nothing more than the sum total of the measures and operations that are used to measure it.

Incidentally, it seems almost as difficult to define behaviorism as it is to define behavior. For example, Zuriff (1985), suggested the word "behaviorism" accrues meaning as the science grows. What the behaviorist measures, the observed laws governing behavior, and the theories that are generated, collectively become the currently accepted definition of behaviorism (pp. 30–31).

4.3.10 Can a Behaviorism Ever Not Be a Mentalism?

The next issue with which we must deal concerning the future of behaviorism is—can it ever be other than a crypto-mentalism. Many critics of behaviorism and even some of its supporters feel that most instantiations of this approach always retreat to a vocabulary that is not objective and operational in the way I proposed earlier. Rather, it is sometimes argued, all behaviorisms always invoke concepts that are not functionally distinguishable from the hypothetical constructs of any mentalism. We have seen how this was true of Tolman's "behaviorism." As we have also seen, some critics (e.g., Chomsky, 1959) made the same argument even with regard to Skinner's much more extreme and radical behaviorism—accusing it of being as much a mentalism as any other psychology.

Obviously, all psychologists are humans and all humans are aware of their mental states. The question here is: Is it, therefore, inevitable that all psychologists will ultimately interject their own private mental experiences into their public science? In other words, will psychologists be doomed to perpetually commit what William James referred to as the "Psychologist's Fallacy"? The answer to these questions, as to so many others, are elusive, but it is clear that it may not be as easy as some behaviorists would like us to believe to exorcise the "ghost in the machine" in order to generate a purely scientific behaviorism.

4.3.11 Is the Invocation of "Mind" Necessary?

It is universally assumed on the basis of first-hand experience and on the basis of our ability to consistently intercommunicate with each other that we each presumably have a rich mental life of some kind. Our only window into the mind is through verbal and other behavioral indicators. Unfortunately, as we have already discussed, this window is, in the main, undependable and not just obscurational but also transformational. That is, it not only hides, but also alters. Furthermore, mind is functionally a closed system (in many senses of the word) and, according to many modern theoretical perspectives is unanalyzable in principle and not subject to the discovery of unique reductionist theories. Human beings, being curious theory builders, will always want to tell stories and "explain" mental processes, but what the mind is, what it does, and how it does it are probably best left to the novelist or poet. Therapeutic theories such as psychoanalysis can be invented in unending succession. Although the process of talking out one's problems or finding social support may be palliative, there can be no assurance that any such therapeutic approach is "correct" in any scientific sense.

It should also be noted, however, this presumed palliative value is not universally accepted. Littrell (in press), for example, joins other social scientists such as Dawes (1994) in pointing out that classical catharsis and the expression of emotion may even be damaging. This is particularly likely to be the case if the unearthed emotions are negative or if adversarial relationships are generated that could well have been avoided or ignored. Setting up a psychological "template" in which the patient becomes vulnerable may do more harm than one in which negative experiences remained buried. It is only when the cathartic technique of psychotherapy leads to the substitution of a new adaptive behavior for an old maladaptive one that the process is useful. Perhaps there is no field in which the penalty for forging false hypothetical constructs is as great as in psychotherapy.

4.3.12 What Happens to All the Experimental Psychological Literature That Has Been Collected Over the Last Century?

With the exception of the special problems I have already discussed concerning fragility, variability, and validity, the phenomena, the findings, and the observations of scientific psychology remain the empirical foundation of our science. Even accepting the fact that our methods may sometimes mislead us about the nature of human behavior and that the brain is remarkably adaptive, there still is a wealth of knowledge in the literature describing the relationship between situational and stimulus factors, on the one hand, and the responses made by humans, on the other. We know how long it takes to forget something; we know the relationship between the information content of a complex stimulus and reaction times; and we know the thresholds for the various wavelengths of light; we know that a straight line of evenly spaced dots is detected more easily than a curved one, to list but a few of the incontrovertible "facts" and "laws" of behavior.

Thus, the raw data and the descriptions of the transforms between stimuli and responses are the essentials of our science. It is in terms of how these transforms and findings are *interpreted* that any revised behaviorism must diverge from the contemporary cognitive mentalism.

4.3.13 What Happens to the Social, Clinical, and Personality Areas of Psychology?

A substantial portion of the last century's efforts in applying psychology has gone into what has been assumed to be analyses of how and what people think individually and in groups? A closer inspection of what is happening when social, clinical, and personality psychologists go about their business suggests, however, that they are not actually studying the mechanisms of mental activity directly but, rather, they are studying *what people think they are thinking.* The actual mental processes being inaccessible, much of what these areas of psychology are examining are the heavily transformed and modified interpretations of thought processes by the individual.

The argument that humans simply do not have direct access to their own cognitive or neurophysiological mechanisms and processes is now gaining credibility. I discussed some of this evidence in Chapter 2. As introspective observers, it was concluded that we individually probably have as little access to the underlying transformations and processes as does the external observer—the psychologist observing our behavior. Instead, whatever is actually going on in the mind is perceived by the self-observer as a mentally unanalyzable whole. To add to this natural obscuration, our thoughts about our thoughts are heavily penetrated by cognitive processes that have evolved to protect the individual's self-esteem and to organize thoughts into coherent stories. These transformations are sometimes instantiated into post hoc theories and convenient myths by psychologists and other practitioners interested in intervening in the social and personal behavior of their fellows. In the final analysis, however, most of the work using verbal reports has provided only cloudy indications of the actual mental processes at work when we solve problems.

4.3.14 Should We Drop Everything That We Are Doing?

The most likely message to be misconstrued of all of those I am sending in this book would be that I am advocating a major change in the course of what is now being done in a variety of psychological, neuroscientific, and computational laboratories. Rest assured, that is not my intent. Rather, the main point I am making is that some of the interpretive and theoretical constructions that are being used to bridge between the various sciences may be implausible and misleading. As a psychologist, I am concerned that computational models, however well they may effectively describe, are often stretched beyond plausibility in the pursuit of some unrealizable hope of becoming reductive explanations. I am concerned with neurophysiological data that is only remotely analogous to some psychological finding being used as a neuroreductionist explanation of that phenomenon. In the specific context of this book, I am even further concerned with the creation of ad hoc hypothetical constructs that purport to explain mental processes when those processes are demonstrably inaccessible.

However, these concerns should not be misinterpreted to imply that I am recommending that each of these sciences should not go on with the empirical and descriptive studies they have traditionally pursued. This work, however, should be continued without the frail, if not false, bridges that are so often invented to link the several levels of discourse. Neurophysiology, computational modeling, and psychology are each able to justify their continued existence in their own right. Neurophysiologists have helped us to understand the functions of individual neurons and synapses as well as of larger chunks of the brain. Computer models have allowed us to test theories for plausibility in a way that could never be achieved by verbal speculation. Psychology, not the least of the sciences, has allowed us to map out the ways in which we transform information and thus to determine lawful relationships between the stimulus environment and the normative human's repertoire of responses. Although I believe this latter body of knowledge cannot be analyzed into cognitive components nor can it uniquely define the processes and mechanisms that account for these transformations, I am convinced we have learned much about the laws governing how organisms behave in various situations. This, itself, totally justifies all of the previous investment in research and vigorous support for the future.

Thus, my message is that we must collectively minimize the quests for the unknowable and maximize the use of an objective scientific method to achieve understanding of the knowable. We must continue to describe transformations and relationships even though we are unable to dissect them into fanciful theoretical explanations or nonunique components. In summary, I expect that even if the arguments I present here should by some small miracle become generally accepted, there would be little change in the specific empirical research agenda of all of the involved sciences. Hopefully, what would emerge would be a greater appreciation of the limits of what the obtained data mean.

4.4 SOME CONTEMPORARY BEHAVIORISMS

Now that I have considered some of the principal characteristics of a 21st-century psychophysical behaviorism and have answered (at least partially) some of the posed questions, it is appropriate to seek out what current steps have been made in the revitalizing and renewing of behaviorisms. I have found only a few who have made explicit attempts to formalize their view. One, in particular, required that I look no further than the next building on my campus to find one of the most complete models. My colleague in the psychology department at Arizona State University, Peter Killeen, presented one of the most interesting and systematic views of behaviorism. Many years ago, long before I arrived on the scene, this campus had been known as "Fort Skinner in the West." It appears that the behavioral tradition has lived on here in a way that I had not appreciated until recently. Killeen's model deserves a great deal of attention.

I was also able to find a few others who had provided an organized and coherent view of what a behaviorist psychology should be (or rather what psychology should be from the point of view of behaviorism). The following section describes a few of these exemplar modern behaviorisms.

4.4.1 Killeen's Mechanical Metaphor

Throughout its history, psychology has sought to improve its scientific status by emulating some of the methodological techniques of the physical and biological sciences. The experimental method, itself, became an explicit component of psychological research only a little more than a century ago. Psychology's transition from a component of philosophy to a part of physiology and then to an independent enterprise of its own was accompanied by an increasing utilization not only of the tools, but also of the methods of physics, chemistry, computer science, and statistics.

In only rare instances (e.g., Lewin, 1933), however, had any psychologist attempted to imitate physics to the point of incorporating physical principles into their model. Lewin's approach, unlike that of a hyperdimensionalized physics, was based on a nonmetric topology in which there were no fixed directions or for that matter no rigidity to the space in which the subject was operating. Topology permitted formalization of such factors as *vectors* and *tensions* operating in a field he referred to as the *life space* of the individual.

Killeen (1992, 1995) carried the physical metaphor far further than Lewin's vague analogies. Killeen incorporated not only the specific vocabulary of dimensions and forces into a model, but also some of the specific laws of physics. In Killeen's (1992) behaviorism "behavior is treated as basic physics" (p. 429). It is interesting to note that despite the fact that we are in the midst of a great electronic age, Killeen chose the field of mechanics as his heuristic. In developing this model, therefore, he dealt with behavior and its dimensions in much the same way that Newton dealt with the mechanics of physical objects. The processes are described in words and mathematical expressions, but no attempt is made to analyze the observed processes into their underlying mechanisms. In this regard, Killeen's system is very much in the descriptive mode I have championed throughout this book. He leaves it to future scientists to explain (if that is ultimately possible) and to add the details of the actual mechanisms that produce the functional relationships described by his system. By adequately describing behavior in this physical language, Killeen hoped that laws describing relations can be discovered even though we do not know exactly what the underlying mechanisms may be. This is the essence of a pure behaviorism.

The properties of behavior invoked by Killeen are familiar. They include the *dimensions* of space and time, *trajectories* in the behavior space, *potential fields, trajectory geodesics* produced by conditioning, and, of course, *forces* produced by both internal needs and the value of external incentives.

The trajectories to which Killeen alludes may be the actual physical paths of the organism (including, of course, the human being) in some well-defined physical space such as an experimental apparatus or the playing field. It may, also, however, be a trajectory in time with loops representing circadian rhythms or even more tightly defined curls representing regular events within the day. Formal relations of the effectiveness of an incentive are offered as a function of the spatial or temporal relations, or even the psychological distance (attributable to the degree of learning) between the organism and an incentive. Incentives, like physical forces, can attract or repel, but whatever the direction of the force, it is assumed to be able to change the trajectory of behavior in a way *analogous* to the way that gravity can change the trajectory of a comet.

There is also an analogy to a minimum energy principle in Killeen's system much as there is in the solution of certain dynamic equations in physics. When the shortest or least energy trajectory is achieved during a learning procedure, anything else would be more or less useless overlearning. This is comparable to Hamilton's principle of least action in physics and mathematics or contemporary models of thermal annealing in which the solution to an ill-posed problem can often be progressively achieved by an iterative series of successive approximations to the least stressed final configuration. The analogy is between a behavior discrepancy between the stimulus and response and the physical stain introduced by a deformed and thus stressed physical system. Interestingly, this same principle of least action was also offered as an alternative to and, thus, as an argument against teleological evolution by Voltaire. Goalless behavior driven by natural forces was substituted for innate purpose.

Killeen's 1992 model was considerably strengthened and broadened in a subsequent paper (Killeen, 1995). It would have been easy to criticize the original as being nothing more than a verbal metaphor. In the 1995 article Killeen, however, gets down to the details of the formal relations among response rates, number of reinforcements, satiation, deprivation, and incentive magnitudes among other variables.

Killeen's (1992, 1995) model, though highly ingenious and potentially very valuable, is not without its limitations. First, as he wisely acknowledges, it is a metaphor at this stage of its development. Although, the language and terms of physical science have been absorbed into his description of behavior, it is by no means certain the specific functional relationships between the various components are remotely similar to the relationships between the parameters of a physical system. For example, physical systems are characterized by simple forces; gravity is trivially simple compared to the complex and multidimensional effects of neural activity that define the relation of an organism to an incentive. A simple inverse square law may be replaced by a functional relationship that is far more complex. The variability of behavior also raises questions about the usefulness of a metaphor taken from a science in which variability of measures is so slight that it is often not even considered to be an issue. What astronomer, indeed, expects his calculations on the trajectory of a comet to vary sufficiently so that it will not be in the expected place the next day? What psychologist, on the other hand, would not be delighted to find some measure of behavior constant two days in succession or from subject to subject?

The difference between the physicist's trivial perturbations and the psychologist's substantial intertrial variability must be considered to be far more than just a minor quantitative difference. Similarly, there is in the physical world a strong tendency to be continuous and linear. Although, there certainly are nonlinear and discontinuous systems in physical nature, the likelihoods that any psychological force would be a smooth function (prior to data pooling) or that mental activity is linear in any sense of the word are much lower than in the physical domain. Other kinds of deviations from regularity and simplicity can certainly be observed in human ambivalence—a term that would drive molecular chemists wild even if quantum physicists might find it acceptable in their strange world. Yet, many behavioral incentives can simultaneously repel and attract.

Second, I believe that Killeen (1992) backslides a bit from his original molar descriptive stance when he begins to discuss "hierarchies of action patterns." This is an analytic approach that should not be, in my opinion, a part of a pure behaviorism. The search for the "units of behavior" (p. 433) and his Figure 4 slip away from what I consider to be one of the main advantages of his system—the molar approach that characterizes almost all of the rest of his discussion.

In these articles Killeen proposes a systematic approach that has much to offer to an objective scientific psychology. His approach to scientific behaviorism, as he indicates himself, is of a form characteristic of a science that has not yet arrived at a reductionist phase. Clearly, his metaphor is one that will offer the opportunity to conceptualize behaviorism in a novel way, and it certainly provides a framework for the formulation of general laws should they appear in the experimental laboratory.

An important general point for me is that Killeen's insightful model clearly illustrates the neutrality of mathematics. The same formulas used to describe planetary motion are used to describe the interaction and outcomes of behavioral forces. No one, particularly Killeen, is suggesting that the actual biological or physical forces at work are the same. Rather, both the power and the great weakness of mathematics is that it can represent each system with equal ease.

4.4.2 Rachlin's Teleological Behaviorism

Earlier in this chapter I specified that one of the most important characteristics of a valid renewed behaviorism will be its eclecticism. So far in this book, however, I have been hardly eclectic when it comes to any reconciliation between what I see as the diametrically opposed positions of mentalism and behaviorism. My opinion in this regard is not universally shared as is clearly illustrated in the work of Rachlin (1992, 1994). From the point of view of his deep respect for history and philosophy, he attempts to do what I, frankly, do not believe can be accomplished—to reconcile the search for the internal mechanisms of mind carried on by modern cognitive and neurophysiological reductionists with the essentially nonreductive molar approach of behaviorism.

Rachlin's approach is based in large part on traditional (i.e., Aristotelian) ideas that teleological or goal oriented forces are exceedingly important to psychology. As Rachlin (1994) pointed out, "For Aristotle, the question *why* necessarily precedes the question *how* in order of investigation" (p. viii). Such a teleological approach is not popular in modern scientific circles. Contemporary theory sees nature characterized by an almost random, adaptive, naturally selective, goaless movement forward in response to natural forces interacting in a complex web according to such principles as the "least energy" one previously mentioned. Nevertheless, such a classic teleology is the essential premise of Rachlin's eclectic behaviorism. Indeed, it is the basis of his argument that both the reductive cognitive and neurophysiological search for the mechanisms of *how* behavior is created and the teleological behaviorist approach to understanding *why* behavior is created must both be important parts of the current science of psychology. Rachlin argues that both approaches are converging on the same answers and models.

For Rachlin, the apparent contradiction between the two parts has been a longstanding misunderstanding of the difference between the proximate or efficient, on the one hand, and the ultimate or final causation, on the other. In short, the former is concerned with the definition of *how* behavior happens, the latter with *why* behavior happens. Cognitive and neurophysiological psychologies seek to answer the former question, teleological behaviorism the latter one.

There is no way better to probe the intent of an author than to use his own words to describe what he means when he uses a particular term. In this case, he has been very specific in defining the fundamentals of the philosophy of his psychology. Therefore, let Rachlin (1994) speak for himself with regard to the essential meaning of his version of behaviorism.

> Teleological behaviorism: The belief that mental terms refer to overt behavior of intact animals. Mental events are not supposed to occur inside the animal at all. Overt behavior does not just reveal the mind; it is the mind. Each mental term stands for a pattern of overt behavior. This includes such mental terms as "sensation," "pain," "love," "hunger," and "fear" (terms considered by the mentalist to be "raw feels"), as well as terms such as "belief" and "intelligence" that are sometime said to refer to "complex mental states," sometimes to "propositional attitudes" and sometimes to "intentional acts." (pp. 15–16)

Rachlin then made the same point even more succinctly: "According to teleological behaviorism, love like all other aspects of the human soul, is a complex pattern of behavior" (p. 17).

The nature of Rachlin's proposed rapprochement now becomes clear. It is not that the internal mechanisms of mind are revealed by behavior, but rather that behavior IS mind! It is a rapprochement in which one point of view does not fuse with the other but in which one is devoured by the other. Rachlin is, from this perspective, an extremely radical behaviorist. From another perspective, that of the different goals of answering the *how* and *why* questions, he appears to be much more eclectic accepting these as the twin motivating questions of two kinds of compatible psychology.

My disappointment with Rachlin's interesting approach is that he does not make clear how the two kinds of psychology can be combined. Although lip service is paid to the value of each, most of his effort is directed at the justification of the Aristotelian, final cause, or teleological aspects of the problem of mind. Although fully committing himself to a teleological point of view, he pays scant attention to the value of a purely behavioral analysis. Furthermore, when identifying mind with behavior, Rachlin also seems to revert to a peculiar version of the automaton version of organisms. One is left to wonder how he would deal with covert behavior-free mental acts such as imagining and day-dreaming? Thus, his model appears to be incomplete.

4.4.3 Timberlake's Modular Behaviorism

Not all behaviorisms are quite so molar. Some, like the "behavior systems" approach of Timberlake (1994) assume that behavior can be explained by a system of interacting modules that are either built into the organism's genetic heritage or are quickly learned. Timberlake refers to the former as "highly preorganized" and the latter as "less preorganized" modules. The key difference is that the former are virtually automatic whereas the latter may require some conditioning for their expression. These behaviors controlled by these modules can be very variable and may include such functions as memory, timing, motor sequences, and motivational states.

The behavior systems approach offered by Timberlake assumes that the molar behavior of the organism is controlled by a sequence of interactions among the modules. The output of one module serves as the input to the next. Groups of modules are called into action in different modes of behavior. For example, he suggests that the feeding behavior of an animal may be divided into three modes—general search, focal search, and the handling and consuming mode. Each mode is carried out by a particular subset of the modules of the system. The focal search activity, for example, is presumed to be based on the operations of chase, capture, and test modules, respectively. Each of these modules is associated with a specific set of observable stimuli and behaviors. The capture module, therefore, controls "tracking and running after" a moving stimulus and then "grabbing with mouth and paws."

Timberlake's behavior systems approach is obviously based on the model developed by control systems engineers. It permits the precise specification of the sequence of behaviors and the stimuli that elicited each of those behaviors. It permits us to apply concepts from engineering that potentially include some powerful mathematical and computer methods. However, the behavior systems approach suffers from the same difficulties that more explicitly mentalist psychologies confront. The modules that are invoked are actually hypothetical constructs! If this be behaviorism, then so too is Sperling and Lu's (1998) model. They are all based on inferences drawn from the behavior that cannot be unique explanations of what is actually occurring internally.

4.4.4 Staddon and Zanutto's Behavioral Model

There have been many models of behavior. Some have been neuroreductionist in that they sought to explain some aspect of behavior in terms of its neuronal underpinnings. Others, such as Timberlake's (1994), attempted to explain behavior by invoking hypothetical modules that were assumed to control and integrate the specific response components of such a complex act as feeding.

An alternative approach is to try to describe the behavior itself in a model that does not assume the existence of any internal modules or components that are assumed to be carrying out intermediate stages of the molar behavioral response. It is the reef of this analysis into hypothetical components onto which so many theories have foundered.

Staddon and Zanutto (1998) have chosen the nonreductive direction on which to build their model of feeding behavior. The important point their behavioral model exemplifies is that it does not invoke any physiological entities nor any hypothetical internal and unobservable modules. Their model, to the contrary, is based purely on the behavioral data. As an initial step they describe a physical metaphor for the behavior in the form of a cascade of overflowing buckets. Of course, this is but a metaphor and not intended to be a reductive explanation, however useful it may be in formulating their mathematical expression for this behavior.

The behavior of this analogous system is sufficiently close to the feeding behavior in which Staddon and Zanutto are interested to provide the basis for a mathematical equation that describes the original feeding behavior. The metaphorical overflowing buckets now become cascaded integration processes in the equation. The main nonobservables entering into the equation are functional concepts of satiation and other positive incentives such as the taste of the food.

The equation suggested by Staddon and Zanutto, thus, includes terms not linked to any physiological, anatomical, or functional units in any reductive or analytic sense. It is purely a description of the observed behavior using a metaphorical intermediary to help in the construction of a descriptive mathematical expression. Although the eating behavior they have chosen to model is not all there is to behavior and/or mind, their approach seems to be a step toward a completely objective theory that does not violate any of the caveats discussed in this book. This work is an excellent exemplar of the way in which a mathematical description that is not reductive, but only descriptive can be used to illuminate and enhance our understanding about our psychological nature.

4.5 A SUMMARY

In this chapter, I extracted the essentials of the arguments made against behaviorism and cognitive mentalisms. The arguments made against behaviorism can be seen as being mainly extrascientific. On the other hand, those raised against mentalisms of all kinds are much more serious matters of scientific logic and methodology. In my opinion, the invocation of a mentalism requires suspension of some of the most important assumptions of empirical science.

This next chapter fleshed out the bare skeleton of the revitalized behaviorism I think is required to guarantee that scientific psychology has a future, infiltrated as it is with computational modelers and incipient neuroreductionists and latent eliminativists. Based on this foundation, I then provided some tentative answers to the fundamental questions posed in Chapter 1. These answers are presented with great trepidation and hesitancy. Most of these questions are so profound as well as being so controversial, it is unlikely that any consensus will be reached in the foreseeable future concerning their acceptability.

Finally, I reviewed a few of the other versions of behaviorism that have emerged in recent years to replace the classic behaviorisms of the past.

The next step for the present enterprise is to distill all of this down to a behavioral credo—a set of principles that condenses and highlights the essential ideas of a revitalized behaviorism. That is the purpose of the next chapter.

Chapter 5

Epilogue: Conclusions and Emerging Principles

And so we come to the end of our inquiry into the behaviorism–mentalism controversy. A variety of viewpoints have been considered, analyzed, evaluated, and summarized. The nature of the two contending sides has been clarified so that readers should now be aware of what I believe are the salient issues and what are the irrelevant ones. However, it would be ostentatious to even suggest the matter has been settled. It is still the case that not everyone will agree with anything, much less everything, that has been concluded so far. The war between mentalism and behaviorism is not going to be resolved by this book or by any other. It remains a battle between deeply held positions that has been continuing for centuries.

The material reviewed and discussed in this book makes it clear that this fractious debate is based on issues of deep philosophical import and human self-esteem that in many cases antedate scientific psychology. The modern scientific status of the debate is, however, new.

It is important as I begin this final chapter to highlight some viewpoints and perspectives that are especially liable to misinterpretation.

1. This book is written from the point of view of a scientific psychologist. It is only one of many ways the behaviorist–mentalist conundrum can be approached. I am sure that some social philosophers would find my arguments unsatisfactory because they do not adequately take into account the impact of science on society, or even more important, the impact of society on science. Certainly, both cognitive and behavioral psychologists have been criticized for their "mechanistic views" by scholars from other fields. However much I am sympathetic to and personally interested in the role

that science plays in society and vice versa, my concern here is with the objective and empirical criteria that will help us to resolve the mentalism–behaviorism controversy.

2. Similarly, this continuing controversy has drawn the interest of other kinds of philosophers and historians who are currently interpreting what has happened in psychology. The human mind is certainly not the sole business of psychologists. Insights can in many instances come better from novelists and historians than from the laboratory. However, these are topics I also leave to others.

3. Nothing I say here is intended to suggest anything other than a materialist monism underlies mental processes. Their inaccessibility notwithstanding, these processes are the result of real brain mechanisms. One's epistemology must be kept separate from one's ontology.

4. Other authors have converged on the same argument I made in this and my previous book—that we are limited to description and that reductive analysis and mental accessibility are difficult, if not impossible, to achieve. This argument is then used by them to suggest that the mysteries one is left with reflect something metaphysical and theological. Nothing could be further from my personal philosophy! The remaining mysteries to me are nothing more than the result of complexity and reflect nothing more than another combinatorial barrier to the acquisition of knowledge.

5. From the outsider's point of view, behaviorist and cognitive psychology may seem so much alike that this controversy may appear to be empty. However, a valid question may be raised concerning the objectivity and validity of the positivist position—is it really so naïve and inadequate that it was properly rejected? My view is that there were few sound reasons for the shift from an operational, positivist, behaviorism 35 years ago and that the case should be reopened. Indeed, not just with regard to psychology, but for all sciences, the appropriateness of inferring from observed measurements to underlying mechanism should be reconsidered.

6. Philosophers have long debated whether or not a science can be fully "objective." Of course, all forms of science are influenced by nonobjective forces and influences. However, when it comes down to the nitty-gritty of specific issues, it should be the empirical and technical matters that dominate the discussion—to the maximum extent possible. I argue two points here: First, the accessibility question is not one that should be resolved on the basis of such secondary issues as elegance, parsimony, or pragmatic societal needs, and second, it can be so resolved.

7. There are many other important controversies in psychological science and many other forces that have driven its evolution. I do not reject

their importance. This book is mainly concerned with the core matter of accessibility and its implications.

8. Finally, a point that may be surprising to some of my readers. I believe a strong argument can be made that many of my suggestions for a renewed behaviorist approach to psychology are, in fact, already being used in contemporary scientific psychology. It seems to me there has been a progressive reduction in putative neuroreductionist models in some parts of the literature. Examination of the contents of journals published by the American Psychological Association and the Psychonomic Press reveals far less neural and somewhat less cognitive reductionist theorizing than in the past. Similarly, the methods of contemporary cognitive mentalism are evolving to be closer and closer to the simple, direct, psychophysical, Class A, procedures that seem most appropriate to me. The major necessary change I foresee will be a reevaluation of the validity of the interpretations and the extrapolations from data collected in this way. In short, we should change our goal from pseudoreductive explanation to adequate description.

With this preamble of caveats in hand, it must also be appreciated that we are converging on answers to some of the key questions and that an enormous amount of progress has already been made. The positions and arguments presented by psychologists these days are very different than those of 17th or 18th century philosophers or even the psychologists of the 1960s or 1970s. My goal in this book has been to examine these new perspectives and to draw from them a contemporary approach to scientific psychology that satisfies both modern science's view of the nature of human thought and its criteria for objective credibility.

One of the best ways to concretize any school of thought is to collect together in a single list, the main points that have been made but which may have been submerged in the details of the discussion. That is the purpose of this final chapter. Here are summarized the principles and conclusions I have drawn from the studies on which this book was based and from my work on previous volumes in this series. These principles are presented with a minimum of additional discussion and unencumbered by details of the arguments that led to each of them.

There are several purposes of a summary list of conclusions and emerging principles. One point is to assure that readers who might pick up this book but are not willing to wade through it in its entirety might still have a means of absorbing the essential message. Another purpose is to provide a more formal taxonomy of the ideas that emerge when someone, perhaps too ambitiously, tries to cover a field as complex and as loaded with vested interest and importance as is this one. The formulation of such a credo *in abstracto* also helps to concretize the message that is being sent after many pages of "on the one hand" and "on the other." Needless to say, the development of a list of concluding principles also helps an author to firm up his own conclusions and to identify any logical inconsistencies in the arguments presented.

This book is somewhat different from the previous ones I have written. It is a much more historical and philosophical interpretation and much less a review of the empirical literature. Perhaps, because of this difference, the idea of a crisp tabular summary of drawn conclusions may be even more important. There is no question that in many cases, the goal of achieving a fair and balanced account may actually have obscured the conclusions that were intended from the discussion. Furthermore, there are some conclusions that, no matter how often repeated, may still be misunderstood by even an attentive reader. By highlighting them in the form of explicit statements of principle, it is sometimes (but, alas, not always) possible to avoid the inevitable misreading of one's thesis. It is for these reasons that an epilog and a set of emerging principles is extremely useful.

Perhaps the most important summary point is that there really is no conclusion in sight to the great debate between cognitive mentalists and nonreductive behaviorists. There is nothing in this book that provides the ultimate "smoking gun" that will convince all cognitivists to become behaviorists. As we have seen the arguments presented on each side often transcend the logical and empirical and involve matters of personal values that are extremely compelling and very, very important to each individual's sense of self.

To state the obvious, the war between mentalism and cognitivism rages on and from some points of view may be no closer to a conclusion than it was 70 years ago when Watson crystallized the historical antecedents that led to the modern behaviorist revolution. His enunciation of a new psychology itself was swept away by another sea change in which a new and congenial version of mentalism—cognitivism—became the standard approach of psychology. Yet, in spite of the substantial commitment of contemporary scientific psychology to the new cognitive version of classical mentalism, there remains a substantial corpus of behaviorist thinking.

An interesting retrospective review (Friman, Allen, Kerwin, & Larzelere, 1993) of the citation rates and "impact factor" (defined as the frequency of citation of the average article in a given year) of cognitive and behavioral journals respectively, speaks directly to this question. Although four of the most prestigious cognitive psychology journals did show a gradual increase in both the number of citations and the impact factor from 1979 to 1988, there was virtually no decline in the corresponding values for four equivalently important behavioral journals. Indeed, as late as 1988, the citation numbers for the four behavioral journals were still numerically higher than those of the cognitive ones. Of course, this comparison might have been biased by the number of available journals in each field (cognitive journals proliferated much more vigorously than did the behaviorist ones in the previous decades). I was also somewhat surprised to recently note that the Association for Behavior Analysis also draws more than 2,500 attendees to its annual meeting.

Obviously behaviorism has not yet been completely replaced by cognitivism even if the main stream of scientific psychology seems to be going in the cognitive direction. Perhaps the pendular analogy presented in Chapter 1 describes not so much the absolute amount of commitment to one point of view or another as the "appearance" of the commitment. Friman and his colleagues (1993) made this point well when they said ". . . the repeated declaration of a [cognitive] revolution may be more a reflection of the enthusiasm many cognitive psychologists have for their discipline than of actual events" (p. 662).

In another interesting and relevant paper, Boneau (1992) collected the impressions of 48 distinguished psychologists about the state of contemporary psychology. He reports verbatim (but anonymous) quotes from their comments concerning two posed questions: What had surprised these scholars most in the past 25 years? and What did they expect to happen in the next 25 years? The most notable thing in the present context about these responses was the remarkably large amount of criticism directed at mentalistic cognitivism. Perhaps, the negativity is not too surprising given that most of the respondents were senior scientists who had been trained in the days in which behaviorism was very strong. Nevertheless, among those scholars who Boneau did list as participants in his survey were many who have remained very important in contemporary academic psychology and, indeed, some who were clearly in the cognitivist camp. Unfortunately the specific authorship of the specific responses was hidden and there is no way to correlate particular answers with particular scholars. Nevertheless, it seems evident that an undercurrent of antimentalist (presumably also anticognitivist) criticism is still surprisingly strong among leading experimental psychologists today. That undercurrent is an important additional piece of evidence that although behaviorism may be subdued, it is not extinct, and that the key controversy has certainly not yet been resolved.

Be that as it may be, it is clear that the majority, if not dominant, school of thought in contemporary psychology is cognitivist and generally mentalist. Equally clear is the fact that there remains a substantial and productive group of deeply committed behaviorist psychologists as well as other psychologists who are not so doctrinaire but who still are uncomfortable with the contemporary mentalism.

In the following sections, I present two lists of emerging general principles. The first includes some that are so important or so likely to be misunderstood I have designated them as *metaprinciples*. The second is a longer list of more specific conclusions or principles that I see emerging as a logical consequence of the discussions presented in this book. Whether or not they are distorted by my personal predilections is not an issue. Of course they are! That is the point of this book. Each represents my interpretation of the appropriate outcome of some of the more extended discussions presented in the pages of this and my earlier books. However dogmatic some of these statements may seem in isolation, I hope they have been adequately justified in these books and will not be rejected out of hand.

5.1 EMERGING METAPRINCIPLES

By a metaprinciple I am referring to a generalization of such breadth and universal importance that it must be considered fundamental to any discussion of the great controversy between mentalism and behaviorism. These are not just the answers to technical issues that have been or can be resolved by empirical studies or logical argument. Rather, these are the foundation premises on which all other conclusions must be based. If they are not accepted, then the rest of the discussion becomes moot.

5.1.1 The First Ontological Metaprinciple—Psychoneural Equivalence

The first ontological metaprinciple states simply and directly that neural activity is the sole basis of mental activity. Mind is a function of the brain and without a comparable material substrate, the function could not occur. Nevertheless, the most likely misinterpretation of my position to emerge from the preceding discussions is that by suggesting there are limits to our understanding of mental activity I am championing something that is essentially dualistic—that either knowingly or unknowingly I have actually adopted a cryptodualism. The expression of an "in principle" barrier between our *intra*personal mental states and our *inter*personal ability to communicate ideas is not, however, a dualistic assertion. I am not invoking a mysterious mental domain that is of a different kind of reality than the physical universe of which we (and our brains) are a part. Nothing could be further from my intent. I am, have always been, and expect I will always be a materialist monist regardless of the "foxholes" in which I may find myself in the future.

Scientific psychology would make no sense unless mental processes were a part of the natural world. The basic nature of the reality of the mind is that the brain is both necessary and sufficient to account for it—in fundamental and axiomatic principle. That is the essence of this first metaprinciple. If it is not accepted a priori, then there is little hope that any progress can be made in this scientific endeavor. To not accept this principle is to push psychology, either cognitive or behaviorist, out of the realm of science.

A corollary of this metaprinciple is that the essential level at which mental activity must be represented is the ensemble activity of many neurons, not in the representation provided by single neurons. But, that is another story.

5.1.2 The Second Ontological Metaprinciple— The Reality of Mind

Regardless of how inaccessible mental activity may or may not be to the scientific observer, nothing said in this book should be misinterpreted to mean that mental processes are less real than the function of any other organ of the body, in particular, nor of any machine, in general. Not only are we each aware of our own consciousness (even if we cannot always correctly interpret the motivating forces or logic that drive our behavior) but the very variability and adaptability of human behavior indicates that stimulus information is operating on what must be considered to be, at least, an extremely complicated system and which, at best, is of such complexity that something very real, which we denote by the term consciousness, has emerged. To assume that mind and its associated self-awareness is not real is to assert that all is illusion. Unfortunately, there is ample enough feeling about these days that mind is extrascientific or supernatural that this metaprinciple must be explicitly enunciated. To do otherwise than accept this second metaprinciple would mean we would have to ask—whose illusion? This brings us to the boundaries of the ridiculous as it would inevitably challenge the reality of everything else.

However important it is to accept mental activity and even consciousness as real, there is no question that their exact definitions, if not explanations, remain extremely refractory problems.

5.1.3 The Epistemological Metaprinciple— The Inaccessibility of Mental Processes

I have just expressed full commitment to the ontological reality of both the relationship between the brain and the mind, on the one hand, and mental activity itself, on the other. Now it is possible to enunciate a third metaprinciple concerning possible limits to our understanding of that very real mental activity. It is here that I diverge from what is generally accepted in the psychological, if not the wider, scientific community. I have concluded, particularly as discussed in Chapter 2, there is an abundance of logical, theoretical, and even empirical evidence to support the assertion that mental processes are inaccessible. The arguments are of three kinds.

First, because of the extreme complexity of the neural networks in which mental processes are instantiated, they are not amenable to neuroreductive analysis. That is, the probability of developing a reductive explanation for the detailed interconnections of large numbers of neurons (the essential level at which the origins of mind must be sought) is extremely low, if not an outright impossibility.

Second, because of the fundamental limits of input–output techniques that must treat the brain–mind as a black box, the likelihood of using psychological techniques to analyze or describe the actual inner workings of the mind is also vanishingly small. Cognitive reductionism is as remote a possibility as is neuroreductionism.

Third, individual subjects do not have any special insight into their own cognitive processes. Any new technique that purports to allow such insight is actually only a resurrected version of classic introspection. Such a technique must ultimately also fail for the same reasons its predecessors did.

Therefore, notwithstanding the fundamental ontological reality of both the brain and the mind, it is maintained that there are epistemological barriers to accessing and then analyzing mental activity. These barriers arise from criteria of both deep principle and empirical fact. It is this *epistemological* principle that has been violated by mentalisms, cognitive or otherwise, throughout the history of our science. It is here that behaviorism and mentalism find their most crucial and essential differences. It is on the foundation provided by this metaprinciple that a revitalized scientific psychology must be based if it is to have any chance of providing a valid understanding of the human condition in the future.

These, then, are the three main metaprinciples that have led me to champion the return of behaviorism as the best possible psychology for the next century. But, there are also a number of other general conclusions and general principles of only slightly less importance that have to be highlighted to fully understand the need for this new approach to psychological science. Some are derivative of the three metaprinciples, but there are others that help to flesh out the logic of the revitalized behaviorism. These principles are enumerated in the following section.

5.2 EMERGING CONCLUSIONS AND PRINCIPLES

1. Behaviorism has been under attack for the last 40 years often for reasons that lie far outside the acceptable boundaries of scientific discourse. Some of these wounds are self-inflicted.

2. Behaviorism has been criticized for being “antihumanism,” “anti-free will,” “antireligious,” and “uninteresting” as well as “authoritarian,” “mechanical,” and “trivial.” It is criticized for rejecting “inner feelings” or for

not allowing us "to enjoy music." These are all value judgments that are irrelevant to the real scientific issues.

3. Behaviorism has been poorly served by ill-fated attempts to extrapolate its scientific findings into the social, educational, or cultural domain. First and foremost, it must be evaluated as a science, free of vested interests and secondary goals concerning matters about which it has little to say.

4. Behaviorism has its own history but it also has a rich background of influence from other fields of science and philosophy.

5. Some behaviorisms are actually mentalisms. An objective empirical approach is not the same thing as a behaviorist approach to the study of organisms.

6. No behaviorist psychologist has ever rejected the fact that people think, feel, emote, and reason. All accept the basic idea that the brain–mind is an active element in adaptive behavior.

7. Theological issues have often played an important role in an individual's acceptance of either mentalism or behaviorism. One of Boneau's (1992) anonymous respondents was quoted as saying "Another [factor in cognitivism's rise] was ideology—the influence of believers in soul and spirit defending the homunculus and thereby its Creator, even if they didn't realize they were doing so" (p. 1590; brackets added).

8. Pragmatic concerns about psychology's potential contributions to human welfare have often misled theory building. Where objective empirical or logical arguments should take priority, utility has sometimes been used to justify parascientific silliness.

9. There are powerful vested interests (e.g., the psychotherapeutic industry) that draw their sustenance from mentalist theories and approaches to psychology. To met their needs, they have often ignored the basic scientific issues and findings.

10. New empirical and theoretical information from the other sciences returns the debate between behaviorism and mentalism to the scientific domain.

11. Some behaviorists as well as most mentalists have been "in principle" reductionists. Behaviorists, however, have generally taught that a holistic, molar approach was preferred when approaching experiments or theories.

12. Behaviorism and cognitivism both are alternative approaches to the study of human thought and behavior and, thus, must cover the same range of topics. It is the interpretation of the significance and meaning of experimental findings, not the topics they choose to study, that distinguishes the two kinds of psychology.

13. Contemporary cognitivism is closely associated with information processing, computer analogies, and neuroreduction of psychological processes.

14. Contemporary behaviorism is closely associated with a nonreductive study of observed responses in a way that eschews the creation of unwarranted hypothetical constructs. Its forays into verbal behavior have been met with strong resistance.

15. The main difference between behaviorism and cognitivism, however, has been their respective answers to the question—is mind accessible? Cognitivists assume that it is; behaviorists that it is not because of the limits of introspection, the fallibility of verbal reports, and the fundamental constraints on input–output analyses. *Intra*personally privileged awareness is not tantamount to *inter*personal communication.

16. A second major difference between behaviorists and cognitivists is their respective answers to the question of analyzability. Cognitivists believe that mental behavior can be reduced to a system of "internal information processing states." Behaviorists believe this is not possible. Arguments supporting the behaviorist position come from thermodynamics, complexity theory, chaos theory, automata theory, and many other facts from other sciences.

17. As with any other field of science, scientific psychology must include both empirical and theoretical approaches to understanding its content matter. What psychologists mean by an "acceptable" theory, however, is highly variable.

18. Theory in science can be reductive or descriptive. Cognitive psychologists lean toward the former; behaviorists toward the latter.

19. Quite different questions of science are often confused with each other. Localization of a particular region of the brain that seems to have some behavioral effect is not the same as a detailed analysis of the network of neurons that represents or encodes that function in that location.

20. There is no question that organism plays an important role in determining what kind of a response will be made to a stimulus. Organisms are, however, not simple automata. At the very least, they are very complicated systems. The difference in complexity between organisms and automata is of such a great degree that there is currently a qualitative difference between artificial and natural intelligence.

21. Extreme versions of conflicting theories are both usually incorrect. Compromises enjoying features of both extremes are more usually accepted in the final analysis.

22. Many of the standard criteria for choosing a scientific theory are inappropriate for psychology. Parsimony, simplicity, elegance, practical utility, and exact repeatability become irrelevant in a system made up of so many parts that they can be wasted or a system that is so adaptive that it usefully changes its behavior from trial to trial. Even what is "objective," therefore, becomes a matter of opinion.

23. Because of the adaptability and variability of the component mental processes (even if one accepts for the sake of argument that they, in fact, exist), a cognitively reductive approach is unlikely to succeed.

24. Fundamental physical principles such as Moore's (1956) Theorem and the engineer's black box constraint preclude any kind of stimulus–response approach from providing access into the inner workings of the brain or the mind.

25. Both behavior and mathematics are essentially descriptive approaches and are neutral with regard to internal mechanisms, structures, and processes.

26. Computational models, however well they may describe the behavior of a system, are also neutral with regard to internal mechanisms, structures, and processes.

27. Humans have a very poor appreciation of their own motives, logic, and other forces driving their behavior. They cannot analyze the processes that lead to their behavior nor are they aware of any part of their mental activity except the final outcome. When their introspective explanations agree with independent measures, it is often coincidental or based on a priori predilections, prejudices, and opinions.

28. Human memory is extremely fallible. False memories are easily implanted.

29. Scientists generally underestimate the importance of exceptions to rules. The logic of syllogistic reasoning asserts that exceptions can completely disprove overgeneralized hypotheses.

30. Analogies are not the same thing as homologies. Isomorphic response trends in data and in theories may be accounted for by totally different internal mechanisms.

31. Because of the limits on accessibility, there are inadequate constraints on the construction of hypothetical constructs. Mentalist theorists are, therefore, free to invent an infinite variety of ad hoc explanations of human behavior. Behavioral theories honor these constraints to a greater degree.

32. Because of the complexity of human mental activity experimental results may often be qualitatively altered by slight changes in experimental design.

33. Subjects often do not play the game that the experimenter wishes them to play.

34. Humans should enjoy no special role as the subject of psychological or any other kind of science. The principles and factors that drive organic behavior are common to all organisms even though the level of sentience may vary greatly.

35. There remains an enormous unanswered question, of such magnitude as to potentially change humanity's view of its own nature. It is: Is mind epiphenomenal or does it exert a direct force on the body–brain or behavior? The ultimate answer to this question, if it can be answered, will have a drastic effect on human affairs both in science and other domains.

36. There is no need for a major change in the kind of research that is carried out by psychologists, neurophysiologists, and computer scientists. Each of these fields is of value and stands in its own right. Changes, however, are necessary in our interpretations of the relations between these field.

37. A radical environmental or learning explanation of human behavior is as inappropriate as a pure genetic determinism. Both are rigid and dogmatic scientific doctrines that do not accept the obvious interplay between heredity and environment. The selection of an appropriate response may be a very complex process depending on the experiential history and development of the organism as well as the current stimuli. The only acceptable approach to studying human mentation and behavior must take into account genetic and experiential factors.

38. Because of the difficulties in teasing apart the internal structures of mental activity, and the neutrality of behavior and mathematics, mental activity and behavior must be studied from a molar point of view.

39. A revitalized behaviorism must be psychophysical. That is, to the maximum extent possible, it must anchor all responses to some measure of the physical or situational stimulus. A psychophysical approach makes the least demands on its subjects (and thus distort the findings the least) by requiring the simplest possible (i.e., Class A) responses. The quality and the longevity of the acceptance of empirical results declines in inverse relation to the complexity of the cognitive decisions that must be made in formulating a response.

40. A revitalized behaviorism must accept the fact that most psychological theories are, in principle, descriptive in a mathematical, computational or even a verbal sense. Truly reductive theories (i.e., ontologically reductive) are rare and, except in some special cases, impossible.

41. A revitalized behaviorism must eschew any physiological reductionism. There is ample evidence now that the search for neuroreductive explanations at either the neuron or neuronal network level for complex cognitive processes is an unachievable goal.

42. A revitalized behaviorism must dote on its empirical and experimental roots. Direct contact with nature by objective exploration and experimentation is the *sine qua non* of this or any other science.

43. A revitalized behaviorism must accept the eclectic position that both logically mediated and automatic factors jointly affect behavior.

44. Finally, it must be appreciated that many of the questions that psychologists have raised have not been answered and may not be answerable. Distinguishing the possible and achievable from the will-of-the-wisps is an important task for any future student of this very important field of science.

The main goal of this book has been to clarify the nature of the issues, compare the arguments from either side, and draw forth what appears to at least one experimental psychologist a new synthesis that better meets the needs of a valid scientific psychology than the current one. For me, the future of scientific psychology lies in a renewed and appropriately modified version of behaviorism. To the degree that I have identified the issues and clarified the positions of the two contending perspectives, this effort may have achieved a partial success. I have no great expectation that the viewpoint expressed in this book will immediately change contemporary scientific psychology. However, it is my hope that this has been a worthwhile effort and that it may play a role in a reconsideration of the basic principles of our science some time in the future.

References

Amsel, A. (1989). *Behaviorism, neobehaviorism, and cognitivism in learning theory.* Hillsdale, NJ: Lawrence Erlbaum Associates.

Anderson, J. R., & Lebiere, C. (1998). *The atomic components of thought.* Mahwah, NJ: Lawrence Erlbaum Associates.

Attneave, F., & Arnoult, M. D. (1956). The quantitative study of shape and pattern perception. *Psychological Bulletin, 53,* 452–471.

Bargh, J. A. (1997). The automaticity of everyday life. In R. S. Wyer Jr. (Ed.), *Advances in social cognition* (pp. 1–47). Mahwah, NJ: Lawrence Erlbaum Associates.

Bargh, J. A., Chen, M., & Burrows, L. (1996). Automaticity of social behavior: Direct effects of trait construct and stereotype activation on action. *Journal of Personality and Social Psychology, 71,* 230–244.

Bartlett, F. C. (1932). *Remembering: A study in experimental and social psychology.* Cambridge, England: Cambridge University Press.

Black, M. (1967). Induction. In P. Edwards (Ed.), *The encyclopedia of philosophy* (Vol. 3, pp. 169–181). New York: Macmillan and The Free Press.

Boneau, C. A. (1992). Observations on psychology's past and future. *American Psychologist, 47,* 1586–1596.

Boring, E. G. (1933). *The physical dimensions of consciousness.* New York: Appleton-Century-Crofts.

Boring, E. G. (1950). *A history of experimental psychology* (2nd ed.). New York: Appleton-Century-Crofts.

Boyd, R. (1980). Materialism without reductionism: What physicalism does not entail. In R. Block (Ed.), *Readings in the philosophy of psychology* (Vol. 1, pp. 67–107). Cambridge, MA: Harvard University Press.

Bridgman, P. W. (1927). *The logic of modern physics.* New York: Macmillan.

Brindley, G. S. (1960). *Physiology of the retina and the visual pathway.* London: Edward Arnold.

Brown, D. R., & Owen, D. H. (1967). The metrics of visual form: Methodological dyspepsia. *Psychological Bulletin, 68,* 243–259.

Casti, J. L. (1996). Confronting science's logical limits. *Scientific American* (October), 102–105.

Chomsky, N. (1959). Verbal Behavior—A review. *Language, 35,* 26–58.

Chomsky, N. (1972). *Language and mind.* New York: Harcourt Brace Jovanovich.

Churchland, P. M. (1988). *Matter and consciousness: A contemporary introduction to philosophy of mind.* Cambridge, MA: MIT Press.

Dawes, R. M. (1994). *House of cards: Psychology and psychotherapy built on myth.* New York: The Free Press.

Day, W. F. (1980). The historical antecedents of contemporary behaviorism. In R. W. Rieber & K. Salzinger (Eds.), *Psychology: Historical theoretical perspectives* (pp. 203–262). New York: Academic Press.

Dennett, D. C. (1988). *Brainstorms.* Cambridge, MA: MIT Press.

Dennett, D. C. (1991). *Consciousness explained.* Boston: Little, Brown.

DeValois, R. L., & DeValois, K. K. (1988). *Spatial vision.* New York: Oxford University Press.

Dienes, Z., & Berry, D. (1997). Implicit learning: Below the subjective threshold. *Psychonomic Bulletin and Review, 4,* 3–23.

Donders, F. C. (1969). On the speed of mental processes (W. G. Koster, Trans.). *Acta Psychologia, 30,* 412–431. (Originally published 1868)

Ericsson, K. A., & Simon, H. A. (1980). Verbal reports as data. *Psychological Review, 87,* 215–251.

Feyerabend, P. (1963). Mental events and the brain. *Journal of Philosophy, 60,* 295–296.

Friman, P. C., Allen, K. D., Kerwin, M. L. E., & Larzelere, R. (1993). A citation analysis of the Kuhnian displacement thesis. *American Psychologist, 48,* 658–664.

Gardner, H. (1985). *The mind's new science: A history of the cognitive revolution.* New York: Basic Books.

Gilovich, T. (1991). *How we know what isn't so.* New York: The Free Press.

Graham, N. V. S. (1989). *Visual pattern analyzers.* New York: Oxford University Press.

Green, C. D. (1992). Of immortal psychological beasts: Operationalism in Psychology. *Theory and Psychology, 2,* 291–320.

Hanfling, O. (1989). *Wittgenstein's later philosophy.* London, England: Macmillan.

Hanson, N. R. (1958). *Patterns of discovery.* Cambridge, England: Cambridge University Press.

Hebb, D. O. (1949). *The organization of behavior: A neuropsychological theory.* New York: Wiley.

Heisenberg, W. (1927). Uber den anschaulichen Inhalt der quantentheoretischen Kinematik und Mechanik. *Zeitschrift Physik, 43,* 172–198.

Holt, E. B. (1914). *The concept of consciousness.* London: George Allen.

Hull, C. L. (1943). *Principles of behavior: An introduction to behavior theory.* New York: Appleton Century Crofts.

James, W. (1890). *The principles of psychology.* New York: Holt.

Jenning, H. S. (1976). *Behavior of the lower organisms.* Bloomington, IN: Indiana University Press. (Originally published 1906)

Kahneman, D., Slovic, P., & Tversky, A. (1982). *Judgment under uncertainty: Heuristics and biases.* Cambridge, England: Cambridge University Press.

Kandel, E. R., & Kupfermann, I. (1995). From nerve cells to cognition. In E. R. Kandel, J. H. Schwartz, & T. M. Jessell (Eds.), *Essentials of neural science and behavior* (pp. 321–346). Norwalk, CT: Appleton and Lange.

Kantor, J. R. (1971a). Behaviorism: Whose image? In *The aim and progress of psychology and other sciences: A selection of papers by J. R. Kantor* (pp. 521–533). Chicago: The Principia Press.

Kantor, J. R. (1971b). Behaviorism in the history of psychology. In *The aim and progress of psychology and other sciences: A selection of papers by J. R. Kantor* (pp. 534–548). Chicago: The Principia Press.

Killeen, P. R. (1988). The reflex reserve. *Journal of Experimental Analysis of Behavior, 50,* 319–331.

Killeen, P. R. (1992). Mechanics of the animate. *Journal of the Experimental Analysis of Behavior, 57,* 429–463.

Killeen, P. R. (1995). Economics, ecologics, and mechanics: The dynamics of responding under conditions of varying motivation. *Journal of the Experimental Analysis of Behavior, 64*, 405–431.

Kimble, G. A. (1996). *Psychology: The hope of a science.* Cambridge, MA: The MIT Press.

Koch, S. (Ed.). (1959). *Psychology: A study of a science. Vol. 1: Sensory, perceptual, and physiological foundations.* New York: McGraw-Hill.

Koch, S. (Ed.). (1962). *Psychology: A study of a science. Vol. 4: Biologically oriented fields.* New York: McGraw-Hill.

Koch, S. (1964). Psychology and emerging conceptions of knowledge as unitary. In T. W. Wann (Ed.), *Behaviorism and phenomenology.* Chicago: University of Chicago Press.

Koch, S. (1992). Psychology's Bridgman vs Bridgman's Bridgman. *Theory and Psychology, 2*, 261–290.

Lashley, K. S. (1942). The problem of cerebral organization in vision. *Biological symposia Vol. VII, Visual mechanisms.* Lancaster: Jacques Cattell Press.

Lashley, K. S., Chow, K. L., & Semmes, J. (1951). An examination of the electrical field theory of cerebral integration. *Psychological Review, 58*, 123–136.

Leahey, T. H. (1997). *A history of psychology: Main currents in psychological thought.* Upper Saddle River, NJ: Prentice-Hall.

Lee, V. L. (1988). *Beyond behaviorism.* Hillsdale, NJ: Lawrence Erlbaum Associates.

Leeuwenberg, E. (1971). A perceptual coding language for visual and auditory patterns. *American Journal of Psychology, 84*, 307–349.

Lewin, K. (1933). Environmental forces. In C. Murchison (Ed.), *A handbook of child psychology* (2nd ed., pp. 590–625). Worcester, MA: Clark University Press.

Littrell, J. (1998). Is the reexperience of painful emotion therapeutic? *Clinical Psychology Review, 18*, 71–102.

Lockhead, G. (1992). Psychophysical scaling: Judgments of attributes of objects? *Behavioral and Brain Sciences, 15*, 543–601.

Loeb, J. (1909/1964). The significance of tropisms for psychology. In D. Fleming (Ed.), *The mechanistic conception of life* (pp. 35–63). Cambridge, MA: Belknap Press.

Loftus, E. F. (1979). *Eyewitness testimony.* Cambridge, MA: Harvard University Press.

Loftus, E. F. (1994). *The myth of repressed memory.* New York: St. Martin's Press.

Loftus, E. F. (1996). Manufacturing false memories using bits of reality. In L. M. Reder (Ed.), *Implicit memory and metacognition.* Mahwah, NJ: Lawrence Erlbaum Associates.

MacCorquodale, K., & Meehl, P. E. (1948). On a distinction between hypothetical constructs and intervening variables. *Psychological Review, 55*, 95–107.

MacKenzie, B. D. (1977). *Behaviorism and the limits of scientific methods.* Atlantic Highlands, NJ: Humanities Press.

Mark, J. (1930). Behaviorism and religion. In W. P. King (Ed.), *Behaviorism: A battle line.* Nashville, TN: Cokesbury Press.

Marx, M. H., & Hillix, W. A. (1973). *Systems and theories in psychology.* New York: McGraw Hill.

Matlin, M. W. (1994). *Cognition.* Fort Worth, TX: Harcourt Brace.

McFall, R. M., & Townsend, J. T. (1998). Foundations of psychological assessment: Implications for cognitive assessment in clinical science. *Psychological Assessment, 10*, 316–330.

McGeoch, J. A. (1942). *The psychology of human learning: An introduction.* New York: Longmans Green.

McGinn, C. (1989). Can we solve the mind-body problem? *Mind, 98*, 349–366.

Miller, G. A. (1962). *Psychology: The science of mental life.* New York: Harper and Row.

Miller, G. A., Galanter, E., & Pribram, K. H. (1960). *Plans and the structure of behavior.* New York: Henry Holt.

Minsky, M. (1963). Steps toward artificial intelligence. In E. A. Feigenbaum & J. Feldman (Eds.), *Computers and thought.* New York: McGraw-Hill.

Moore, E. F. (1956). *Automata studies.* Princeton, NJ: Princeton University Press.

Moore, T. F. (1939). *Cognitive psychology.* Philadelphia: Lippincott.

Nagel, T. (1979). *Mortal questions.* New York: Cambridge University Press.

Nagel, T. (1986). *The view from nowhere.* New York: Oxford University Press.

Neal, A., & Hesketh, B. (1997). Episodic knowledge and implicit learning. *Psychonomic Bulletin and Review, 4,* 24–37.

Neisser, U. (1967). *Cognitive psychology.* New York: Appleton-Century-Crofts.

Nisbett, R., & Ross, L. (1980). *Human inference: Strategies and shortcomings of social judgment.* Englewood Cliffs, NJ: Prentice-Hall.

Nisbett, R. E., & Wilson, T. D. (1977). Telling more than we can know: Verbal reports on mental processes. *Psychological Review, 84,* 231–259.

Pachella, R. G. (1974). The interpretation of reaction time in information processing research. In B. H. Kantowitz (Ed.), *Human information processing: Tutorials in performance and cognition.* Hillsdale, NJ: Lawrence Erlbaum Associates.

Penrose, R. (1989). *The emperor's new mind.* New York: Oxford University Press.

Perruchet, P., & Pacteau, C. (1990). Synthetic grammar learning: Implicit rule abstraction or explicit fragmentary knowledge? *Journal of Experimental Psychology: General, 119,* 264–276.

Popper, K. (1959). *The logic of scientific discovery.* New York: Harper & Row.

Pribram, K. H. (1979). Behaviorism, phenomenology and holism in psychology: A scientific analysis. *Journal of Social and Biological Structure, 2,* 65–72.

Pribram, K. H. (1985). 'Holism' could close cognition era. *APA Monitor, 16,* 5–6.

Pribram, K. H. (1991). *Brain and perception: Holonomy and structure in figural processing.* Hillsdale, NJ: Lawrence Erlbaum Associates.

Putnam, H. (1973). Reductionism and the nature of psychology. *Cognition, 2,* 131–146.

Pylyshyn, Z. W. (1986). *Computation and cognition: Toward a foundation for cognitive science.* Cambridge, MA: MIT Press.

Quine, W. V. (1969). *Ontological relativity and other essays.* New York: Columbia University.

Rachlin, H. (1992). Teleological behaviorism. *American Psychologist, 47,* 1371–1382.

Rachlin, H. (1994). *Behavior and mind: The roots of modern psychology.* New York: Oxford University Press.

Rakover, S. S. (1990). *Metapsychology: Missing links in behavior, mind, and science.* New York: Paragon House.

Ratliffe, F. (1965). *Mach bands: Quantitative studies on neural networks in the retina.* San Francisco: Holden-day.

Rawl, H. F. (1930). What does behaviorism mean for religion? In W. P. King (Ed.), *Behaviorism: A battle line.* Nashville, TN: Cokesbury Press.

Rey, G. (1988). A question about consciousness. In H. Otto & J. Tuedio (Eds.), *Perspectives on mind* (pp. 5–24). Dordrecht: Reidel.

Robinson, D. N. (1976). Thomas Reid's gestalt psychology. In S. F. Barker & T. L. Beauchamp (Eds.), *Thomas Reid: Critical interpretations* (Vol. 3, pp. 44–54). Philadelphia: Philosophical Monographs.

Robinson, D. N. (1995). The logic of reductionistic models. *New Ideas in Psychology, 13,* 1–8.

Roediger, H. L. (1997). Implicit learning: A symposium. *Psychonomic Bulletin and Review, 4*(1), 1–133.

Rogers, C. R. (1964). Toward a science of the person. In T. Wann (Ed.), *Behaviorism and phenomenology* (pp. 109–133). Chicago: University of Chicago Press.

Ryle, G. (1949). *The concept of mind.* New York: Barnes & Noble.

Searle, J. R. (1992). *The rediscovery of the mind.* Cambridge MA: MIT Press.

Sagan, C. (1995). *The demon-haunted world.* New York: Random House.

Shannon, C. E., & Weaver, W. (1949). *The mathematical theory of communication.* Urbana: University of Illinois Press.

Shaw, M. L. (1978). A capacity allocation model for reaction time. *Journal of Experimental Psychology: Human Perception and Performance, 4,* 586–598.

Skinner, B. F. (1938). *The behavior of organisms: An experimental analysis.* New York: Appleton-Century.

Skinner, B. F. (1953). *Science and human behavior.* New York: The Free Press.

Skinner, B. F. (1957). *Verbal behavior.* New York: Appleton-Century-Crofts.

Skinner, B. F. (1963). Behaviorism at fifty. *Science, 140,* 951–958.

Skinner, B. F. (1974). *About behaviorism.* New York: Alfred Knopf.

Skinner, B. F. (1975). The steep and thorny way to a science of behavior. *American Psychologist, 30,* 42–49.

Skinner, B. F. (1987). Whatever happened to psychology as the science of behavior? *American Psychologist, 42,* 780–786.

Smith, E. R., & Miller, F. D. (1978). Limits on perception of cognitive processes: A reply to Nisbett and Wilson. *Psychological Review, 85,* 355–362.

Smith, L. D. (1986). *Behaviorism and logical positivism: A reassessment of the alliance.* Palo Alto, CA: Stanford University Press.

Sperling, G., & Lu, Z.-L. (1998). A systems analysis of visual motion perception. In T. Watanabe (Ed.), *High-level motion processing: Computational, neurobiological, and psychophysical perspectives.* Cambridge, MA: MIT Press.

Sperry, R. W., Miner, R., & Meyers, R. E. (1955). Visual pattern perception following subpial slicing and tantalum wire implantations in the visual cortex. *Journal of Comparative and Physiological Psychology, 48,* 50–58.

Staddon, J. E. R. (1993). *Behaviorism: Mind, mechanism, and society.* London: Duckworth.

Staddon, J. E. R., & Zanutto, B. S. (1998). In praise of parsimony. In C. D. L. Wynne & J. E. R. Staddon (Eds.), *Models for action: Mechanisms for adaptive behavior* (pp. 239–267). Mahwah, NJ: Lawrence Erlbaum Associates.

Sternberg, S. (1969). The discovery of processing stages: Extension of Donder's method. *Acta Psychologia, 30,* 276–315.

Stevens, S. S. (1935). The operational definition of psychological concepts. *Psychological Review, 42,* 517–527.

Stevens, S. S. (1961). The psychophysics of sensory function. In W. A. Rosenblith (Ed.), *Sensory communication* (pp. 1–34). Cambridge, MA: MIT Press.

Surprenant, A. M., & Neath, I. (1997). T. V. Moore's (1939) cognitive psychology. *Psychonomic Bulletin and Review, 4,* 342–349.

Tanner, W. P., Jr., & Swets, J. A. (1954). A decision-making theory of visual detection. *Psychological Review, 61,* 401–409

Thorndike, E. L. (1907). *The elements of psychology.* New York: A. G. Seiler.

Timberlake, W. (1994). Behavior systems, associationism, and Pavlovian conditioning. *Psychonomic Bulletin and Review, 1,* 405–420.

Titchener, E. B. (1899). *An outline of psychology.* New York: Macmillan.

Tolman, E. C. (1932). *Purposive behavior in animals and man.* New York: Appleton-Century-Crofts.

Townsend, J. T., & Thomas, R. D. (1994). Stochastic dependencies in parallel and serial models: Effects on systems factorial interactions. *Journal of Mathematical Psychology, 38*(1), 1–34.

Underwood, B. J. (1972). Are we overloading memory? In A. W. Melton & E. Martin (Eds.), *Coding processes in human memory* (pp. 347–372). Washington, DC: Winston.

Uttal, W. R. (1973). *The psychobiology of sensory coding.* New York: Harper and Row.

Uttal, W. R. (1978). *The psychobiology of mind.* Hillsdale, NJ: Lawrence Erlbaum Associates.

Uttal, W. R. (1981). *A taxonomy of visual processes.* Hillsdale, NJ: Lawrence Erlbaum Associates.

Uttal, W. R. (1988). *On seeing forms.* Hillsdale, NJ: Lawrence Erlbaum Associates.

Uttal, W. R. (1990). On some two way barriers between theories and mechanisms. *Perception and Psychophysics, 48,* 188–203.

Uttal, W. R. (1998). *Toward a new behaviorism: The case against perceptual reductionism.* Mahwah, NJ: Lawrence Erlbaum Associates.

Watkins, M. J. (1990). Mediationism and the obfuscation of memory. *American Psychologist,* 328-335.

Watson, J. B. (1914). *Behavior: An introduction to comparative psychology.* New York: Henry Holt.

Watson, J. B. (1924). *Psychology from the standpoint of a behaviorist.* Philadelphia: Lippincott.

Watson, J. B. (1930). *Behaviorism.* New York: Norton.

Wegner, D. M. (1994). Ironic processes of mental control. *Psychological Review, 101,* 34–52.

Wiener, N. (1948). *Cybernetics.* New York: Wiley.

Wilson, E. O. (1975). *Sociobiology: The new synthesis.* Cambridge MA: Harvard University Press.

Wittgenstein, L. (1953). *Philosophical investigations* (3rd ed.). New York: Macmillan.

Wittgenstein, L. (1958). *The blue and brown books.* New York: Harper Colophon.

Woodworth, R. S. (1938). *Experimental psychology.* New York: Holt.

Zuriff, G. E. (1985). *Behaviorism: A conceptual reconstruction.* New York: Columbia University Press.

Author Index

Subject Index

H

I

J-L

M